D1365286

CHAMPLAIN COLLEGE

SO TO SPEAK

SO TO SPEAK

Interviews with
contemporary Canadian writers
Edited by Peter O'Brien

Véhicule Press

MONTRÉAL

This book is for Lee O'Brien, *in absentia*, with whom I often speak.

Special thanks to David Manicom for his conscientious hard work, and to Richard Hamilton, Barbara Leckie, Raina Feldman, Ann Scowcroft, Ann Hamilton, Su Schnee, Stephen Brockwell, Peter Legris, Maggie Berg, Harold Heft, Mary Stinson, Paul John, Peter Malden, Teresa Marquis, Elizabeth Maloney, and the rest of the staff of *Rubicon* magazine. Thanks also to Adrian King-Edwards and Simon Dardick for their enthusiastic support.

Published with the assistance of The Canada Council.

Cover design by JW Stewart.
Typeset in Bembo by Zibra Inc.
Printed by Les Éditions Marquis Ltée.

Dépôt légal, Bibliothèque nationale du Québec
and the National Library of Canada, 4th trimester 1987.

Canadian Cataloguing in Publication Data

Main entry under title:

So to speak: interviews with contemporary Canadian writers
ISBN 0-919890-84-9
Bibliography: p.
1. Authors, Canadian (English) — 20th century —
    Interviews. I. O'Brien, Peter, 1957-
PS8081.S68 1987   C810'.9'0054   C87-090340-3
PR9189.6.S68 1987

Address all Canadian orders to:
University of Toronto Press
Publications Department
5201 Dufferin Street
Downsview, Ontario M3H 5T8

Address all U.S. orders to:
University of Toronto Press
340 Nagel Drive
Buffalo, NY 14225-4731

Véhicule Press, P.O.B. 125, Place du Parc Station,
Montreal, Quebec, Canada H2W 2M9

Printed in Canada.

CONTENTS

INTRODUCTION

All of these interviews have appeared (or, in the case of Nicole Brossard, will soon appear) in the Montreal literary journal *Rubicon*. This collection of eleven interviews makes no claim to being either inclusive or exhaustive. It is a relatively random selection of Canadian writerly voices: established and new, female and male, poet and fictioneer. Although this rough grouping of interviews does not propose a particular thematic or chronological perspective, it does demonstrate the disorderly richness of current Canadian writing. Canada has too often demonstrated a misplaced need to categorize its writers, to appropriate their activities and to say that they therefore speak of a tradition rightfully and distinctly Canadian. Yet writers are, by nature, much more cantankerous than that. They would prefer to speak in their own voices and let the traditions fall where they may. The country that writers see today is disparate, vibrant, democratic in its limbs. Some of this is seen in the following pages.

Over the latter half of this century, interviews have become more important as a source of literary documentation. This is a direct result of the rise in the use of telephones and computers, and the consequent decline in letter writing by authors. In a recent issue of *The New York Times Book Review* James Atlas laments this decline: "What will biographers of our contemporaries find when they arrive, notebook and pen in hand, at the library where their subject's papers have been deposited? A packet of letters, a few scribbled postcards and a box of tape cassettes. Will they have any advantage over the biographer whose only source was the written word? I doubt the garrulous archive bequeathed us by the tape recorder will prove as memorable as Henry James's thank-you notes." The humourist Ian Frazier is a little more philosophic about the demise of letter writing. In a recent story of his, "Igor Stravinsky: The Selected Phone Calls," Frazier pretends to use old telephone bills as a way of investigating the great composer's life. Although biographers and readers certainly lament the diminishing number of literary letters, interviews will inevitably help to fill this gap.

Interviews can never supply all the information we may desire about a writer, yet they can pique interest and provide biographical and literary background to the author and the work. At their worst—as in magazines like *People* and *Vanity Fair*—interviews are only gossipy and titillating. At their best—as in some of the better *Paris Review* interviews, and in books such as *Labyrinths of Voice: Conversations with Robert Kroetsch*—interviews provide portraits of the writer that are both fascinating and illuminating. They demonstrate that both lived experience and language—often slippery and temporal—are the bases of that more permanent animal, writing.

Within these pages you will discover some loose connections between markedly different writers. Jack Hodgins talks about the coastline as "a place of magic, transformation," and of the fantastic assortment of characters that is present in the average Vancouver Island town. Roo Borson talks of the "mood of a place" coming out of "emotional nuance," and how it is also possible for her to write not using landscapes at all. Both of these writers have some of the same sympathies, some of the same concerns about writing and the imagination. Yet they achieve and perhaps work toward different ends. It seems to me that Hodgins discovers something of himself in the characters that he creates or documents, and that Borson discovers the world of others by digging deeper into her own emotions.

You may also discover a healthy overlapping of disciplines. For Rudy Wiebe, history—both that which has been recorded and that which escapes the history books—plays a seminal role. Mennonite family relationships and the Métis and Big Bear all speak through Wiebe's writing. "When there's nothing to say anymore, when language breaks down," says Wiebe, "that's when you reach for guns." In Christopher Dewdney's work you are likely to enter the world of quantum physics and synaptic spine theory, where there are vast quantities of the unknown filtered through infinitely small elements of the brain and the heart. For Dewdney, "there doesn't have to be any contradiction" between the magical and the scientific, since "science is magic" and "there's no need for anything to be more miraculous than it already is." In the Mavis Gallant interview you will read about the events of May 1968 in Paris—the student revolts and the first inklings of a new philosophical understanding of the twentieth century, however short-lived these sentiments might have been. As she says, "the tension, the ugliness, the materialism" of the post-war era disappeared and the world "suddenly looked good for one afternoon."

What is also evident throughout these interviews is a sense of the political, and how the worlds of politics and literature are inextricably yoked together. In Nicole Brossard's writings and in this interview, feminism is her "*politique*": "As for the spiral, it is a metaphor used to talk about the type of position we as women, not only lesbians, are placed at in the world. I don't think that we can confront logically what I call the thick wall of lies of patriarchy. We would be hurting ourselves unnecessarily. So I think that we have to curve reality, re-mind, re-call our energy, go forth, move in such a way that our thoughts make a spiral." For Josef Skvorecky, politics informs everything else—not the politics of any given party so much as the politics of daily life. Skvorecky's experience in 1968, when the Russians invaded his native Czechoslovakia, and perhaps his subsequent experiences in Canada, are reflected in his distrust of any definitive ideology. The duty of the writer, he says, is "to try as hard as he or she can to separate himself or herself from preconceived ideas." One of the antidotes to preconceived ideas is storytelling, in which you mix "reality with your imagination."

Erin Mouré builds her poems out of the politics of work, of community, of time: "The little people, who do not know themselves, keep the world from being annihilated . . . I feel sometimes, somewhat, like I'm writing other people's poems, as if fulfilling a responsibility towards them." For Mouré, the apocalypse "has been happening all this time." It becomes an "ordinary act" that most of us have overlooked. Within these pages you'll find Margaret Atwood referring to her recent activity with PEN International, and its activities with writers in prison. She also brings politics right down to earth: "Politics in the widest sense affects everybody. So writers write about human thought, behaviour, action, even when they're writing fantasy. Some of the most political writing in the 1950s was done by science fiction writers because people then didn't feel safe enough to do it openly. That's politics."

Peter Van Toorn and Leon Rooke each give, in their own idiosyncratic and tactile way, an idea of what happens in the imagination of a writer. Van Toorn says that sometimes, "if you're lucky, in a poem—or at least I feel this way—the first line will come sailing in like a ship, with all the fullness and promise and strength. Then the intuition gets lost. So you hold on to the first line, the sound of it, or the image, or the brightness of it, and you try to tune every other line, like the other strings on a guitar, to that first line (or string)." Rooke, throughout his stories and this interview, is host to a wealth of voices and images. When asked about symbols he responds that he's "not outlandishly symbolical . . . Symbol is fine, useful, and dandy, when true to a work's texture. I wouldn't want to hoist it up on a pole and have it wave about like a red flag. If symbol is a thing to be noticed in the first place, I'd want to kick a big pile of dirt up over it. Then throw on leaves so you wouldn't know for sure that the dirt was there."

Together with the multitude of topics referred to in the following pages—landscape, science, music, history, politics, the act of writing—you'll also be able to hear voices speaking, for writers are notoriously talkative. This is not to say that they always talk about themselves. They sometimes seem more comfortable when talking about their fictional selves, or their lyrical selves, or their potential selves. And, of course, this talking goes on in a variety of places—sometimes in the writing itself, sometimes in conversations, sometimes within the imagination of a created persona or character. Yet there are voices within these pages, voices that think and write and speak about things that matter to them.

Some of these interviews, the Gallant and the Van Toorn among them, have been entirely taped; the Borson and the Rooke have been the product of letters; others, for example the Mouré and the Dewdney, are the melding together of taped sessions and letters. Within all the interviews, however, there is a sense of the spontaneous intelligence at work, of the voice working through some of the similar concerns that are present in the poems and stories that these writers create. Gathered together, this group of voices helps to document the wealth of images and concerns that exist in the heart of writing.

Photo by William Yang

JOSEF SKVORECKY

Even though it was only the thirteenth of March (1987), it seemed like the first day of Spring; the air was warm, the snow had melted, vendors were selling flowers on the corners of Yonge Street—an appropriate day for an interview with the author of The Swell Season. *Skvorecky was busy: he had just been on* The Journal, *he had to write an article for* The Globe and Mail.*

I arrived at the door of his small Cabbagetown house on a quiet, dead-end street at two o'clock in the afternoon. Despite the hectic nature of Skvorecky's schedule, there was nothing hurried or impatient in his manner. He answered my questions thoughtfully, with the precision of one who has considered a daunting range of issues. When I asked questions about which many volumes had already been written—how does one define "truth," and "ideology," for example—he rose to the challenge without blinking an eye. Only when I asked about "realism" did he raise his eyebrows—I expected him to explain that?—and laughed before launching into a coherent account of the issue.

At the end of the interview, which had already extended well beyond the allotted time, he offered to tape me some of the songs to which he refers in The Engineer of Human Souls. *The depth of the emotion in these songs parallels a certain aspect of Skvorecky's work: the music is lively, but there is deep sadness there too. And it is impossible not to listen, not to be captured by the music.*

Skvorecky's fiction derives from its Eastern European context a rare combination of humour and seriousness. Born in Nachod, Bohemia, Skvorecky emigrated to Canada in 1968. In 1980 he was awarded the Neustadt International Prize for Literature, and in 1985 he won the Governor General's Award for The Engineer of Human Souls. *He is presently a professor of English at Erindale College, University of Toronto. Those of his books which have been translated into English are as follows:* The Cowards *(1970),* The Mournful Demeanour of Lieutenant Boruvka *(1974),* The Bass Saxophone *(1977),* Miss Silver's Past *(1975),* The Swell Season *(1982),* The Engineer of Human Souls *(1983), and* Dvorak in Love *(1986).*

13

How do you begin writing? Does the novel begin with some idea or character or desire . . . ?

That's hard to answer because it's different with different novels. Sometimes you have an idea which you carry in your subconscious mind, probably for years, and you realize that you are not ready for it; and then one day you feel that you are. That happened with *The Bass Saxophone*, for example, which was based on something that happened to a friend of mine in the war—I conceived the idea in the war actually—but it took me over twenty years to really write it. So sometimes it's like that. It depends on the character of the novel.

The Engineer of Human Souls which is, in a way, a summing up of my life experience, did not originate with any particular idea. I just had so many experiences and stories to tell. I was looking for a form—how to put it all together. Whereas "The Legend of Emoke," the story of a Hungarian girl, more or less actually happened. All the characters are based on real people; they behave very much like these real people behaved in the real world. It's almost a photographic copy.

The Cowards obviously took place during one week of May 1945, and it was based on the war experience. To me, to everybody, it was a very strong experience because we came in touch with the real thing. We were young teenagers, and I was full of emotions; the idea for that novel was that I wished to live through the events once again to somehow preserve the magic of the time. I was thinking of magic realism. Unfortunately, as with so many things, the South Americans stole that from the Czechs; Ricardo Reyes stole the name of our great 19th century poet Jan Neruda, and the term magic realism was really introduced into literature by a Czech poet in the 1930s. Josef Hora used it in an essay where he speaks about the magic realism of prose; by which he did not mean what Marquez thinks—"magically" adjusting reality for one's—usually political—purpose. He meant the introduction of poetry into prose, not in the sense that the prose would be lyrical but that the writer should take meticulous care with every word in the way that a poet does. Prose then would shine just as good poetry does.

So that was *The Cowards*. I simply wanted to write something that would have a sort of magic about it as I was remembering those days so many years later. Everybody likes to remember his or her teen years unless they were lived under very bad circumstances. I realized that I had quite a few more stories to tell about that period in my life with the same characters so, many years after *The Cowards,* I started *The Swell Season.* The idea for that came from a wish to tell the rest of the story, and also to prove to myself that I could write a well-constructed traditional story with a twist in the tail—that was also a form of inspiration.

INTERVIEWER

In *Engineer* Danny says that almost everything is nicer when it's told in a story. How does storytelling make things better?

SKVORECKY

I think storytelling has always made things nicer than they were in reality because you mix reality with your imagination. If the story is written well it is much more powerful than the actual event, I think. You don't simply tell things as they actually happened because then you would be writing reportage; every writer infuses the memory with imagination and the story becomes better. There are aspects of this process that are strange and perhaps even reprehensible because a good writer can make almost anything sound nice and interesting and enjoyable. You may have a novel about concentration camps which you read and you are aesthetically aroused. That is why some people, such as George Steiner, say that when writers are faced with this sort of reality they should keep silent. But then, of course, powerful novels have been written about very tragic events and they have influenced the course of history even if only in a minor way. When John Steinbeck wrote *The Grapes of Wrath* it led to the U.S. Senate passing certain laws to support itinerant farm workers. This is a very complex thing; I think there are some studies on it, or there should be anyway.

INTERVIEWER

You frequently refer to a pursuit of truth—Hemingway's quotation "A writer's job is to tell the truth," for instance—but what do you mean by truth?

SKVORECKY

I define truth as Hemingway defines it. In fiction truth means the truth about your own feelings at the moment they exist. That's a very orthodox definition. But of course since we are people we don't only have feelings, we also have a brain. It's fine to have the truth about feelings but it depends on what kind of novel you are writing. If you write a simple love story with no real social background then feelings are all that count. But if you write a novel about Vietnam and limit yourself just to the

15

feelings of the rank-and-file soldiers then it may be a disaster. What comes out of it may be a gross caricature of history, and that is dangerous.

When you write on any historical theme you have to take into account what you know about the historical situation and not just what you feel about it. And in fact Hemingway did precisely that; if you read *For Whom the Bell Tolls* you find it's not a novel just about the feelings of Maria and Robert. There is a lot more to it. But what Hemingway meant by his definition simply is that you shouldn't fake feelings. Patriotism, for example. Some people have no patriotic feelings, but they are expected to have them, so they pretend. Nowadays the opposite is often true; its very fashionable not to be patriotic. You can see it in the United States, even in this country. You might have really nice feelings about Canada but you don't show them if you are sophisticated. A genuine writer simply must express his honest feelings but, it doesn't mean that he should ignore his thoughts.

INTERVIEWER

You also suggest that something written well may have many meanings. Would this be something that gets close to your understanding of truth?

SKVORECKY

Ah, well that's another quote from Hemingway. Hemingway was dead-set against preconceived symbolism. I am too, in the sense that you can first think about possible symbols to use and then build a story around the symbols. I, too, think if you describe a thing well it may have many meanings. If I may point to my own book, *The Bass Saxophone*, for example. Many people have talked to me and they have their own interpretation of the meaning of the story and to be quite honest I am not absolutely sure what the story means. But there is a strong feeling about it; it is based on an actual event, and I was in a state of mind that was probably conducive to improvisation and to inspiration. That's what I mean when I say if you write something really well it may have more meanings than just one.

INTERVIEWER

In the essay "Red Music" you talk about fidelity to your craft. One of my favourite passages from your essays is: "I was writing about fidelity, about the sole real art there is, about what one must be true to, come hell or high water; what must be done to the point of collapse . . ." Could you comment on this?

The Bass Saxophone was written under very specific circumstances. At the time there was a counter-reaction to the Stalinist years when only socialist realism was permitted. In those years if you didn't write so that every half-literate could understand you then you were bad. And then when Stalin died there was this upheaval and suddenly everyone became terribly snobbish. Unless you wrote things that nobody could understand you were regarded as passé. This is a simplification, naturally, but it gives you the gist of the matter. I was always a more or less traditional storyteller and I read about myself in articles and they said: "Oh, he's a good storyteller, he has humour and so on, but he hasn't really anything new to say. He's a traditional storyteller." People were praised when they just imitated Kafka or Beckett; they were all imitations of these absurdist writers. I don't think there was ever any genuine Czech Kafka except Franz Kafka, but many people started writing very convoluted stories that were so hard to penetrate and if you did penetrate them you wondered whether they were worth telling. Most of them had been realists like myself and traditional storytellers. I simply refused to do that. I don't believe in that sort of literature. I respect Kafka very much, but to him it came naturally. He didn't say to himself, "I must write like nobody else." He was being faithful to himself. It was then that I wrote The Bass Saxophone, which is my response to the snobbishness of the times.

INTERVIEWER

What do you mean when you use the term "ideology"?

SKVORECKY

I just use the word ideology as Friedrich Engels used it. It's what Engels defined as false consciousness. It means you believe in a certain vision of society or life and you think it's an objective vision, the way things are; but, in fact, you are a prisoner of false consciousness. In actual fact things are different because they are more complicated than in your ideological vision. An ideological writer adjusts his experience to his preconceived ideas. The typical product of ideology is socialist realism. In the fifties if you wanted to write a novel all the working class characters had to be nice people, all the capitalists had to be just lousy crooks, and the bourgeois could be wavering characters, mostly bad; but there could be some bourgeois in whose mind the good and the bad fight. Either the good wins, in which case the bourgeois also becomes a positive character, or it loses and he becomes a negative character. This is preconceived literature.

My god, I know many working class people—I have worked in several factories—and some are great and some are crooks. And I have known some very good manufacturers. There was one right here in Toronto who helped us very much when we started a publishing house—Mr. Prokop Havlík. He owned a factory in the war. They made propellers. He was a rich man and a very nice man and he was a capitalist, and so if I put him in a novel in Czechoslovakia I would have to change his character into an exploiting monster because otherwise it wouldn't be published. That is what I mean by ideological writing. It doesn't just have to be socialist realism. It can be anything. If you are a black man or a feminist and you write a novel about whites and all the whites and all the men are bad, for instance—those are simply preconceived ideas. Not all gentlemen prefer blondes.

INTERVIEWER
Can you ever separate yourself from ideology then?

SKVORECKY
I think that is the duty of every writer: to try as hard as he or she can to separate himself or herself from preconceived ideas. I will have a new novel translated called *The Miracle Game* and it is about the year 1968 primarily. I had a very deep distaste for Communism and the Communists but I tried to present them as they really are, some of them are bad and some are good. One of the central characters is a headmistress in a school. She talks like Stalin and is a pillar of orthodoxy, but when it comes to concrete things she suddenly melts and sees the other side of the story and usually tries to help the "class enemies" among her students. What happens to her is that when faced with gross injustice against those "class enemies" her real consciousness makes a hole in her false consciousness and she sees like the child in the Andersen fairy tale about the Emperor's new clothes.

It is absolutely false to believe that you can't extricate yourself from ideology; you *can* extricate yourself from ideology. If not 100 percent then 99 percent. And also consider what people usually say here about exiles: "Well, I can understand why you are anti-Communist but you must realize that you are biased." But if they murder half of your family, and if they put one hundred thousand people into concentration camps, and execute five hundred innocent people then, my god, you aren't really biased; you are being very objective. It's the anti-Communists who are biased. By their false consciousness.

Would you say that ideology is always negative for you?

SKVORECKY
Certainly in art it is a negative thing. In politics it is probably sometimes necessary and even useful because you cannot arouse people by appealing solely to their pure reason—very few people are able to do that—you have to influence them somehow. But fiction is not for that.

INTERVIEWER
What do you see as the difference between implicit ideological structures (in the West for example, in feminism) and explicitly repressive regimes?

SKVORECKY
I would say if you are an intelligent person the implicit ideologies can motivate you only to some extent. We are intelligent people. Every second person has a university education; why should he or she fall blindly for an ideology? Some people do that. Feminism or whatever. Like any such movement it has its extremes. On one extreme you have these fanatics who simply hate men as such and who would prefer to have them put away; and on the other extreme you have women who are dead-set against any feminist movement. But life is a compromise; the truth is usually somewhere in the middle. Much of what the feminists have been saying, and they have been saying it for two hundred years probably, is true, and much of what the extreme spokespersons say is silly. That's what we have a brain for, and we should use it as much as possible.

INTERVIEWER
You have suggested that we must distinguish between ideas and ideology. How does one do so?

SKVORECKY
There is, for instance, an idea of social justice which may be formulated in different ways in different societies but which essentially means that people who are honest and people who work should not be desperately poor, for instance. The rest of society is then obligated to take care of people who can't support themselves for some reason—sick people or

19

people who live a more miserable life than they deserve—and that's the social justice idea. But once you change it into an ideology and say that capitalism is exploitation and therefore there should be a dictatorship of the proletariat then you very soon create another set of injustices.

In *Engineer* Danny suggests that every serious novel has the same thesis. I take it then that you are not opposed to messages in novels—something that is somewhat out of favour these days?

No. But again the message is something like symbolism. The message has to come out of what is being narrated. If you were to ask me about the message of *Engineer* I wouldn't be able to define it precisely. I think that it is simply humanity. I think that the basic message of all good novels is that they make the readers feel what the human situation is in various societies at various times. If you read an excellent early nineteenth-century novel set in Ireland you know what the human situation was at that time. If you read a bad novel, a Harlequin romance for example, then I don't know if you get any feeling for the human situation. And so I think that is the basic message. And novels have of course specific messages; the war novels do, for instance.

How would you define realism? In a number of places you seem to suggest that there is a close connection between realism and the dream.

I don't think that anybody has ever been able to define realism. There are many very scholarly works on realism and obviously it means different things in different times, but I simply think that if the reader reading your work feels that this is how it is, then it is realism. And it may be Kafka. Think of *The Castle*, for instance. What does it mean? It is very difficult to say, but if you read it you feel that there is some aspect of reality there. It isn't just fantasy. Any book by Kafka. There is one story called "The Burrow" which is an absolutely unrealistic story about an animal which is never described, and that animal tries to build a burrow for himself because he has an enemy who is after him and wants to eat him. The story is about how this poor animal devises various corridors so that the burrow would be absolutely safe; it has nothing to do with reality and yet you feel something of reality in it. I read the story at a time in my life when I really read it as a very real story. It was during the war when I committed that piece of sabotage and I felt caught because I knew that if they came for me there was nowhere to hide. I read this unrealistic story and yet at that moment I read it as utter realism. And so I think if you read something and you recognize: "this is how things are," then it is realism. It may not be presented as realism, but if it's really strong you always have the feeling of recognition. It isn't just a flimsy fantasy; it has roots in something that is real.

INTERVIEWER

One of the epigraphs to a chapter in *Engineer* is from Colin Wilson. He suggests that the daydream is the true basis of all literature. Do you agree?

SKVORECKY

He of course didn't mean that as an argument against realism. He simply believed what Freud and Goethe and Mark Twain believed although they put it in different ways: the novel is always more real than reality because it is mixed with imagination. *Dichtung und Wahrheit*, Goethe said.

INTERVIEWER

To what extent do you think that people who haven't experienced war firsthand can understand it from secondhand references; stories we are told, television, movies?

SKVORECKY

If you haven't experienced something it is much harder for you to get a meaning, but it is possible. For instance it drives me mad that some people never read anything on things they don't know about from personal experience, and yet they express opinions, even pass judgments. Last week in *Maclean's* there was a letter to the editor which said: "How do we know the Nicaraguan regime is Communist?" My god, how do we know it is? The Sandinistas make no secret of it, all you have to do is read the speeches of their leaders. And it makes no difference that some wear dog collars. A novel written under a Communist regime is likely filled with allusions you don't understand if you haven't lived there. So you have to read some books on it. *One Day in the Life of Ivan Denisovich* by Solzhenitsyn, for example. It is a very powerful story even if you know nothing of the background but it becomes much more significant and comprehensible if you read things on Soviet history and Stalin and so on.

It is very difficult, and few people can understand things that are not part of their personal experience. That is the unfortunate fact. You cannot even blame them very much because it takes hard work to understand things that do not affect you. But it can be done. I think in the case of intellectual people, people with a university education, it should be done, because it becomes criminal to be naive at some point. Mr Chamberlain in September 1938 returned victoriously from Munich with the peace treaty and said, "Why should we go to war for a people we know nothing about?" He should—and could—have learned something about those people he may have then avoided the war by not signing the Munich Agreement. The German army, at that time, was not yet fully under Hitler's control.

INTERVIEWER

Do you see your own novels as advancing an understanding of various different experiences?

SKVORECKY

Well I think people that are interested in this sort of thing, in life in other countries, may profit from them to some extent. You have read some of my books so you know they are not so much about politics. For instance, *The Engineer of Human Souls*. Many reviews say that it is about Communism but there is so little about Communism in it. There are, of course, some passages but it's not about Communism. It's simply a novel about life. The hero only happens to have lived under three different regimes.

INTERVIEWER

Kundera has complained that his novels are always read politically—even if there are only three political lines—and the rest is overlooked. Have you encountered a similar problem?

SKVORECKY

It could also be said that his novels are taken apolitically by many people if there are three apolitical lines in them. His novels are very political. He said that just to defend himself, to present himself as a real writer and not just a political propagandist—which he is not, of course. If you read his novels *only* as political messages then you read them wrongly, but you can't take out the politics. Take the last one, *The Unbearable Lightness of Being*, there can't be anything more political, but it's a good novel. Again it gives you some feeling about a human situation.

It is not a general trend that my own novels are treated politically; that depends on the reviewer. I was interested in the fact that no one treated *Dvorak in Love* politically . . . although it contains certain political things. But they are probably too hidden.

INTERVIEWER

Do you find that your work is treated differently by Czech reviewers?

SKVORECKY

Czech reviewers know much more about the background and also they read the Czech original and so they can appreciate the language of the dialogues. I like to play with the Czech language and I use various regional dialects and slang. Some of those things simply cannot be translated. Paul Wilson is an excellent translator, but there are things that are technically impossible. For instance, in *Engineer,* you know that loquacious young woman Dotty. In the original she speaks American Czech which is a language that cannot be translated into English; it could be into French or Italian or other non-English languages. That's the way that Czechs speak in North America—Czech corrupted in a very funny way by English, and you can't translate that. How can you corrupt English by English? I think Paul Wilson did it very well—the character is still quite funny but in the Czech original she is much funnier because of her language. It happens to every non-English language in North America because people live in surroundings that force them to speak English all day. Then they get home and talk in their own language to their family but they can't remember some words—usually those in daily use—in their own language. Their mother tongue becomes a mixture of English and Italian and Japanese or whatever, which has a terrific humorous potential.

INTERVIEWER

Havel mentions that Westerners have a very different understanding of certain words—like freedom or democracy—than Easterners. Do you ever feel that you have problems expressing what you want to express because of limitations in the language?

SKVORECKY

Well frankly I don't think that people understand such words as freedom or democracy differently. They simply appreciate them differently. Freedom is freedom; you are free to say what is on your mind. That is

23

the same in the East and the West. But in the West anybody can do it so you don't think so much about it because you have it. And in the East you don't have freedom so you think much more of it. I think it's not a matter of different understandings of words but often a different awareness of their value. If you can breathe normally then you don't think about air. But when they lock you up in a gas chamber and suddenly you are in trouble because of a lack of air you think about it. That is my understanding, but I am a very pedestrian man you know. Havel is a philosopher.

INTERVIEWER

When Danny is talking about reviewers of his novels he says that they are literate but they don't understand literature. To what extent does this apply to reviewers of your novels?

SKVORECKY

In this instance he talks about the exile reviewers and that is a different thing because in exile there are very few literary scholars. In all the many various papers published all over the world in Czech, books are usually reviewed by people who have no idea what literature means. If they like the book it's nice and if they don't like it it is terrible. Their criteria are sometimes extremely funny. For instance, I wrote a novel which is very popular among the Czechs called *The Tank Corps*, a satire on the Czech army. One reviewer here in Toronto said that you cannot eat while you're reading such a novel because it is full of disgusting four-letter words. Well, soldiers don't talk like seminarians, at least not like the seminarians of yesteryear. Is that a literary criterion? Food is not edible while you are reading? That is an example of how these amateur reviewers do it. But there are by now quite a few good literary scholars in exile—we have just published a book by a woman, Helena Koskova, who lives in Sweden and she is an excellent scholar. She wrote a book of essays on contemporary Czech writers which is as sophisticated as anything you can read in English. But there are so many small regional papers published in Czech and they simply don't have people to review the books, people that would understand them.

INTERVIEWER

How does one understand literature then?

SKVORECKY

First of all, I think very few people would dare to criticize music if they didn't have any idea about harmony, point-, counter-point, the theoretical basics. But literature is made of words and most people can read so they think they understand it even though it is probably more complex than music. The technical basis for music is much better defined than the technical basis for literature. There *is* a technical basis, though. For instance, I wrote the script for a Czech film which is called *End of a Priest*, and it is the only film ever made in a communist state that is pro-Christian. We even had the script read by the archbishop of Prague before it went into production, secretly you know. But when this film was shown in Toronto to the Czech community there was an explosion of resentment. "This is another Communist, anti-religious slander . . ." And there were articles in the Catholic papers that condemned the movie as Communist trash. They didn't get the meaning because it is a comedy and these are simple people mostly who never associate humour with religion. Religion is something deadly serious and when you have a priest who is comical then you are against the priest and consequently against religion. That's because such people don't know the A-B-C of art. They don't know that a comic portrait may be very flattering, it may be a tribute to someone, and yet it may be very funny.

INTERVIEWER

In *Engineer* Danny privileges a form of literary interpretation that concentrates on the concrete. An example of the opposite of this is the exploration of colour in *The Scarlet Letter* . . .

SKVORECKY

The Scarlet Letter was obviously meant as a symbolic novel but it is not the most important thing about it. It is not what is beautiful about it. I have met people in Prague who have read *The Scarlet Letter* who knew nothing about the Puritans and who didn't really notice any symbolism. But they loved the novel because it is a human tragedy. It's a moving human tragedy. That is what I mean when I say that concrete reality is always primary. *The Scarlet Letter*, for instance, has a very beautiful symmetrical structure but how many people notice it? And it's not necessary to notice it because it is so powerful in its, if you wish, message. It portrays the human situation at a certain time in history. The symmetrical structure and the play with colours is something that is added to it; it makes it even more enjoyable for those who notice it. But even if you don't notice it, it is still a powerful novel.

At another point Danny says of his novels: all his protagonists are losers in one way or another. Do you think that the same holds true for your own novels? If so, what do you mean by a loser?

SKVORECKY

Well, I think that Danny, at least when he was younger, didn't have any luck with women; he always lost in the battle of the sexes. He was always exploited by all these girls and, in that sense, he was a loser. But, you know, I think that everybody is a loser in the sense that you never achieve really what you want to achieve. When you are young you may think about becoming a great rich famous person. Then you may become a rich famous person. But you also expect absolute happiness. Then you are rich and famous and suddenly you find out it's nice, it's better to be rich and famous than to be poor and unknown, but it's not pure happiness. So in that sense everybody is a loser. People have illusions due to a lack of experience and that is as it should be. If you didn't have any illusions why care? But absolute happiness is something that can never be achieved.

INTERVIEWER

How influenced are you by Nietzsche? Other philosophers?

SKVORECKY

I don't think I have ever been influenced by Nietzsche. The only philosopher who interested me to some extent was Schopenhauer—not that I would know him by heart—but I have read some books of his and he was quite an influence—a very depressing influence. It comes up in *Dvorak*, in Dvorak's discussion with Seidl. He uses Schopenhauer against Dvorak's optimistic Christian view that all is right with the world. Other than that I don't think I was influenced by philosophers. I like to read histories of philosophy, especially Greek philosophy. When you read old Greek philosophers you can see how the human mind emerges from the chaos. Aristotle, for example, is the father of science, but he had so many things wrong. But he had a systematic mind and that is remarkably refreshing. Or Socrates. And if you realize this was two thousand and— how many?—three hundred, four hundred years ago, you see that people were intelligent even in those dark ages.

INTERVIEWER

The eternal return comes up in both your work and Kundera's. At one point in *Engineer* Danny says: "Not changing means remaining faithful. And seeing things always with fresh, unexhausted eyes. The only change is towards the worse. It's a law of nature." To what extent do you agree with this?

SKVORECKY

By that I think I mean that one should remain faithful to certain dearly held ideas that you formulate when you are young and that you should not betray them without a *real* reason. So, for instance, in my case it is writing and jazz music. I had certain ideas about writing — how one should write and how one should be honest in writing — and I have never changed. Many of my colleagues have changed terribly and several times. Some became socialist realists and as soon as it was over they became Kafkaesque and now they are somewhere in between maybe. I have never changed in that respect.

INTERVIEWER

Do you follow the latest trends in literary theory? Deconstruction and so on?

SKVORECKY

I don't understand them. There may be very clever ideas but it's so hard to plod your way through these articles. Henry James is a man with a literary theory and he is not so easy to read — I mean his introductions — but they always contain some useful ideas as to how to write which I don't find in Derrida and others.

INTERVIEWER

Danny states that "all art that makes us think is valuable." How do you define thinking here?

SKVORECKY

I mean that if you finish a book and close it and you still have it with you then you are thinking. You think about the book and the problems it addressed and somehow it stays with you. Whereas some books you forget and you can't recollect anything.

INTERVIEWER

Is there any way to get Irene to think, for instance?

SKVORECKY

Well, I think she is not a stupid girl; she is quite intelligent and when

she wants she can write even good papers. She is just a bit lazy. She is
very young of course.

Do you think that reading can somehow compensate for the
unquestioning and forgetful history that she assimilates from her environment?

SKVORECKY

I think it can. Because nobody can experience everything. And if you
read a convincing, good book you learn about things that otherwise
would never become part of your experience. So certainly it can. For
sick people literature means much more than for healthy people. I
remember one of my books, *Miss Silver's Past*, was published in braille
and I once got such a moving letter from a girl who had been blind since
birth and she obviously had no experience of this sort. She wrote about
twenty pages and she was raving about the novel. I could see that to her
it was not just literature, it was a life experience, and she lived with it.
Literature can compensate for very much.

INTERVIEWER

Danny says, "I don't have such an absolute faith in the power of words
to believe that what we do not say does not exist." But do you believe
that some things exist simply because they are said? Would you agree
that a novel doesn't just translate experience, it also creates it?

SKVORECKY

A novel certainly contributes to experience, because it is a mixture of
observation and imagination. You know many people are not moved by
reality — they may be incapable, insensitive — and these people, when
they read a really powerful novel, *Madame Bovary* for example, are moved.
The novel does something for them. There is a Milos Forman movie,
Loves of a Blonde, about a common, ordinary factory girl – there are
thousands of them just working in factories – and suddenly you get a
very moving story. She is a simple young girl who is so full of complexity;
but she can't verbalize it, of course. Faulkner does this all the time. Many
of his characters are very simple people and yet he attributes to them
such a complexity of mind and he verbalizes it. They themselves don't
so you could say that he is not realistic because they really don't think
in these long complex sentences. But it is a verbalization of a complexity
that exists even in very simple people. In that sense, literature creates or

contributes to our knowledge of reality.

In *Miss Silver's Past* Lenka rejects what she calls "philosophical twaddle" on the basis of her contact with Hemingway's work. Would you reject it on the same grounds? How do you distinguish between art and philosophy?

SKVORECKY

She probably says that in one of the conversations with Leden. The point of *Miss Silver's Past* is that Karel Leden, who is supposed to be an intellectual, simply cannot comprehend that this brilliant girl marries a simple-minded physical training instructor and not him. And this indicates that there are other values in life besides brilliance and the ability to talk philosophically. It is a very moralistic novel. She represents something very healthy in life, something very traditional, but very healthy. Karel Leden, as you know, is very superficial. He is a product of a superficial milieu but he is not so superficial that he doesn't see himself in the correct light in the end.

INTERVIEWER

Did you suggest the English title for *Miss Silver's Past*, which differs somewhat from the Czech?

SKVORECKY

No, that was suggested by the American publisher originally. It is probably a good title commercially but it gives away too much. The Czech title translates as "The Lion Cub" because Lenka's real Jewish name is Leona which means a lioness.

INTERVIEWER

Do you get the same pleasure from writing your detective stories as you do from writing novels? Do you take them as seriously?

SKVORECKY

I don't know if I get the same pleasure but I certainly get pleasure. If I may I will quote Dvorak; he says: "You know, I enjoy doing a symphony in the same way that I enjoy doing a silly polka." Music was simply an obsession with him. Writing detective stories, for instance, does not have to be cheap or demeaning. You write them as well as you can. They can rarely be as complex and profound as serious novels because it is a formula (i.e. a genre) and the formula must be respected. If you don't respect it then you are not really writing a detective story. *Miss Silver's Past* is technically a detective story because there is a murder and clues and so on. For that matter, Faulkner wrote detective stories like *Intruder in the Dust* but nobody reads them in the same way that you read Agatha Christie. I have great respect for detective story writers because they fulfill a very useful function in life.

INTERVIEWER

Would I be right in thinking that Lojza in *Engineer* is the sort of Communist you would define as "a Communist but otherwise a decent sort"?

SKVORECKY

He is nothing; he is neither a Communist nor an anti-Communist. He is a very simple person; he is quite mentally limited. For example, he never realizes that this daughter of his could not possibly be his although he could have very easily found out because he first slept with his wife only after the wedding. He is a simpleton. He is a good person, a hard worker, and he loves his family, but he is terribly simple. He can be misused by any regime that is bent on misusing him. In the course of the novel he constantly changes; he starts by being grateful to the SS General Heydrich for being sent to the spa. Then he's deadset against collective farms and eventually he becomes an enthusiastic member of a collective farm. By the way, he is based on a real character. I still keep getting letters from him like the ones that are printed in the novel.

INTERVIEWER

One of his letters is both the first and the last in *Engineer* — in fact one of his letters closes the book. Do you pay a lot of attention to the structure of the book in this way?

SKVORECKY

Oh yes, certainly. That is not haphazard.

INTERVIEWER

How do you go about structuring one of your longer novels like *Engineer* or *Dvorak*?

SKVORECKY

Well, *Engineer* was a special case. It was similar with *The Miracle Game*.

I had so many stories to tell. The traditional way of writing a long novel chronologically requires too many people. Somerset Maugham, for instance, uses a philosophical term called *pons assinorum* (assinine bridge, bridge for asses). He applies it to the necessity of writing what sometimes is referred to as continuity passages, passages that don't have any aesthetic appeal but just connect sequences. But you can do away with them. Here fiction learned a lot from the film. Short cuts. In the old films there was always a transition, a dissolve perhaps, and you saw a calendar with the leaves falling which indicated the passage of time and then again you dissolve to another sequence. Things like that. My problem was how to put this rich material together without having to write lots of these transitional passages and arranging them chronologically. Chronology does not really connect things except in a very mechanical way. If you leaf through various experiences you find that they are connected by other means than time. That was one thing.

The other thing was that I wanted to express the chaotic view of modern life. We are bombarded by impressions. People in the nineteenth-century were not bombarded by so many things. But now you come home and you turn on the TV news and *boom* comes something from Africa. I got this idea when I flew from Prague to London in 1969 after the invasion. I left Prague on a very gloomy day after the funeral of Jan Palach, the student who immolated himself, and it was a very dreary gloomy winter day. Everybody was depressed. And then forty-five minutes later we landed in London and it was a very bright sunny winter day. There were jolly people walking around and it was divided by only forty-five minutes. That is what gave me the idea for this structure.

INTERVIEWER

When you accepted the Neustadt Prize in 1980 you were compared to Dvorak. Do you think the comparison apt?

SKVORECKY

They did compare me to Dvorak? I think that in the sense that Dvorak liked to write everything. He wrote very light polkas, little pieces, bagatelles, and also great symphonies and operas. He just liked music on all levels. He said: "My heart is never so happy as when I hear a good brass band." I don't think that a modern serious sophisticated composer would say that. Perhaps he would, I don't know. But not many composers would say that. He was happy with any good and genuine sort of music.

31

If "premature cynicism is not a characteristic of young Canadians"—
and I see no reason why it would be—what is?

People are so different, I hesitate to make any generalizations. One
quality that is obvious is simply the political naïveté. But they are not
to blame for it because their elders are as naive as them. At least they
are seeking and I think they are open-minded. I am quite frank about
my political opinions, in class for instance, and I have never encountered
a really vicious opposition from students. I'm sure that many of them
were leftist or maybe even radicals and they did discuss things with me
but it was never vicious. A real ideologue, when he doesn't like
something, condemns you and leaves the class. That has never happened
to me.

I especially enjoy the creative writing courses because they are small
and you get to know the people and they write stories which reveal a
lot about them and about their lives and about Canada as they see it.
These are very enjoyable classes and I must say that technically there are
a surprising number of Canadian students who have the potential to
become really good writers. The trouble is it is a very difficult thing to
become a good writer in a country where nothing very drastic happens.
That's why I admire Henry James. He was a gentleman of leisure and
probably nothing very drastic happened to him and yet he was such a
great writer. It is very easy to write an acceptable novel if you survive
a war in which you were a soldier. You have to be very untalented not
to produce something readable about that experience. This year I have
an excellent class, people who can write delightful stories. Of course,
the stories are not very, what we would call, significant, because they
are about very minor problems and they are young people. It's always
much easier to become a readable writer if you live in a dictatorship.
Provided you get out in time and publish what you know.

Nevertheless you do suggest that there are a number of similarities
between people despite historic and cultural differences. The parallels
between Nadia and Irene—both repeat "that's delicious"—are only one
example. How do these similarities fit with the differences?

SKVORECKY

That's the point. All these young people remind me so much about myself and my friends when we were eighteen or nineteen. Basic things are common everywhere. I remember that Egyptian Pharaoh Tutankhamen. He was a Pharaoh who was quite insignificant but somehow his grave remained intact. When they excavated the grave they found a gold coffin and then there was another coffin—there were about four of five coffins—and when they got to the mummy they found a bunch of field flowers on the chest of the Pharaoh. He died very young, at nineteen, but he was already married to a very young girl. With all the splendour and gold and diamonds, she put a bunch of field flowers on him, which is so . . . up-to-date. So things don't change, the basic things don't change. Obviously there was affection between the two; she could have put a diamond necklace on him and instead she put simple flowers. That is, for me, a proof that the basic things in life don't change. And it's not different with different races. That's why I called *The Swell Season* a text about the most important things in life. It's about love, and about flirting and things connected with human relationships of a very basic nature because I think they are the most important.

INTERVIEWER

It is pretty clear what you are able to give your students here; I am wondering what you get in return?

SKVORECKY

Well, I don't know what I can give Canadian students. But Canada gave me one thing and that is freedom. And that is what I still appreciate. I will never get used to it to the point that I forget about it. This society does not oppress me and there is no legal danger if you don't commit crimes, unless there is a big judicial error, so you can feel safe. The most precious thing for an intellectual is to express himself freely, in print or in public. And that is taken away from intellectuals in dictatorships. They can express themselves freely only in private, carefully checking whether there are any bugs and things like that. In the long run a lack of freedom almost always leads to crimes, I mean crimes committed by the government. If you can't criticize, if you have no free press, anything may happen. If you have no free press and a strong well-paid police force the establishment can do anything they want.

INTERVIEWER

In what sense do you think "so what?" is the "question of the century"?

33

SKVORECKY

That was, of course, a reflection of the times. It was a cynicism that befell most people after the Soviet invasion in 1968. You know that song where Hana Ulrychová sings: "So what? I say, so what? /When headlong down the days / The universe is rushing, rushing on / At the crossing of absolute ways . . ." That's the cynicism of the times. This was a very specific sort of cynicism born out of desperation. These people had just been through a very hopeful period based on the Dubcek reforms and suddenly the Soviet army came and everything was crushed so they suddenly said that nothing has any sense. Everything is hopeless and dark. And so what?

Interview by Barbara Leckie

ROO BORSON

In the wake of her highly praised 1981 book A Sad Device, *Timothy Findley remarked that Roo Borson "creates a compelling sense of wonder in all her work." Since then, Mark Abley has called her "the first major poet to emerge in Canada in the '80s," and Fred Cogswell has placed her "firmly in the front rank of younger Canadian poets."*

Roo Borson was born in Berkeley, California in 1952, and studied at the University of California at Santa Barbara and at Goddard College in Vermont, before doing an MFA in Creative Writing at the University of British Columbia. She lived for some time in Vancouver and Toronto, working at a variety of jobs between bouts of full-time writing, before returning to live for two years in Oakland, near Berkeley, and another in Los Alamos, New Mexico. In September 1986 she moved back to Toronto. Borson's first book, Landfall, *was published by Fiddlehead in 1977, and was followed by* In the Smoky Light of the Fields *(1980),* Rain *(1980), and* Night Walk *(1981). Since* A Sad Device, *Borson has won the 1982 CBC Literary Competition and has published a major collection,* The Whole Night, Coming Home, *(1984), which was a finalist for the Governor General's Award. A recent collection,* The Transparence of November/Snow *(1985) is co-written with Kim Maltman.*

This interview was conducted entirely by mail in March and April of 1986. The questions are posed in a semi-basement flat in downtown Montreal, where an overfed snowbank blocks all views from the front window. Borson replies from the dining room table of an apartment in old government housing in Los Alamos, looking out on Ponderosa pines, a narrow canyon, and the pink-orange volcanic wall of the adjoining mesa. Behind her is a Navajo rug bought by her grandmother before Borson's birth. "Los Alamos," Borson writes, "is one of the stranger towns on earth. It came into being only because it was the site chosen for the secret development of the bomb. Before that, it was a boy's school. It's a ghetto of scientists and spouses (mainly non-working wives) and children. There is an amazing proliferation of churches. There are discretely placed fallout shelters. The undercurrent of life is coloured by the major employment—classified weapons research—while on the surface there are Kiwanis Club pancake breakfasts and high school sports. *The town is built on three mesas connected by bridges, at 7,500 feet. Nearby, the landscape is spectacular, and dotted with Hispanic towns and Indian pueblos, including San Ildefonso Pueblo, where my grandmother bought Santa Clara pottery from the famous potter, Maria."*

As Borson answers the questions, Kim Maltman is at work at the lab (not on weapons), and their elderly cat is complaining or sitting on the papers. There is a pile of well-read issues of the Saturday Globe and Mail nearby. Outside, spring is trying to come to the old apricot tree. During the course of the interview there is a cold snap, flurries among the blossoms. As the last questions are sent out, the pile of snow in front of the interviewer's window is smaller and blacker, divulging the grime it has been saving up all winter. Meanwhile, in Los Alamos, the apricot tree is now in full bloom, and the air has turned soft.

You must have been pleased by the reception of *The Whole Night, Coming Home.*

BORSON

Ah. The true answer is yes and no. Several individuals whose work and judgement I respect felt very good about the book, and, for me, that's the best measure and one of the best rewards. The poems moved people in readings, too, and that matters. Also, it was reviewed enthusiastically for the most part, though two of the reviews happened to fall into categories that infuriate me: in one, the reviewer actually didn't think it was necessary to read the second half of the book before pronouncing on it, and in the second, my work was attributed, in style, to authors I hadn't read. Also, I'm sad that it hasn't sold more copies. I did manage to say some things in that book that I really wanted to say—not "discursively," but intuitively, by understatement—and I hope they're things people would appreciate hearing.

INTERVIEWER

You mention readings. Do you like doing them, are they important to your work? Do you sometimes find you learn a lot about your work when you read it out loud? A different perspective perhaps . . .

BORSON

Lots of writers say that they can tell what works and what doesn't work when they read aloud to an audience. That hasn't been my experience. Sometimes I learn which poems people like to hear out loud, but I learn nothing about the page. I already know which phrases run less than trippingly over the tongue because I speak aloud when I revise. Sometimes such phrases do work well silently on the page, and other times I simply can't find a less awkward way to say the thing I want to say. Consonants butt up against one another and get garbled.

I like doing some readings better than others. When I can tell that people are really listening, I like it. Then there's a force that binds me to the audience and to the oral space I'm filling. Although I don't improvise when reading—I read directly from the page—there's an improvisational quality to the pacing and the relationship with the audience. Emotionally, it's a conversation.

Reading is also valuable because it's a way of introducing one's work to people who aren't familiar with it. It's doubly rewarding when someone comes up afterwards and says "My wife/husband dragged me to this and, to be honest, I was expecting to be bored—I hate poetry—but

I really enjoyed this . . ."

INTERVIEWER

I'm interested in what you've been working on since *The Whole Night*. I notice that the poems in your recent Quarry book, *The Transparence of November/Snow*, are signed by neither you nor Kim Maltman. How did these poems come about? Is each poem co-authored?

BORSON

The poems in *Transparence* are more or less contemporary with those in the first half of *Whole Night* and in Kim's book *Softened Violence*. As often happens, the timing of publication doesn't precisely reflect the time of composition. As for the matter of signing of poems, it's interesting that none of the poets to whom I showed the book when it first came out were able to see the identifying mark on each page—but it took a glass blower, a visual artist, approximately two seconds. He saw the page as a field, with everything on it, while the more verbally-oriented readers burrowed straight into the meat of the poem. Kim and I talked about the question at length, and finally decided that the best thing would be a pair of unobtrusive marks, such as the ones the publishers chose. We felt the authorship of the poems was secondary to the poems, and, on the other hand, we didn't want people to spend all their time trying to second-guess the poems as to their authorship rather than reading them! The book isn't a conversation between two distinct voices or two distinct roles like the one Pat Lane and Lorna Uher [Lorna Crozier] wrote together. There are shadings of voice, sometimes reflected in imagistic echoes, but it's not a series of letters back and forth.

So the poems aren't co-authored, but, as always, they are to some extent collaborative efforts. The way Kim and I work is that one of us writes a poem until it seems like it could be close to finished, or else until it's so frustrating that an outside eye or ear is needed. We work on poems privately and then show them back and forth, through many revisions, trying to iron out problems. We are each other's first and toughest critics and most enduring supporters. That is, we each believe totally in the other's vision, and yet—or because of that—we see the failings in each poem, or we try. Sometimes we just talk about what's wrong, other times we rewrite each other's lines. We have complementary weaknesses. I'm best at seeing the skeleton of a poem inside the flesh of too many words—I cross out chunks from my own poems and from Kim's. Kim is best at seeing where ideas have become didactic, and also at recasting syntax. We have different ears for rhythm but can hear each other's music. Amazingly, after all this, our poems are usually very different from one another's. We do have different overall visions of the world.

The way *Transparence* got started was that we both found ourselves writing wintry lyrics now and then. I was working on the first half of *Whole Night* and Kim was working on *Softened Violence*. We were both writing about people, and Kim's poems especially were very socially-oriented. I think we each had to "let off steam" or relax by writing something completely different. We were working on these big solitary projects, and part of their imagery was hot, summery weather. So a few of these short wintry lyrics started happening, alongside. They obviously didn't fit in with what we were each doing—and we'd had the idea some time before to write a book together. The poems were very close tonally, and they seemed to combine easily. So then we had this side project which either of us could work on when the other stuff became claustrophobic. We were then writing poems intentionally for the book, a few of them oblique response poems in terms of image. Echo poems. It was lots of fun. Someday we'll do another book together.

INTERVIEWER

Sounds like an ideal working relationship. In what direction do you feel your new work to be going? Are there certain things you will be trying to accomplish in your next book, new subjects to tackle, new regions to articulate?

BORSON

My next book is going to be a miscellany. *Whole Night* was united thematically, and I intended it to be read from beginning to end, like a novel, not by skipping around. *Transparence* is united tonally and imagistically, though it moves through phases. The next book will be more of a straight collection. I think it's over half-finished now, so I can give you an idea of what's in it so far. There's a section of Ontario poems and prose poems, set in and outside Toronto. There's a longish piece I wrote last year in an alien state of mind. There are occasional pieces, set here and there, some short narratives and some imagistic lyrics. At the moment I've hit on a new cadence which can accommodate lists and rotating facets of a single subject. This phase will last for a spell and then change again. I've been writing almost a poem a day for a week, which is almost unheard of for me.

I'm not writing with any goal in mind at present. Actually, I can only discern my goals once I'm part way to having reached them. With *Whole*

Night, I finished a process of moving from writing about pure abstract landscape (as in my first book, *Landfall*)—well, abstract landscape *and* abstract formulations of emotions—to placing "real" people in a "real" landscape. In the long poem I mentioned before, called "Intent, Or the Weight of the World," I did away with landscape and tried to illumine a state of mind. I'm no longer troubled by those particular lacks in my writing—I feel I've filled them. I'm free-floating again.

And yes, there are always new regions to articulate. With me, this means changing styles, syntax, cadence. A new way of talking brings in new subjects, or vice versa.

INTERVIEWER

How *can* we illumine the mind without a landscape of some kind, without any reference to the physical? Words like "happy" or "sad" or "love" obviously aren't much help. I guess I'm just not sure what you mean by abstract landscape.

BORSON

By abstract landscape I simply mean generic landscape. Unidentified by specific flora, etc. To say "trees" instead of "alders" or "firs." To say "rock" instead of "sandstone." And there are gradations of course. You can still write a pretty generic landscape using firs and sandstone, but the more detail, the more identifiable the place becomes. It's important to some poems to take place in a certain locale; in others it's the general sense of a landscape that's important—a mountainous place or a beach, rather than Banff or Kitsilano.

I don't know of any poems that make no use of the physical, except maybe nonsense verse—but even there there's a sense of solidity, of a fantasy realm reassuringly familiar because the cadences make it so—the physical is what grounds us. But the setting can be more or less incidental to the action, and a setting can be represented by, say, a bough of blossoms rather than by a highly articulated scene which includes passing cars and a man in a tweed cap.

INTERVIEWER

Going in the opposite direction, are there particular ways in which you now find your early poetry, in books like *Landfall* or *Rain*, to be unsatisfactory?

BORSON

Yes, but no more so than I did at the time of writing them. What's

42

amazing is that there are a few poems in each book that I like, beyond just feeling an affection for the process of writing them. In each book a few poems are representative of the style I was trying to get at, and other poems indicate how I failed.

INTERVIEWER

In an interview three or four years ago (with Bruce Meyer and Brian O'Riordan) you spoke of the influence on your work of people like Louise Glück and especially Robert Bringhurst. What other writers, poets or otherwise, have you been reading lately? Have any of them been particularly important to the development of your own work?

BORSON

Though I've never been able to write like him, my current hero is Peter Handke. He speaks for the twentieth century. I'm not sure what I speak for, but it's not the whole tenor of our time.

Books I've loved lately: *The Book of Ebenezer Le Page* by G. B. Edwards, *The Master of Go* by Yasunari Kawabata, *The Engineer of Human Souls* by Josef Skvorecky. All of those are novels. Kim and I just went through the manuscript of a magnificent translation of Neruda's *The Heights of Machu Picchu* done by a physicist! In poetry, I'm dabbling and rereading. As I think I said in the interview you mentioned, I'm not sure who I'm influenced by, I just know who I'm crazy about. I've been away from Canada for so long that I feel a little out of touch with what's going on up there. I've been anxious to see the new Canadian books. I'll get my chance, now that we're moving back to Toronto.

INTERVIEWER

Funny, I just finished *Ebenezer Le Page* myself. It seems a neglected gem. I didn't think anybody else knew it existed! Do you know Neruda's little essay on "Impure Poetry"? It's always been a favourite of mine. "Let that be the poetry we search for: worn with the hand's obligation, as by acids, steeped in sweat and in smoke, smelling of lilies and urine, spattered diversely by the trades we live by, inside the law or beyond it. . ."

BORSON

No, I don't know it. I'll have to look it up. The sample sounds typically Nerudaesque.

INTERVIEWER

I was wondering about your work habits. Is there any particular time

43

of day when you write, or particular places? Do you work on your poetry quite regularly—almost every day—or in spurts?

It depends on whether I have a job or not. When I do, I have to fit writing in as best I can. When I don't, I often start off in the morning. Some mornings I'm not in the right frame for writing, so I do other things until I'm drawn to it again. I usually work in the living room or dining room in whatever place we're in—Kim and I move a lot. I type in the writing room. Whenever I can I work near a window. I spend a lot of time just gazing. I do work almost every day, often for most of the day, punctuated by a walk or a squash game or some cooking or letter-writing. Most days I read a little. Some days I just tinker, on and off, with a few lines. I have an attentive, jumpy mind. I move from poem to poem and back again in the course of a day. There's always the chance that when you look at a poem again you'll suddenly see the answer to a problem, or see a new problem. I hate referring to writing as "working," but it seems to be the verb in current use and of current pretensions. For me, it's playing.

Also, it can depend on what kind of poems I'm writing. Some are best suited to morning light and freshness (and blankness), others to afternoon and others to evening. I like to write poetry as a break from other things and vice versa. I do admire those writers who become obsessed with what they're working on and write night and day until it's done. If I concentrate too long on one activity I begin to hate it or else my mind goes blank.

Often I don't sleep well. Once in a while I note something down in the dark. When I'm sick I write in bed. Sometimes I dream in poetry.

I go through periods of despising all poetry, all literature. Then I play squash and bake pastries and wander the streets or the hills and wish I were travelling. And wish I could make lots of money. And read nothing but recipes and newspapers, *Natural History* and *National Geographic*.

You dream in poetry?!

Certainly. Usually I can only remember the last few lines when I wake up. Often in such dreams it's not my own poetry. I'll dream that I'm reading someone's new book or sitting in a reading hearing poetry that has of course never been written in real life. I remember two very vivid examples: in one, I was reading the first two poems in a new book of

Robert Pinsky's that he's never written; in the other I'm looking over Phyllis Webb's shoulder as she's reading aloud to an audience. In dreams the poetry is always superlative and startling. When I wake I try to write down what I can remember, and it's always startling, though not necessarily superlative. Sometimes I'm composing my own poetry. And sometimes there's a running narration to the action. I only dream in poetry once a month or so.

INTERVIEWER
Do you write in longhand or at the typewriter?

BORSON
Always in longhand, through several drafts. I type only when I think I may have a nearly "final" version, to see what it looks like. I revise until I pull my hair out, then send to magazines, then, after months have passed, revise some more. I revise again before a book is published. I have not yet written the final version of any poem. Unless I get the chance to do a revised edition of a book, I won't touch poems after book publication. I move on.

INTERVIEWER
You've been living back in the U.S. the past few years, in California, in New Mexico. Does this affect your poetry? Does it affect it mainly because of the differing physical landscapes, or more because of differing communities, societies?

BORSON
It affects it in that I do use landscapes in my writing. When I moved from Vancouver to Toronto, I wrote *Rain*, about Vancouver, then began writing about a city landscape rather than wilderness or countryside. In Toronto, I began *Whole Night*, looking back on the landscapes/lifescapes of my birthplace. In California I finished *Whole Night* and then wrote about Ontario. For a long time, as you can see, I wrote from memory. I'm no longer doing that—but I'm not using landscapes at the moment. It takes a while for a landscape to sink in. New Mexico probably won't appear in my poems until I move back to Toronto. Each morning in California I was shocked to step out the door to find the hibiscus bush, the freeway overpass, the shorts and T-shirts in February and the fog in July.

The poetry community around me has no effect on my output as far as I can see, but it makes a difference in other ways. Toronto is a fantastic literary centre for readings, particularly at Harbourfront. It's easy to hear a wide variety in a short space of time—it's a good way to decide if I'm interested in reading more of an author or not. In California, the Bay Area has been a premier literary spot for years. My grandmother, who died before I was born, knew Jack London slightly. There are wonderful poets there, Robert Pinsky, Robert Hass and Peter Dale Scott, who Kim and I met with over Canadian beer and poetry—a mini-salon. He was writing a fine book, a long sectioned poem in tercets. The Bolinas gang (including Bobbie Louise Hawkins, and Robert Creeley in earlier days) lives just up the coast. There's plenty going on in San Francisco. In Berkeley there are still half-crazed, drugged-out street poets, and there are the academics. There are fewer readings there than in Toronto, and they aren't free, so we kept yearning for Tuesday night at Harbourfront! Most of New Mexico, though unreal-ly beautiful, is a desert, literally and literarily. There's one fellow trying to make a go of a genuine bookstore in Santa Fe, and there are a few outlets for readings. Los Alamos itself is a ghetto of scientists.

There's a mood in every place. Partly it's the landscape, partly the people, the ways they live. I've never done travellogue or documentary poems, so, for me, the mood of a place comes out more in emotional nuance, in syntax and music. With California, there was restlessness and lushness. Actually, a few people have complained about the lushness in my prose poems; other people love it. When Susan Glickman came to visit me in California, she said something like "Roo, I admired those prose poems so much—I thought you made it all up—but you were just writing down what's there!" In Vancouver it was rain, rain, rain. The quick, beautiful passing away of things. In Toronto there's the incredible vitality of people packed close together, and outside the city there's all that mute, overfarmed countryside, lovely and calm and in decline. For me, the landscape is not separable from our life. Lives are not separable from the apartments and farmhouses they take place in. Societies are not separable from the land.

INTERVIEWER

Are there dangers in a literary community becoming too centred, too entangled? I've lived in Toronto, and it seems a bit overly-incestuous sometimes, everybody reading and reviewing and publishing each other. There was a stretch where half the poems in *Canadian Forum* seemed to be by one Toronto poet and dedicated to another Toronto poet. Can't writers lose their perspective and objectivity in a situation like that?

BORSON

It hasn't been a problem for me. I enjoy the liveliness generated by cramming many poets into a few square miles. It feels like a community, not a close community or an untroubled one, but it's like a small town within the larger city. Full of petty jealousies and great love and feuds and common purpose.

Since I read a smattering of the magazines that come out all across the country I don't get an insular feeling about who's published where or reviewed by whom. I guess there's no getting away from the fact that Toronto houses the largest number of English-language poets in the country, so it's natural that many of them should know one another and become friends or enemies and dedicate poems to one another and review one another. The antidote is simply to read an issue of *Dandelion* or *Malahat* or *Rubicon*. Or read Transtromer or Michaud or Hass.

As for perspective and objectivity, I'm afraid those are pretty well lost anyway the moment we plunge into writing.

INTERVIEWER

I certainly agree with what you said earlier about societies and poets not being separable from their land, their landscapes. I notice you haven't mentioned reading the contemporary Irish poets—Heaney, Medbh McGuckian, John Montague. It seems to me you'd find them interesting from that point of view.

BORSON

Of those, Heaney is the only one I've read a sizeable chunk of. He writes beautifully, but almost in another language. It takes a while each time for my North American ears to adjust to the bevies of consonants.

INTERVIEWER

Speaking of landscape, how *do* poems generally begin for you? With an image, a setting, with a narrative situation? Or with a more abstract idea?

BORSON

Usually with an image, or images, or a phrase. The poem starts speaking, or starts with some remembered sensory experience, a scent or vista, or the feel of a situation between people. Or something in the present catches me and I want to compose an informal fugue on that theme.

An "informal fugue": that seems to point to the heart of the dilemma of how to write poetry that is both poetic and modern. Why does the fugue have to be "informal"? Can a fugue be informal and still be a fugue?

BORSON

I'm speaking very loosely here. In the strict sense of the word a fugue can't be informal. However, the rhythms and timing can be loose and conversational while the "thought" in the poem, the larger content, can form patterns with a fugue-like feel. I often think of Bach in relation to poetry, to the intricacies, highly articulated variations, circularities of certain patterns of thinking, unfolding. And then again sometimes I think of Beethoven's seventh symphony, or of Satie . . .

INTERVIEWER

Do you tend to write spontaneously, letting the poem take its own direction, or do poems get some advance planning? Do you ever know when you start how a poem will end?

BORSON

There's no premeditation when I start to write. At most, something that "caught" me will stay with me for a time before I write anything down, but it's never worked out beforehand except in the cases when a poem starts speaking and I have no way to write it down and have to recite it over and over to myself until I can get to a pen and paper. Then I feel like Wordsworth marching up and down country lanes. Usually I have no idea how a poem will end. Now and then the beginning and the end come together, not in words, but in a rounded-out feeling.

INTERVIEWER

You said there that something "catches" you. You seem to instinctively see your material, the world, as an active force, something that you have an encounter with.

BORSON

I guess so. I can't imagine it any other way.

INTERVIEWER

In another interview you've used the word "conjure" in relation to your poetry. Does poetry seem in some way "magical" to you, a plumbing of the irrational?

BORSON

Almost everything we think and do is a plumbing of the irrational. The only exceptions I can think of offhand are the hard sciences. There are rational processes in mathematics. And in astronomy and chemistry and physics, whose language is mathematics. Rational thought proceeds by induction. Sherlock Holmes tries to be rational in the human realm, but he's a fictional character. Sociology and psychology try to be pure sciences and by doing so sometimes come to silly conclusions. Grand folly! Really, they're empirical studies, like medicine. Read a few paragraphs in a first-year sociology textbook and you can see the faulty mechanism at work. Poetry is an empirical study and psychiatry is a fine art. Psychiatry often falls wide of the mark because it adopts biased theories to begin with and then overanalyzes along those lines. Which isn't to say it isn't useful: like poetry or astrology or tarot or a career or a romance it can give one the sense of travelling forward, and of the worth of the journey.

INTERVIEWER

That's interesting, what you said about poetry as an empirical study. But surely the fundamental difference is that science is relentlessly amoral. Not *scientists* of course. But science is the last form of knowledge that hasn't been disillusioned yet, isn't it? Science seems to be the last form of "philosophia" that still believes in the inherent virtue of "progress." I've often thought that's what makes it so dangerous, the fact that it still hasn't undergone the disillusionment, the questioning of foundations, of the post-enlightenment . . .

BORSON

I think poetry, as a field of discipline, is relentlessly amoral also. It is akin to pure research, or at its best it is. The results are unpredictable and exciting.

I don't believe that what makes science dangerous is the assumption that progress is virtuous. The only things I find dangerous are certain inventions, or rather, the uses that can be made of them. I don't call knowledge dangerous, I call people dangerous. I call greed, loathing, race and gender prejudice dangerous. I suppose you could say curiosity is risky in that you never know where it will lead you, but when you get there there are always choices to be made. As Oppenheimer knew. And without intense curiosity we would not be the creatures we are. As for the questioning of foundations, science is usually the first to question the prevailing model of the universe, and the other disciplines follow, borrowing metaphors from science and/or technology.

INTERVIEWER

I believe you've written somewhere, perhaps in *A Sad Device*, that "the ideas we carry around in our pockets are terrible precipices." Should we read the word "ideas" there as being directly contrasted with the magical, as being a warning about the dangerous flaws in rational thought?

BORSON

I don't want to tell anyone how to read my poems. If you stand on an idea, no matter what kind, believing it to be solid ground, you might eventually find yourself peering into the chasm or falling into it.

INTERVIEWER

Ah, but there you *are* suggesting how to read it! And why not? Surely the intention is clarity, not confusion. Of course we understand *your* reading isn't a be-all and end-all, but . . .

BORSON

Gosh, I thought I was just reiterating the line in more words! So much for the illusion of clarity in poetry . . .

INTERVIEWER

You were in Religious Studies, weren't you, in California?

BORSON

Yes, that was my major at Santa Barbara. Not a theological course, but comparative religion. Religion versus science, religion versus philosophy, religion versus religion. I was interested in the origins of different religions and how revelations of an individual or personal nature become canonized and are finally turned into commodities.

INTERVIEWER

Are the mysterious, magical elements that are so prominent in your poetry religious in the larger sense of the word? I'm thinking particularly of passages such as, "Sometimes I would rather step between slices of dark rye and be taken in by some larger beast." A delightful line: witty metaphysics!

I'm not sure. As I think about it, I'm not sure what the larger sense of religion is. If it is awe, then yes. But awe has to do with the origins of religion, and is just barely kept alive in the final forms, which have more to do with human communities than an individual's sensations of life. I guess I don't want to comment on the particular lines you quote; they could be interpreted in several ways depending on the predilections of different readers.

As for awe in our age, I'm surprised at the numbers of people who seem to think that awe and technology are opposed in some sort of contest and that technology is winning. The computer is little different from the wheel. I'm charmed by the horror with which some people who have no background in the sciences view them, actually thinking that the mysteries will be bared one by one and that there will be nothing left that's not understood. A very good scientist actually said the same thing to me one day, except that his attitude was blasé, not horror. I'm not sure whether he was being ironic.

Awe and atheism are not opposed either. Passionate atheism doesn't deny the insuperable mystery of life or of physical nature. It exalts it by taking it out of the realm of intention.

INTERVIEWER

I'm interested in the short poem "Abundance" that you use to preface *A Sad Device*. I wonder if I'm right to see it as emblematic of much of your work. In it you talk of the "wasted intricacy of each snowflake." Do you perhaps have a sense of that natural world as an over-abundance of beauty and complexity that requires the poetic imagination to *see* that intricacy, to change the "waste" into part of the human world by becoming aware of it, by making it part of us? Since the poem's next "example" is "A field without a man in it" . . .

BORSON

I felt "Abundance" was emblematic of the poems in that book, which is why I put it first, as a sort of overture. Actually, I only discovered that it worked that way when I couldn't find the right spot for it in the sequence, it didn't seem to fit between any of the poems and it certainly didn't work at the end, as a summation.

I'm not sure that it's emblematic of most of my work. Only of some.

I interpret the "waste" a little differently than you do. This just indicates different preoccupations. I hope every poem can be unlocked with different keys—and lead into different rooms. Anyway, in that poem I

51

feel the "waste" to be related to linear time and to loss, while you see it as related to a lack of things being perceived. I see the intricacy of the snowflake—the subtle, elegant build-up of a complicated pattern—simply going to "waste" because the snowflake melts. Let me correct myself: I see it your way too, in some combination with my way. Remember that after the field without a man in it there's a rusted plough filling with snow. My feelings about loss within linear time have changed somewhat since then, but that poem does encapsulate those feelings for me, feelings like: what use is all the knowledge that a person has learned in a lifetime when that person dies? I've started to come up with some answers to that, but at the time I wrote the poem, I hadn't.

To answer another aspect of your question, I don't think the beauty of the natural world requires us or our perception of it to not be "wasted." The bear needs the berry, the leaf needs the sunlight, the seed needs the soil. And we need the natural world and some of us, most of us, need our perceptions of it.

INTERVIEWER

In the poem "Talk" in *A Sad Device* you write that the old women "had to learn everything on their own," and that the young women haven't been shown anything. What sorts of things did you have in mind? What are young men "shown"?

BORSON

That sure has been a controversial poem. It even caused a furor in a high school English class.

The things that are "shown" or "not shown" are not cut-and-dried. I wanted to point to a sense of confidence in being in the world versus a lack of confidence. A sense that one can get along, knows how to do things, how to survive on one's own, versus a feeling that one couldn't survive on one's own, wouldn't know how, what things to do—that one must be dependent upon another's know-how for survival—or else, in the case of the old women, to have to learn on one's own because, ultimately, one is not taken care of by anyone else. To pin it all down to particular items in a list would be to do an injustice to the poem and to trivialize and invalidate the experience it's trying to convey. But I *can* say a couple of things to help elucidate it.

In the years when I was growing up, where I was growing up, and previously, and in other places, and still, today, in many places, boys have a stronger sense of their very presence in the world, their physical presence, than girls do. When a boy is taught to throw a ball, he learns

52

the feel of muscle and skin against air, and the feel of personal power, of physical mastery. When a girl is taught to put eyeliner on and to match her shoes to her dress, she is learning how to make herself desirable, not to feel her own presence. Girls around the world are taught to wait for a man, and, in our Western tradition, for a romance, an ideal. When a boy learns how to construct a model airplane, to do something with his hands for his own pleasure, he finds out the sorts of things he likes to do and how to do them. When a girl is taught to bake muffins she learns how to provide for others within a certain context, but without the sense of doing something for herself as well. Girls are taught to wait to be taken care of. And that they have certain duties to perform in exchange for their overall protection.

So you can see the nature of the things that are shown or not shown, or learned on one's own. Very personal things, having to do with a sense of one's existence as a discreet entity (see Mary di Michele's poem "Proof That I Don't Exist"). (And of course it's not the airplanes or the muffins that dictate all this—it's the way things are taught, by whom, to whom, for what purpose—and these things are so much a part of the fabric of our culture and perception that they're hard to isolate or itemize without making them sound superficial.) It's a sense of doing things because you like to do them versus doing things because it will make you attractive to someone else. And of course I'm not saying these things are black and white between the sexes, I'm pointing to predominant shadings.

INTERVIEWER

Yes—what you say sounds true, yet . . . I don't know. I just think most teenage males would be surprised to learn how confident they are, how independent and sure of themselves and their future. And do you really think adolescent males don't do things to make themselves attractive to females?! At a certain age young males are scared to death of the calm, superior air of the girls they know. I know that sounds like a trivialization.

BORSON

As I said, I'm pointing to predominant shadings. Indeed, I wouldn't want men of any age to get the same impression of what I'm trying to say as you seem to have, it's not that black and white. What most men brought up in our culture and in similar cultures do have is the sense that, despite doubts and uncertainties and often against external odds, they will have to make their own way in the world. Compare this with the sense a woman has that once she has found a man her major work is done. For our parents' generation this was, on the whole, true in an economic sense: the wife was provided for financially. This is less and less so for our generation: wives work too, and, in many cases, are having to learn the tools of a trade at an unusually advanced age, and without the lengthy emotional preparation for it. (Not to mention the lack of political preparation for it—lower wages for the same work, etc.) Strangely, even those women of my generation who are not only talented but putting their talents to use in one form of work or another (public work as opposed to the traditional isolated raising of children and housework) all too often tie most of their energy and *sense of self-worth* to finding a man. It's a ludicrous situation. The ways we have been taught to feel and think are no longer appropriate to the actual course of our lives.

INTERVIEWER

Since we're onto issues of sex and gender, how do you feel about the current explosion of woman-only anthologies? There seems to be a new one every month, and of course now a funding drive for a new fiction award for young female novelists in memory of Marian Engel. Are young male novelists any less impoverished in Canada? Is it easier for them to get published? Is this justifiable in a period when the major new anthologies are at least half female anyway, and many of our best journals, *Descant, Malahat* for example, *Grain, Contemporary Verse 2*, are edited by women? Some female writers I talk to think it's fine, others are finding it increasingly insulting.

BORSON

I don't see it as an explosion in numbers. I don't really think there are all that many such anthologies and magazines. I think it's extremely healthy now and would eventually become unhealthy. I *hope* it will eventually become unhealthy, I hope that one day such segregation will be so unnecessary as to seem ludicrously quaint and silly. So far, many women still need places where they feel they can speak freely and be listened to with interest. There's still a lot of insecurity—and unfortunately it's well-grounded. Imagine: at the League of Poets meeting two or three years ago a woman talking in the Feminist Caucus meeting actually said that for years many of the women members of the League had been too shy to stand up at meetings and say what was on their minds for fear of being laughed at or dismissed. I was shocked. As long as women feel that same way about their poetry, there will be a need for such publications. And as long as certain subject matter is dismissed out-of-hand there will be need for such publications. They are havens.

As long as there are sexist reviews, on either side, we have to be aware of the issue. As long as women can't walk the streets with as little fear as men, we have to be aware of the issue.

What I'm saying is that the problem is large and deep in our society and that poetry can't simply be excluded as being above the problem. I think we are conditioned more deeply than we know, and that it takes a lot to arouse us out of our assumptions. To take the League again as an example: a few years ago, when the issue of the existence of a Feminist Caucus first came up, I was amazed at the ferocity of the response: the response that "we poets are all good guys, naturally" or "poetry is inviolable, it's above prejudice"—above the prejudices of the society in which we live and out of which we write? I doubt it; not entirely. And in any case, it was a revelation to me that when a substantial segment of the group felt put-down, dismissed, voiceless, another substantial segment of the group took this as an attack rather than as a plea, a request for understanding. Whatever happened to compassion?

In principle, I am against gender segregation in publication, just as, *in principle only*, I am against affirmative action—but there are times when higher principles don't serve the actual needs of people. And on this overall issue I am an optimist. I think that for the most part we're moving forward, not backward. I think that once women have as much economic and social power as men, once enough women are in positions of status, power, and authority, we will be less vulnerable and less the victims of intimidation on more subtle levels.

INTERVIEWER

And so you don't think we've reached the point where the segregations seem "quaint and silly"?

BORSON

Unfortunately not, though my thoughts and reactions often leap forward to that time. My longings. Segregated publications still have a role to play. Among other things, they serve as a mode of reportage on the current scene. Phenomena such as the Women and Words Conference are of vital interest to many women and to some men, and so are all-women anthologies and magazine issues. The problem is so large and long-buried and so slow to be unearthed. (In two Swiss cantons—a "sophisticated" country—the women still don't have the right to vote.) And though, as they say, the identification of the illness is the first step toward a cure, it's only a first step, and there are still so many people who don't even recognize that we're sick . . .

I take it that you are able to separate poetry and language cleanly from other social matrices. I can't quite do that. And in any case, it's interesting to see what turns up in books like *Anything is Possible* and *Full Moon*. Partly they are the record of a movement. Partly they are a history (a theirstory?). Also, and this is the main thing, there are good poems in them.

INTERVIEWER

Well, actually, I agree with you that poetry and its social matrices *are* inextricable.

In another interview you've said you find some of the language in *A Sad Device* "paternalistic." I always have trouble seeing this: theorists talk a lot about feminine and masculine voice and so on, but rarely give concrete examples. Beyond pronouns, what *is* paternalistic and patriarchal language?

BORSON

When I said that about *A Sad Device* I did simply mean the pronouns. What surprised me is that I used the male pronoun without thinking, as we all did—but my own obtuseness stunned me. I was a little later than some in realizing what I had done.

Beyond the pronouns, I'm not sure what patriarchal language is. It's a question which fascinates me, but so far the answers point to a vague edifice rather than revealing concrete examples. The first concrete example is, of course, gender pronouns—and the related clichés using "mankind" instead of "humankind." Beyond that I'm prepared to believe that since our society is patriarchal that this is reflected in many ways in the language. I'm willing to imagine that I've overlooked some things, just as I overlooked gender pronouns.

INTERVIEWER

Beyond words themselves, is there a patriarchal structure in our very syntax and grammar that a female poet must fight against? In a recent issue of *Poetry Canada Review*, Erin Mouré writes that "It seems often that language does not allow me *as a woman* to speak, *it* is what forgets my memories." Do you sense this as well?

BORSON

Erin is one of the women to whom I listen for answers on this question. She seems sure of something in an area where I'm not sure of anything. Personally, I don't feel that English grammar and syntax are oppressive to me as a woman; sometimes I feel they are oppressive to me as a child!

But I rarely feel that way in poetry (I have a perverse attraction to formal structures in language, even when I wince at several formal structures in our society)—legal documents and forms of all kind make the child in me squirm and feel despondent. In poetry, syntax can be broken, by women and men, to good effect, and sometimes to confusing effects. The breaking and re-forming of syntax can produce wonderful effects like that of contemporary jazz. I think Cathy Ford is another interesting poet for whom regular sentence structure is oppressive. For me, though this is a private thing, and probably couldn't be guessed from my work, putting inchoate feelings into sentences is a delight—I get a charge out of it, like the charge I get out of that jazz.

Back to Erin's essay. I don't sense what Erin does about language, but I'm interested in what she senses. As far as I've been able to see so far, poets of both genders have problems with trying to speak by means of the language, any language, because what we have to say is not always in words before we put it in words. For a few years I did an informal survey of people I met to try to see how people think. I found that some people always think in words, out loud in their minds but silently, other people are aware only of a blankness full of latent driftings, others think in musical phrases or in images . . . there's an amazing variety. I'm interested in what Erin says about memory, and, if I understand it, it's in direct contradiction to my own experience. My memories are not in language (as I think Erin says hers are—it's another thing again to talk about the memories of the race being in language—but it sounds like Erin is talking about personal memories) and many of my thoughts are not in language. Writing poetry in one's native tongue is often an act of translation. I can understand the idea that language might forget certain memories, if those memories cannot be coded in the system. I'm curious about what sorts of memories she finds can't fit into the language as it stands, and how these are specifically the memories of a woman.

Certainly, if a woman speaks she may not always be heard. I'm thinking now of subject matter. I'm thinking specifically of one of the best books of Canadian poetry in recent years, written by one of the best writers, which was panned in a major newspaper because of its subject matter, notably relationships between women and between women and children and what it feels like to live as a woman. As though any subject matter that is human could be too lowly for poetry, as though such subjects were incapable of the transfiguration that makes good writing.

INTERVIEWER
Do you follow trends in contemporary critical theory much?

Deconstruction and so on? How do you react to assertions such as Derrida's conviction that language always writes the poet, that language is not about an external reality but about its own epistemology, ultimately only about language?

BORSON

No, I don't follow the theories, though I'm always interested to hear about them. Writing by theory is too much like painting by numbers.

I think it's fun to think about language being ultimately only about language, just as it's fun and enlightening to realize that the formulation of our questions influences the answers we get, in anthropology as well as in physics. But the fact is, if I ask you to pick up the potato that's lying on the table, you're likely to pick it up even though you can't see any good reason for doing so other than my asking. And, after all, the physics experiment gets done, and then afterwards people try to analyze how their participation has affected the results.

INTERVIEWER

Yes. It seems to me that language can't be only or even primarily about language even if it tried (and why in heaven's name would it?). Words in people's heads will always suggest objects, emotions, colours and so on, won't they? Our experiences are influenced by language I suppose, but so much of our lives are non-linguistic!

We talked a bit earlier about questions of form for modern poets. Does the poetic line interest you? Do you think the line still has a role in contemporary poetry, as an instrument of tension, of a felt pulse, of rhythm? I guess I'm asking if the musical element of poetry is one of your concerns.

BORSON

Yes, certainly. Music is necessary to all writing, not just poetry. Writing is speech, it's out loud, it makes a noise that's rhythmic or arrhythmic, it forms patterns and breaks them. Whenever I think about rhythm I think of contemporary jazz—Weather Report or Carlos Santana and Alice Coltrane, Jean-Luc Ponty. I had to learn to listen to this kind of music. At first I could only hear a big mass of disorganized sound, unharmonic, crashing, confusing—but then I began to hear individual instruments within the welter and *oh* the pleasure when all the conflicting strains are drawn together into melody again. It's astonishing and fills me with happiness. Coming to a piece of fantastic writing is like that point at which the instruments pull together and everything makes sense—out of the welter of everyday impressions and ups and downs, this clear voice is speaking. It makes the crashing and confusion that preceded it that much more valuable, the contrast is sensual and excruciating and cerebral too.

I had to learn to read contemporary poetry too. It was a similar experience. It's astonishing now that at first I couldn't appreciate the sound of even Sylvia Plath's poems—and her rhythms are so strong. I had to get used to the poetic line without end-rhyme and end-thump and then I could hear what was going on. It's as though one's ears become more finely tuned, more subtle. There is a rhythm used a lot now (and I don't mean you could do an analysis and find the exact same prosodic structures in every poem, but that the overall sound is very similar) which is going to sound just as out-dated as end-thump. You find it a lot in American magazines and books—it's a competent, boring, long-drawn-out structure of sentences, usually complete sentences with many clauses, that sound jaded and vaguely whining while trying to be chatty and profound. I'm talking about the *sound* here, regardless of content. I'm not sure I can describe it in a way that people who don't already know what I mean can hear what I mean. Someone who makes beautiful music out of this general pattern is C. K. Williams; his stands above much of the rest the way Donne's music stands above the rhythms of his time. In Canada, Kim Maltman does a similar thing beautifully in his longer poems. It's a narrative voice. Few people do it really well.

Anyway, yes, I think the line still has a role in poetry. If it didn't, we should all be writing prose or prose poetry. Lines can be used in different kinds of ways. They can accentuate a rhythm of a tension or space between images or ideas. Line breaks can be used as punctuation or as transitional areas. You can use them to make the reader stop or keep going. Line breaks can be used to accentuate the medium of written language—that's how Robert Creeley uses them—or to minimize that and emphasize a natural chanting speech, as W. S. Merwin uses them (his father was a minister). John Newlove is another master of the line. I'm not saying there's only one way, or three ways to master line-breaks; they're one of the components of voice, and everyone's voice is a little different. The most individual voices can be identified by their rhythms, their way of moving. You would never mistake an Atwood poem for a Lee, or a Bringhurst for a Dewdney, or a McKay for a di Michele. Of course, line breaks are only one component of rhythm. Prose has rhythm too. Our rhythms are based on street corners and in poetry—and also on individual temperament. We each have a cadence, or several related cadences.

I'm a bit puzzled by a line in the poem "North Country" about "the eye that is always out searching." The poem comments, "what a terrible loss of an eye." Why? Because eyes should be receptive rather than searching, mirrors rather than lamps? Of course Wordsworth—whom I think you said somewhere was one of the first poets you were familiar with—speaks of a wise passiveness.

The eye that is always out searching is likely to be unusually limited because it's searching for a particular something to fill a particular inadequacy instead of just trying to see what's there. Often we're enriched more by what surprises us than by what we find to fill a narrow need. Or to put it in an old way, when we stop looking, we find. We see what's there instead of what we wish were there.

It seems to me there can be no doubt that you have a particular preoccupation with night in your poems. Why is this?

I don't know. I think of Timothy Findley and his rabbits. In several interviews he's mentioned that publishers have said things like "My God, another rabbit. Where did this one come from?"

All I can think about my case is that it's an ordinary primitive fascination, things unseen in the dark, etc., plus the immense physical beauty of the things you can see: stars, house lights. A primitive attraction to light in the contrasting darkness. To get really mundane about it, I'm always attracted to shiny things—eyes are! And the eeriness of the flat shapes of familiar three-dimensional objects: trees, rooftops, and so on. It's a painterly attraction.

"Night should be fuller than this"?

To me, that line doesn't mean anything outside of the context of my poem, where the speaker feels this way because of the human relationship in the poem, or in conjunction with it.

In "Migrations" you talk about night balancing the darkness inside the body. Is this part of the attraction as well?

BORSON

Yes, I suppose so. I like to think about the dark spaces inside the body and how eerie it is to be opened up in surgery: that there are these crude, strange mechanisms—heart, liver, kidneys—that make all our mental life possible. And I forgot to mention my fascination with outer space, with what's beyond the earth and our life: night is the only time we can easily imagine those physical distances. This is very important to me. I wouldn't say my fascination is symbolic, but imagistic.

INTERVIEWER

In *Books in Canada* Fred Cogswell criticized the prose poem section of *The Whole Night, Coming Home* for its "greater obsessiveness." Do you think he's right? And is obsessiveness a vice or a virtue for a poet anyway?

BORSON

I wish I had seen the context for the comment, because I don't understand what he means. The only thing I can imagine he might mean is that there is an identifiable, more or less unified subject in those poems. I wouldn't call it an obsession just because there are several poems around one theme. In fact, I think those poems are some of the least obsessed writing I've done, in that I knew what I was doing while I was doing it and that's clear, and that a wide open, gentle world view is implied by those poems.

Obsessiveness works magnificently in something like *Coming Through Slaughter*, obsessiveness in the characters and in the author's need to know. It doesn't work so well when there's a self-indulgent focus to the obsessiveness.

INTERVIEWER

Have you been publishing your poetry much in the U.S.? Are you interested in doing so? Why, or why not? Can you see any reason why Canadian poets have been so far behind their prose counterparts in gaining an audience in the rest of the English-speaking world?

BORSON

I haven't published much in the U.S., just a few poems in a few magazines. My literary community is in Canada, so I almost always send to Canadian publishers. I see an oblique dialogue going on in the Canadian magazines that I want to contribute to.

I'm interested in publishing more in the U.S. as well as in the other countries if it becomes possible. I'd love to have my work available in Britain and Australia and in translation in non-English-speaking countries. I'd like as large an audience as my writing will bear, but I spend my time writing rather than trying to promote my work. I think everyone is better served by that.

I think that Canadian poets are behind their prose counterparts not only in the rest of the world but in Canada too. Poetry just doesn't sell as well. I suppose it's possible too that fewer poets use literary agents than prose writers do, and that this has an effect. I don't know any poets personally who use agents. I don't even know whether agents are willing to take on poets. I'm pretty ignorant of the business aspects of writing— well, not writing, but publishing.

INTERVIEWER

I think most agents have "no poetry" signs up—the ones I've seen. Sort of like "no dogs allowed in the restaurant." Of course we can hardly blame them.

BORSON

I'm sorry to hear that. Poetry-loving agents could have a role to play in revving up its popularity. Bruce Whiteman wrote a good essay in *Poetry Canada Review* recently about how a poet today can count on an audience of between 500 and 2000, and that this number has changed little since Chaucer's time, up through Byron and Pound. That there's been no decline. I'd be even more interested if in a future article he would try the comparison again, this time taking into account factors such as the increases in population, education, and literacy, and the change from a largely oral and theatrical art (performance poetry) to a written one, along with technological advances in printing and distribution.

INTERVIEWER

And actually people like Byron, Tennyson, and Pope made large fortunes from selling poetry! Even in Joyce's time, in the '20s, a poet could get five pounds for one lyric in a newspaper, enough to feed a family for a week! We do seem to be in a definite low trough in poetry, in much of the Western world, especially in regards to the audience for poetry. Most of Canada's major poets sell books in the hundreds, rather than the thousands, and let's face it, few books would be published without Canada Council grants. How do you feel about this? Does it

affect your work, this lack of an audience beyond other poets? Are there
ways for poetry to regain a larger readership? Or should poets not concern
themselves with what some people might call "market" forces?

BORSON
Recently I went to a poetry reading by W. S. Merwin in which he
read a poem listing all the various sorts of people—lawyers, accountants,
etc.—who are ashamed of poetry in our time, and the list included poets.
It just isn't a high-status profession among us. I am of two minds about
government support: my gut feeling, conditioned by the capitalistic
system under which we live, and which I am happy to live under, is
guilt: that I produce a product that doesn't sell. On the other hand, I
look at the cute junk produced around me which does sell, and I know
that my product is infinitely more worthwhile, to me, anyway. That in
my life I'd rather have a poem than a pet rock. The end result of all these
deliberations is always that I am glad the government acts as a patron,
that the collective will of the society supports the thing I love even if
most individuals don't.

I don't think of my audience as being composed solely of poets, though
I know it's mainly poets. I often think, when I think of an audience at
all, of the few non-writers who love to read, whose worlds are really
enriched by that. I don't think the audience particularly influences my
writing; certainly the constantly evolving tradition does.

I think there would be ways for poetry to gain a larger audience, but
poets couldn't do it themselves. I believe that the top-notch advertisers
and image-makers can sell *anything*. It would require the remaking of
poetry's image from something dowdy and difficult to something sexy,
and such a facelift would have nothing to do with poetry, only with
marketing. The spirit of poetry might be degraded in the process, but
poets could make more of a living. I do have some specific ideas about
it, but I'm a writer, not an entrepreneur.

I can't answer whether poets should concern themselves with market
forces—it's a question for each poet, how to balance art and business,
or whether to forsake one for the other. The kind of "creativity" needed
to sell something is entirely different from the creativity needed for
composition.

INTERVIEWER
I suppose it's similar to the problem of radical political parties, like
the Greens, trying to decide whether to moderate their policies to get
elected. It's either a sort of prostitution or invisibility, Catch-22. Or does

it have to be that way? It certainly isn't in eastern Europe. Look at Yevtushenko filling hockey arenas, and certainly not because of "official" favour!

BORSON

Yes, I'd love to know more about the status of poetry in other parts of the world. Of course, Bob Dylan can fill hockey arenas, but then his art is not solely verbal. And Yevtushenko, from what I've heard, is quite a performance poet, very dramatic. I've wondered from time to time whether the disrespect shown poetry in North America dates from the original settlers (excluding of course the much earlier native "settlers"), who may not have been of the highly literate upper classes, and certainly had no time for such things while trapping raccoons to eat. But then fiction has made a name for itself here, though the best fiction, what I like the best, rarely makes the bestseller lists. I imagine the situation is similar in Australia, but what is it like elsewhere?

A friend living in England sent me a recent article about the current state of poetry there. It seems that poetry is experiencing a revival. Some of the major literary presses have taken it upon themselves to promote their poetry titles with the same enthusiasm and monetary backing as they devote to other genres, and it's paying off. Authors sent on tour have found large audiences waiting for them. A possible explanation offered by the article is that England is experiencing such a financial and moral slump that people are turning to poetry once again for solace.

INTERVIEWER

While we're on the current state of poetry: the Polish poet Czeslaw Milosz has said, "It is one thing to live in a limbo of doubt and dejection, another to like it." Is it part of poetry's role to *combat* doubt and dejection? To search for some kind of knowledge, some kind of links to dilute alienation? I guess, in the broader sense, does poetry have a moral role?

BORSON

The thought that poetry, or any other art, has a predetermined moral role is abhorrent to me. Look what happened to the arts in China: fine arts were replaced by bizarre forms of folk-art: fascinating culturally, but also a loss. That is, I don't believe that art has a duty, of any sort, to society. To say that it has played a role, in retrospect, is another thing. Does the rose bloom for the bee? No, but their lives are bound together, and they coincidentally, felicitously, serve one another.

It may be one or another poet's role to combat doubt and dejection, but not poetry's. It might be another poet's role to instill doubt in another time and place. I think that a poet can only convey an individual world view, which may or may not have power for others. Since Milosz was speaking of our time, the comment is interesting and appropriate.

INTERVIEWER

No duty of any sort to society? Surely *all* morality isn't relative! Surely art must try—imperfectly of course—to make just those distinctions, to defeat generalizations about behaviour and so on, to do what it can, or to at least express some outrage now and then? I don't really mean a given individual—as you say, we each do what we can do, see what we can see, but . . .

BORSON

No, *morality* isn't relative—or not in all contexts. I speak as one who has certain moral convictions. But I don't believe that the pursuit of knowledge or beauty or happiness is *dutiful*. I'm an individualist in this way, I believe that the best reason for becoming a doctor or a mathematician or a poet is an overwhelming love of the occupation. At their best I think artists are motivated by unsentimental love and by curiosity. Except in the retrospective analytical sense which I already mentioned, to bring duty into it is, for me, to degrade that love. Depending on the personality of the artist, love of the form may be coupled to humanitarian feeling or to misanthropy. Bizarre, warped attitudes can still produce beautiful—and uncomfortable—art. What about a political novel that's humanitarian on a large scale but at the same time implicitly, and by assumption, misogynic? What can be made of that morally? I think artists are by nature individualists, however strongly they may be bound to their milieu, and so it comes naturally to them to comment upon their surroundings, sometimes expressing outrage. But to assign "dutifulness" to art seems to me to be looking at the process backwards.

INTERVIEWER

Does poetry have a *political* function? I realize it's a hard term to define, especially in light of the "troubles," to use a euphemism, at the recent PEN conference in New York.

BORSON

It *is* a hard term to define. If we're thinking of politics as including all affairs between people, yes, of course poetry has a function to the extent that it is written and heard. If we're thinking more narrowly of protest against or support for some policy, then, yes, it can also have a function from time to time: people are more likely to listen if an opinion is elegantly stated. And politicians still quote from poetry in their speeches: it's a strange thing that certain lines are remembered and repeated and held up as models to society, and yet poets can't make a living.

As for the PEN conference, it reminds me of the 1960s in radical Berkeley. In essence, women were told to put aside their own oppression in order to fight for "greater" freedoms. And they did it. And they were again, by implication, asked to do so at the PEN conference. And yes we can rank oppression on scales of one to ten, and fight first in acute life-and-death situations, but there is no reason not to fight all along against the chronic ills as well.

INTERVIEWER

Yeah, you can get tired of people saying don't worry about this evil because look there, that's even worse. But I guess we do have to keep our priorities straight, and choose our language carefully. I remember Skvorecky taking people to task in Toronto for talking about the "oppression" of writers in Canada. We get pretty spoiled.

BORSON

Yes. But it also must be remembered that the oppression of women in our culture is not a "minor" problem just because it operates at a constant level, like a continuous hum that's easy to disregard. It's major and long term.

INTERVIEWER

Do you think there is too much poetry being published in Canada these days? Would we be better off if young poets had a harder time publishing a book but once published were more apt to be noticed?

BORSON

Those are two separate questions. If less poetry were published it wouldn't guarantee that what was published would be read. I think poetry's lack of popularity has more to do with its public image than with the quality of what's being written. Though it's true that there are lots of books published which only show talent but aren't already highly accomplished, every year in Canada several really good books of poetry come out, books worth reading and owning, and that's an excellent track record.

And, although if I were a publisher or a granting agency, my standards for book publication would be considerably higher than most—along the lines of my own taste, of course!—there's something to be said for the great profusion of poetry available. It forms a matrix or a milieu out of which the best poetry can grow. What I mean is that without a vigorous, exciting, open milieu it's less likely that really good poetry will be written. I think of people of Margaret Atwood's generation and earlier talking about the lack of a tradition in Canada, the lack of publishing outlets and role models. How it was a struggle just to realize that one could *do* this, could write, that it was a possible choice. That's no longer the case, both because of the efforts of earlier writers and because the publishing outlets have grown enormously since the early days, even taking into account the fact that hardly any major publishers even touch poetry anymore. There's a generosity in the system now which encourages production.

I suppose I carry around an idea of the ideal situation: fewer, better books would be published, and they would be well-reviewed, cherished, and even talked about by non-writers!—and there would be a healthy magazine market among writers. The magazines could afford to pay their contributors well and they would generate excitement, anticipation, and detailed, interesting shop-talk. They would be the main forum for cross-pollination among poets. In such a world poets could live on their sales of poetry if they so desired.

INTERVIEWER

I'm just worried that too many books *isn't* an exciting, open milieu, that it just makes the situation murky, so that *no one* can really follow the new writing. Heavens, I'm not saying forbid publishing, I'm just wondering if we should rearrange the grant structure—fewer books, *more rewriting* and winnowing, more publicity per book, more advertising. Redistribute the funds, so that it *means* something when you do get published; an event to be striven for.

BORSON

That's an interesting idea. It's amazing to me how many writers get incredibly excited about the publication of a first book and then become frustrated and depressed because nothing seems to come of it. A new book of poetry just doesn't generate much excitement except among the devotees of a particular author's work. None of it qualifies you to make a living, or even to be heard. I wonder what sort of publicity or advertising would work. Publishers keep wondering about that too. Other "archaic" forms like opera and ballet still have comparatively large followings, despite increasing financial uncertainty for the companies. Would it help if we stood on streetcorners reciting Shakespeare's sonnets?

As things stand, there are plenty of people who complain that it's far too hard to get published, that the publication schedules are full up, and/or it's not possible to break through the barrier of the "establish-ment." Granting agencies are tax-supported and so far have felt they have to respond to such complaints from the citizenry. And as soon as there's a committee, compromises in taste have to be made. I wonder what the Canada Council would make of your suggestion. I understand that the Ontario Arts Council now has some funds available for festivals, conferences, and promotion, but I don't know the details.

The best world would be one in which fine poetry made money. A publisher would follow his or her own highly opinionated taste and "pick the winners," really put a lot into promotion and run with it.

INTERVIEWER

If we can end off back where we started, I had a few more questions about *The Whole Night, Coming Home*. There are a lot of "teenage" poems in the book that are very powerfully evocative of the mental and emotional desperation of adolescence. Those poems "taught" me things I felt I already knew—once I read them, that is! Did you have difficulty casting your mind back into those forms, those emotions and situations?

BORSON

No, there was no difficulty, because I simply found myself back in those frames of mind. I didn't set out to write about those characters, I wrote about them out of a state which was imposing itself on me at the time.

INTERVIEWER

Later on in *The Whole Night*, in the second half, you seem fascinated by the recurring image of flowers at night, flowers in the dark. What do they suggest or signify for you?

BORSON

Flowers have a wondrous presence in the dark. Many of them give off stronger fragrances then, and they are living, and yet curiously cool to the touch. Sunlight is what they need to grow, and in sunlight I sense them as rather strenuous beings, manufacturing, building, growing. In the dark they strike me as eerily alive, feeding on moisture, waiting for light, but not waiting anxiously. They seem to enjoy themselves. They remind me of office towers at night, when all the people (the cause of their existence and their continuance) have gone home, and only a few lights burn.

Your poetry seems to dwell a great deal on our relationship with the natural world. Do you think we are generally too cut off from basic physical sensation, cut off from a natural relationship with ourselves, with our bodies? Is this city / nature split not, to a large degree, what the second part of *The Whole Night*, "Folklore," is all about?

You and I, or the reader and the writer, approach the poems from opposite ends of the process of writing. You, as a reader and critic, might draw certain conclusions from my work, but I, as the writer, am not thinking of conclusions at all. All I'm doing is trying to share what I see while making a beautiful sound at the same time. I don't intentionally code messages into my poems; if I had a concrete message I would probably write an essay. I write about the city and about nature because those, combined, are my environment. I write what I see (and hear and smell, etc.) and what I'm thinking / feeling in response to what I see.

I don't feel that we as a group are too cut off from anything, though I'm happy if you, as reader, can interpret my poems in ways that make sense in your own life. Poems have minds of their own and you can engage in a dialogue with them. I do write intensely sometimes about nature because I experience it intensely; that's all.

I hope those prose poems are many things to many people. One of the reasons I wrote them was to preserve something beautiful which is / was not long for this earth. The garden and the natural environments I wrote about no longer existed in those forms even as I wrote about them; I wrote from memory. Not all of the people exist either. Even as I wrote those pieces I knew I was writing an elegy.

Interview by David Manicom

RUDY WIEBE

Rudy Wiebe was born in the Mennonite village of Speedwell in northern Saskatchewan in 1934. Four years earlier, his parents had come to Canada from the Soviet Union. Wiebe's first language was Low German, and he was raised a Mennonite. While he was an undergraduate at the University of Alberta, Edmonton, from 1953 to 1956, Wiebe began to write seriously. He also studied at the University of Tubingen, West Germany. On his return to Canada in 1958, Wiebe taught at the Mennonite Brethren Bible College and edited the Mennonite Brethren Herald. *He received an MA in Creative Writing from the University of Alberta in 1960, and in 1964 was appointed Assistant Professor of English at Goshen College, Indiana. He returned to Canada again in 1967 to teach at the University of Alberta, where he is now Professor of English.*

One of Canada's most highly respected writers, Wiebe's primary subjects have been the Mennonite community and events in nineteenth- and twentieth-century Western Canadian history. He has written seven novels: Peace Shall Destroy Many *(1962),* First and Vital Candle *(1966),* The Blue Mountains of China *(1970),* The Temptations of Big Bear *(1973),* The Scorched-Wood People *(1977),* The Mad Trapper *(1980), and* My Lovely Enemy *(1983). He has published three collections of his short stories,* Where is the Voice Coming From? *(1974),* Alberta: A Celebration *(1979), and* The Angel of the Tar Sands and Other Stories *(1982), and a play,* Far as the Eye Can See *(1977). Wiebe has also edited six anthologies of short fiction.*

This interview took place in Wiebe's University of Alberta office overlooking the South Saskatchewan River on the afternoon of 23 May 1985. In an attempt to convey the multi-layered nature of Wiebe's thinking aloud, the original syntax has been retained as far as possible. The printed page cannot convey, however, the friendly laughter and warmth that well up through Wiebe even during his bleakest contemplations.

INTERVIEWER

Thank you for taking the time to do this. How do you find time, with all your responsibilities, to write? What is your system of priorities?

WIEBE

I don't write during the school year. I used to when I was younger and had more energy, but I don't much anymore. So, what I basically do is try to take time off.

INTERVIEWER

When you're writing, what's your procedure? Do you have a way of getting started, or any rituals about it?

WIEBE

Not really. If something is writing well, if it's going well, you get into it very easily. I don't have much of a superstitious approach about this. If you're a writer, you write. That's one of the things you do: you apply yourself and if it goes well the imaginative turn will be there. It comes after a while. Sometimes it's not worth anything, but then you don't write just to begin with anyway. I mean you write something four or five or six or ten times, so you've got plenty of time to make it better.

INTERVIEWER

So you do a lot of revising?

WIEBE

Oh yes, an enormous amount. I suppose the only time I didn't do a lot of revision—sometimes when you've thought about a story for a long time, or worked on something for a very long time in your head, then suddenly you can write it out quite quickly—I suppose the only time it ever happened for me with a novel was *The Scorched-Wood People*. It went very fast. I began it in the middle of a school year, in January, actually, and finished it completely by the beginning of October; in between I had six weeks holidays in Europe with my wife and children. That's an enormously long book. I still don't know how I did it. I suppose part of it was because I knew the story so well. I'd worked it all through, the history of it, in one sense, with *Big Bear*, and then I'd been working on stories about Riel in another context, so I really knew. It happened very quickly: I would write every morning and teach every afternoon. That was a while ago, when I had a lot of energy.

INTERVIEWER

Your energy is one of the things Robert Kroetsch pointed out in a comment he made in 1980. He said that you are "saved from the cloying stink of piety by your huge energy, the temptation of violence and your erotic relationship to both language and to the process of writing." Are those apt descriptions?

WIEBE

I think for a writer with my background and my predilections, I have to be careful about moralizing. But I've been watching myself for so long with that, that's the easiest thing, perhaps, to avoid, even though I still keep writing a lot about moral subjects. After a while you learn about avoiding the sermon, the preaching, the laying down of the moral dictum. But I don't know about the "erotic relationship" to words. I guess it would take someone like Kroetsch to recognize it.

INTERVIEWER

Of course there are other outcomes to morally-oriented writing than pietism. When you visited the Canadian Literature class here at the University of Alberta to discuss *Big Bear*, you brought Dempsey's biography of Big Bear. You felt that your presentation of Big Bear in your novel had been vindicated by a historian or biographer. Is the real problem with taking a moral position in a book a formal problem rather than a substantive one?

WIEBE

Fiction is not necessarily concerned with accuracy the way history is, with the accuracy of "what happened." And yet, with that book particularly, it's important—especially the way it's seen and the way it's been read, and the way I would like it to be read—that there is a very strong basis in fact. So that I don't argue the way Michael Ondaatje, say, argues about Buddy Bolden in *Coming Through Slaughter*, that he made it all up. Though I don't believe him either. I had a long argument with him once when we were on a panel together at the University of Hawaii, and we actually did talk about the necessity for a feeling of accuracy, some sort of historical truthfulness about what I'm writing about. To me there is a major importance in that. Partly the historical accuracy is important to me in that I see the novel as a social document to a certain extent, as an exploration of society, as an exploration of community, as it is, not as we imagine it to be. The thing I would say about Ondaatje, if you want to contrast, is that his exploration of Buddy Bolden—even though it's set very much in a New Orleans society—

73

demonstrates that in one sense the society disappears and it's more and more Bolden and a couple of individual characters that he relates to. It's a very American kind of novel in its emphasis on the individual and the problem it explores is an inward one, an internal problem.

I think that's one way of seeing it; I think that's a particularly American way of seeing it: where the American writer is exploring almost only the individual. In contrast to that, the great European novels that you think of are novels in relation to a society; they explore man in relation to his society. I guess the greatest of them are Tolstoy and Dostoevsky, the great Russian novelists. That's the way I see fiction also; the individual in relation to a community that can be broken or destroyed, the novel as a political instrument. There you get all the morality you want. It's not so much an individual morality that's being explored, but it is also an individual morality in relation to a community morality of how people *do* live together. The American novel—the United States novel I mean now—is so much an exploration of the individual, and you go in and in and in and in, that at times there seem to be no outward connections left at all. Ondaatje's novel is a classic example of that.

INTERVIEWER
Part of the way you use language in *Peace Shall Destroy Many*—and the point is made by a couple of the conservative characters—is that learning and keeping within the High and Low German languages is not just a tool of communication, but it's a barrier to the outside world.

WIEBE
Oh yes.

INTERVIEWER
Do you feel that with your formal experimentation, which has gone on consistently, that there's any intention of setting up a barrier between the reader and the writer?

WIEBE
No. I would think that my exploration in form is trying to expand and to loosen rather than to set up barriers to protect yourself. In that sense, society, at least the way I experienced it as a kid, used the language actually to keep you ignorant or to restrict what you could know, and to hem in what might have been your natural predilections if you had had a wider, more flexible language in which to embody them. I grew up speaking Low German, which is a very restrictive peasant language:

restrictive in the sense that it has almost no intellectual concepts in it. It's very very rich, very full in expression in terms of humour, of work language, of contact between people, but almost no abstract intellectual language that you can use.

You see, that's where you use a language—unconsciously, I'm sure, for most people—to actually limit what you can think about, because you have no vocabulary in which to clothe it. High German is an incredible philosophic language, but the High German that I knew was strictly the High German that Luther gives us in the Luther Bible, which, again, is a very restrictive language in that it is a theological and narrative language, not an abstract language very much at all. It's very rich in poetry and narrative, but very limited in its abstraction possibilities.

No, what I think I'm trying to do with pushing out and experimenting with form, and the complexities of language which that gives you, is actually to liberate you, to show you more, to give you more possibilities and ways of telling the story, rather than less. Maybe that is, as you say, an unconscious or a conscious response to the way I was, in effect, limited as a child in terms of the world I could manipulate with words. On the other hand, that goes in both directions, because at the same time it gave me an enormous advantage in understanding the differences in what different languages can do for you. Beginning with a peasant language and then working on into the intellectual possibilities of English and High German is not a bad way to go. The thing that I miss most is—I wish I wish I wish I wish I wish; I've always wished—that instead of learning geometry and algebra in high school, I'd learned Latin. That would've helped me a lot more over the years.

INTERVIEWER

Was Russian a part of your vocabulary?

WIEBE

No.

INTERVIEWER

Do you have an image of your readers when you're writing?

WIEBE

Sure I do. I have the image of the perfect reader: somebody who understands exactly what I'm trying to do even better than I do myself.

75

INTERVIEWER

I want to pursue this barrier idea a little further because I know people who find your books inaccessible. You've said that people who complain about the difficulty of your work haven't put any time into trying to learn the conventions of modern art, that coming to art is not the same as coming to a slab of roast beef. And I know that for my freshman class this year the history in *Big Bear* wasn't a problem . . .

WIEBE

I don't think it really is. The one novel that's obviously perfectly easy to read, that's simplest to read, is *The Mad Trapper*. You see, this is what happens when you write for a while: you don't just write one kind of book. If you did, you'd be Arthur Hailey or somebody, which is not interesting. *The Mad Trapper* is the kind of book that kids in grade nine love; it's the kind of book that *Reader's Digest* loves—it's been translated into three or four different languages as a *Reader's Digest* condensed book . . .

INTERVIEWER

And made into a movie?

WIEBE

No. The movie has nothing to do with that book. That was a Hollywood version of the story and it wasn't based on my book. And in France—I just had a statement of sales in France; it was published in Paris—they've sold three times as many copies of *Le Trappeur fou* as they ever have in Canada. It's obviously an easy book to read. So, if you write long enough, presumably you've got a range.

You could say there are some things typically Wiebe about that book; on the other hand, there are a lot of atypical things too: one of them might be such a simple story! Just go from A to Z, right? A writer, if he's half-shakes of anything, should be able to write a good read, just to go through it. I have no compunctions about *The Mad Trapper* at all. I don't pretend it's a great book or an important book, but it's an interesting book, I think, of its kind, so let people read it.

INTERVIEWER

I was surprised to read it.

WIEBE

Why?

INTERVIEWER

Because it's a fast-action book without the richness or depth of your other ones. And I don't find it representative of you. It's certainly a popular book—I wondered if it was your experiment in writing for a large market. I wonder if some people would say that's what you should aim at, writing best-sellers.

WIEBE

Well, sure. A lot of people, including occasional members of my family and close friends, say, "Why don't you write books that sell well, that are on best-seller lists?" To me, that's not important. If I wanted to write those kinds of adventure, north, police—whatever you want to call them—kinds of novels, I'm sure I could do it if I really put a lot of effort into it. (That book didn't take that much effort to write, as you can probably see.) But, it's not something that you're interested in, the way, say, to use a sport analogy, if you were a skier you might not be simply interested in going forever down Rabbit Hill. The analogy isn't quite right, but it's there. You might some day want to ski a really difficult course; you might want to fly a helicopter somewhere and try a mountain that's never been skied before. It's the kind of challenge you set yourself.

I see a purpose in *The Mad Trapper* now that there's a school edition out, for example. McClelland and Stewart have published an edition with maps and pictures and questions for the teacher, and I'm enjoying this more and more. I go to high schools where they read it in grade nine, or in grade eleven by the non-academic stream, say in the technical schools, and the kids love it. We talk about all these problems that are raised there: about who this man was and what happens to you when you hunt someone, if you're a real hunter, what happens. A number of moral questions are raised in the book. And then I can see the real purpose for a book like that. If it is, for example, to provide a good, fast, but well-told read for a non-academic high school grade who never read stories about their own country and their own place and the sorts of things that happen in our North, there's nothing the matter with that book at all.

And that reminds me very much of Tolstoy, who, at a certain stage in his life, suddenly realized that the Russian children had nothing to read. He himself wrote—and many of those fables that we read now were written by Tolstoy simply as a curriculum—for Russian children to hear and to learn to read while having the stories of their own people told. They're magnificent little fables and stories; not so little either!

77

There's nothing wrong with that. At the same time, we don't deny that *Anna Karenina* and *War and Peace* are something of a different quality.

What made me so furious at the beginning of my career was when people said, "He can't write any better than this."

INTERVIEWER

Are you talking about *Peace Shall Destroy Many*?

WIEBE

I'm talking about *Peace Shall Destroy Many*; I'm talking about *The Blue Mountains of China*. They said, "Why does Wiebe make his language so difficult? Seemingly." And I say it's not difficult at all if you think in terms of Faulkner, if you think in terms of Joyce, if you think in terms of Virginia Woolf; it's not difficult language at all. That was my argument then and it still is: that they just weren't willing to give you the benefit of the doubt. Maybe you should be looking at it with a more perceptive eye, the way, of course when you go to Faulkner or Woolf or Joyce, of course — but this is just a kid from the backwoods of Canada, you know.

INTERVIEWER

In *First and Vital Candle* you have the magical return of Abe's lost revolver. I found that event somewhat out of harmony with the realistic aspects of the book.

WIEBE

Because of the hard materialness of the return? We somehow make a difference between an artifact lost in a river to, say, a basic change of heart, a basic change of way of looking at the world. I think it's probably easier to bring a revolver back out of the river than to change a person's way of looking at the world. Take the James Keegstra trial that's going on right now — I mean, you can see how at a certain stage you never change a human being's way of thinking — and the kinds of horrible wars and the kinds of fighting that have been going on in Ireland for how many hundreds of years now, the kind of implacable relationship that Arabs and Jews have, the kinds of unbelievable conflicts that the native people in this country, the Cree and the Blackfoot, had when the white men came here. To change people's ways of thinking, to fundamentally change them, to destroy a prejudice or a hatred in your heart — I think it's easier to bring revolvers back out of rivers.

INTERVIEWER

Sad.

Well it is sad, of course. Perhaps it doesn't come across that well, but that's part of what I'm getting at there. In that sense I don't think it's so much out of keeping, considering what happens in the end. Besides, that whole matter of the shaking tent is a whole different world that we're talking about, in a way. I would've never had the nerve to write that scene if I hadn't read, for example, very coldly analytic, scientific accounts of scientists observing the shaking tent and having things happen to them that they had absolutely no way of explaining that would be acceptable to a modern, scientifically trained person. They say: I don't know how this happened, but it happened. I remember when I was researching that novel working with the University of Pennsylvania anthropologist's reports. The University of Pennsylvania had a whole series of anthropologists who studied the Northern Ontario Ojibway tribe particularly. When I was researching the book I met the last of the great Shaman at Pakanjakam in Northern Ontario. This is what the old man told me. I asked him when he had last done the shaking tent ceremony, and he said he hadn't done it, at that time, for fifteen years—since 1951 or '50—and I asked him why not. He said, there's no more people around. They don't believe it. You can't do it alone. There's no Shaman in the world can do a shaking tent ceremony alone. You have to have a circle of believers. It's okay if some think it's kind of silly and laugh, as he points out in *First and Vital Candle*, but there has to be a community within which it happens. Otherwise the spirits won't come. That's the way he says it. The scientists don't know what to say to that. But in the reports that I read these scientists back in the twenties had very striking accounts of things that happened with the shaking tent, for which there is absolutely no scientific explanation at all. Objective things like this happening.

People who didn't want to believe it too.

Who didn't want to believe it. One scientist in particular had been up north a long time—I don't know if you want to hear this story; it's a very strange one—and he was very concerned because his father was ill. He thought his father was probably dying, but he was far in the bush. In those days you had to get there by canoe; you couldn't even fly. He was very concerned, and the Ojibway conjuror said, "I'm going to be doing a shaking tent ceremony tonight, why don't you ask the spirits a question when they come?" (which is what they did; all of them did that). He said he didn't want to do that. The conjuror said, "Go ahead; if he doesn't know anything he won't tell you." So he did. When the spirit came, he was one of the people who asked the spirit a question. Then the amazing thing happened: he heard, out of the tent, out of the shaking tent, he heard the voice of his father speaking in English. The conjuror couldn't speak English. He heard the voice of his father telling him he was okay, he was all right, he wasn't ill anymore, the illness had gone. He heard it in English. When he came back, he discovered that his father was well. He reported this in the name of science. He didn't know what to do with this, but he said it. He knew his father intimately; it was the voice of his father speaking out of the conjuror's tent. There are a number of stories like this.

INTERVIEWER

So you didn't see it as outrageous, putting this event in the novel.

WIEBE

No, of course not. Not at all.

INTERVIEWER

It strikes us modern scientific types as outrageous!

WIEBE

But there are so many things in this world that are magical — we call them magical or strange or incredible — that we have no scientific explanation for. And if we only had scientific explanations for things, what an impoverished world we would have. The whole point of being a novelist, surely, is that you can think beyond the typical hard facts of what life hammers into you at every turn.

INTERVIEWER

Abe, in *First and Vital Candle,* shows a strong sensitivity to the music of Bach. Has music had any influence on your writing?

WIEBE

Oh, music is there everywhere. As you've read, it's there a lot. I grew up listening to my mother's singing, basically church music, the hymns of the church. My mother had a beautiful singing voice; so did my father. There's a very strong tradition of singing in the Mennonite Church. The two great arts that you could have any contact with at all, growing up as a kid in a Mennonite community, are singing and rhetoric: the rhetoric of the sermon, the rhetoric of storytelling.

I have inherited, in effect, the physical possibilities of singing. For a long time I took a great deal of voice training when I was a young man. At one point, I was pretty close to a career in opera and performance. I won the Winnipeg Music Festival in the opera class, in the oratorio class. I was accepted in one of the major music schools in West Germany. I could have gone there just about the time *Peace Shall Destroy Many* was published. So, I had to make a decision, whether I was going to try that or . . . And the young men and women that I used to sing with in choirs and so on, quite a lot of them have gone on and made professional careers in music. I don't know if I could have or not; I'm not sure. I'm always very glad that I didn't, because performing someone's things is a little different than making them yourself. To use an outrageous analogy, I'd prefer to be Bach than to sing him!

INTERVIEWER

Is he your favourite?

WIEBE

I think Bach is the most consummate artist in the world. He wasn't like Mozart, who just did this out of the — he just had it. At the age of six Mozart was already writing concertos and performing them. That's a particular kind of genius that's totally inexplicable. But perhaps Bach's genius is just as inexplicable. I was in his house when we were travelling in East Germany last summer, and it was strange to see how poorly he began. He had a lot of advantages because his father was a great musician, but he began by studying music, and he was never really at the top of his class, although he was close to it. He worked at learning all the basic things about music and eventually ended up being this incredible cantor at St. Thomas' in Leipzig, where we were too, having to write a cantata for every Sunday in the year, and for the great festivals — Easter and Christmas — you have a special oratorio. This kind of writing and creating on schedule, and at the same time creating probably the greatest music, church music, that's ever been written: that's the most phenomenal kind of artist there can be. He knows that he has to have the thing written by Thursday evening because that's when the first rehearsal is going to be. They run through it on Thursday, and on Friday evening they're already singing, with all the parts, and the orchestra's already practised, and on Sunday morning they perform it. And he does this every week!

A new piece — twenty minutes, thirty minutes. Well, that, to me, is the most incredible kind of genius there is. And besides that, he's writing all kinds of organ pieces, other instrumental music of all kinds — piano — he's writing all these piano pieces because he's teaching piano students and he wants to give them good practice exercises. And he does this with this unbelievable Baroque richness which is quite marvellous. Yeah, to me there is no one greater than Bach. And, at the same time, he's a profoundly religious man who feels very strongly the theological richness of what he's working with. I mean, he's not just doing this as a job; he's doing it to the greater glory and honour of God. You can see where a lot of this reflects everything that I think is important.

INTERVIEWER

Have you ever taken a musical form and worked it into your writing?

WIEBE

I don't know if consciously . . . I'm not sure, I never studied music, the technical aspects of music. That's a crazy thing. I never had a chance, for example, to study piano when I was a kid because we didn't have a piano, nor was there any teacher around, so that I can't play any instrument at all. I started studying the violin one winter when I was a child and we were in Vancouver, but then we left Vancouver and there was no possibility of studying any more. Now my son, who's sixteen, is playing grade ten piano. If the composer lived in the twentieth century or is still alive, he doesn't like him at all. He likes Schubert, Bach — Bach particularly. He's got the same tastes as I have in that sense. But, in a poor farm family, I had nothing to work with but my voice, and by the time you're twenty you can't really start piano; it's a little late.

INTERVIEWER

In practically all of your books there is a sense more of movements rather than chapters.

WIEBE

That could be.

INTERVIEWER

Many readers have pointed out what they call your "artistic maturity" that took place between *First and Vital Candle* and *The Blue Mountain of China*. Do you recognize that step? How do you account for it?

Oh, surely. The individual things that happen, anybody can see for himself. But, at a certain point, I had the confidence to try some more unconventional things. You have a certain kind of confidence in what you're doing. Already in *First and Vital Candle*, you see the attempt to have Abe move backwards in his own thinking about his life and his own experience, so that in the last inserted memory, as it were, you have a number of things layered over each other. He's going further and further back in his consciousness until he finally starts daring to think about some of the things he's consciously held away from his thought for all that time. That's moving in the direction of a more complex structural form than, say, the straight-forward chronology of *Peace Shall Destroy Many*.

I suppose there are a number of things involved with that: just not being content to write another story from beginning to end, the greater awareness of what happens when you think, and memory and the complexities of time in the human being's experience, the nerve to do it, the nerve to actually link — I mean, the story itself demanded that. If you were going to write a huge epic piece on the entire twentieth-century Mennonite history, a four-part, five-part novel — just thinking about that: is there some other way of doing it? And then using the interconnectedness of Mennonite family relationships — there are so many all the time, and especially at that time when mothers died, fathers died, and children were distributed to other families to care for and to raise — so that after a while you get a very complex family relationship. I know that they've worked out family trees for the people in *The Blue Mountains of China*, and yet those family trees are not nearly as complicated as some families literally are. When you're in a time of revolution a lot of funny things like that happen to families. So, there were a lot of reasons why I suddenly had the nerve to do something that wasn't quite as usual. Another was that I was reading more complex novels, and I realized there was no reason for doing it this way. Life moves not only from A to Z.

INTERVIEWER

Speaking of *The Blue Mountains of China*, in particular the ending, Ina Ferris describes your imagination as "secular and novelistic, animated by the here and now, not the transcendent Christian vision": that is, your characters are individuals, not symbols, and your art is existentialist, not structuralist. On the other hand, David L. Jeffery says that you take on a classically prophetic stance in the way of Jeremiah, Amos, Micah, or

Isaiah. Overall, I find Jeffery's view more convincing, but Ferris' does seem to have validity in regard to the ending of *The Blue Mountains of China*, and also, I noticed, with the characters of *My Lovely Enemy*. How do you react to these contradictory positions?

WIEBE

I don't even think in those terms, so I wouldn't care what they say as long as they get their evidence from what's there. It doesn't matter to me what they think. I don't see why it isn't possible, depending on the story and the way it develops and grows, why both aren't possible. I see no reason why one's handling of the story and the way of telling it and letting a story grow within itself, why one story can't tell you a certain kind of thing, and another story tell you another. Consistency on such critical matters, on such philosophic stances, is no great virtue. There are certain stories that I think are prophetic; there are certain stories that are profoundly social in their implications and have the wider echoing concepts of social existentialism, if you want to call it that. On the other hand, *My Lovely Enemy* is a very in-turned book, in-turned kind of story. It concentrates solely on the insides of James Dyck and the ironies and the contradictions and the limitations of the way he is experiencing the world. Is it impossible that I write that kind of novel and also write *The Temptations of Big Bear*? The fact is that presumably it's been done! Maybe it's wrong to set up these kinds of dictums.

If Ferris thinks she has an argument, maybe . . . Her statement was that the last chapter of *The Blue Mountains of China* represents some kind of closure that didn't fit the earlier stance of what was happening?

INTERVIEWER

She says you change to the structuralist conception of characters — they become symbols — whereas, before that the characters developed as individuals, existentially. Perhaps she's complaining about a lack of consistency.

WIEBE

I doubt it myself, but she may have a point there. I don't know; I don't think so. I don't think there's an argument between her and Jeffery in that sense. He argues against her also in terms of what's happening at the end of *The Blue Mountains of China*. I don't think that particular way of dealing with the story is any problem from one book to the other. She might have an argument, if you think that consistency in anything is a virtue to be followed. The same problem was raised to me by a friend who said, in *My Lovely Enemy* you play a trick on us. We begin, and we think, right, this is a straightforward realistic novel. And then, what the heck happens down in the coal mine? I said, have you read the first part carefully enough? I mean, the very first argument, the very first situation is this discussion of whether Louis Riel might not have been hanged, or something. People are so used to reading — and I don't know why — realistic fiction from me — and for the life of me I can't tell why they feel that this is the way they've been programmed to read me — that when I really absolutely throw a curve at them with the bridge, and the church that you can sometimes see there under certain conditions if you're lucky, or get you down in the mine, in the restaurant, then they feel somehow that I haven't been consistent: again, as if consistency is all there is to it. I don't think they're reading carefully enough. There are quite a number of things in *Big Bear*, for example, that are not explainable in the logical, scientific sense of explanation.

INTERVIEWER

I guess it's that they are put into the eyes or the mind of a man who we really are convinced is magical himself.

WIEBE

Who is a Shaman. Okay. Okay. We are willing to accept it from a Cree chief; we might even be willing to accept it from a Jewish rabbi; but not a professor of history at the University of Alberta. That's bullshit! If the possibility is there for human beings at all, it is there for all. It just depends on whether they're opening themselves to it. If it's possible for a man like Big Bear to have a vision of the future, of the future of his people, that's not only — such an experience should not only be — restricted to Indians because they are non-scientific anyway, or the Inuit in *First and Vital Candle*. Civilized (so-called) white people are willing to lean over backwards for them, but you get closer to home, sit in a chair behind a desk: no, no, no. I think those possibilities are there for anybody. It's just that we've deliberately cut ourselves off from it.

INTERVIEWER

Do you regard your writing as a gloss on the Bible? Or does it stand in another relation to the Bible?

WIEBE

The Bible, to me, first is such a magnificent series of stories that explains and tells all the stories; it has all the stories in it that you really need to understand what human beings are about. In that sense, any story that you write is a commentary on what is already there in an archetypal way. But there aren't any new stories anyway. All we do is retell the old ones in slightly different ways.

In a lot of ways, I don't even think I've directly used many stories from the Bible; certainly not as directly as Kroetsch does, or Aritha van Herk does. Maybe if I weren't known as a Christian, people wouldn't think this. But since Kroetsch never talks about himself being a Christian, they don't see it that way. If they looked at his writing from that point of view they might find it anyway.

INTERVIEWER
Would it be accurate to call you a mystic?

WIEBE
Do you want to define it a little?

INTERVIEWER
Someone open to the possibilities of the sort you mentioned in connection with James Dyck and Big Bear; someone who experiences another level of awareness or consciousness different from the logical or scientific, so-called normal one.

WIEBE
Okay. That's where the Indian thing, especially with Big Bear and with Maskepetoon in *My Lovely Enemy* is very clear. At the beginning of that second section of the Maskepetoon story, where he talks about anything being possible in the world, you don't find that strange, because life teaches you that anything is possible. A mystic, if you think of a person who is aware of the mystery of the world — mystery in the sense that the scientist or the existentialist who cannot explain something, and then inexplicable things happen — the existentialist ends up with absurdity. These things are incomprehensible to the logical, reasoning mind, and life ends up being absurd. There are any number of natural phenomena that end up as being absurd. Life as a whole is absurd because there isn't really any logic to life or to being alive. I think the mystic is a person who goes beyond that, who does not see absurdity, but mystery, and that you get further in comprehending what the world is about by opening yourself up to the mystery of it than by saying, "Oh that's absurd; it's illogical; it's something that we just live with but means nothing."

For the mystic, everything means something; it's just that we don't know quite what it is. We never say it's meaningless. There is meaning everywhere; its just that we're not aware yet of what it is. And there are also possibilities everywhere; we just don't grasp what they all are. It's quite a different approach, I think, to looking at what happens in the world with the almost despair that one senses in the absurdist, existentialist ways of looking at the world. If you think in those terms, twentieth-century history is a history you should despair of: the continuing things that happen in the world, all kinds of horrors, like this bomb going off in downtown Beirut and killing all the kids that are going home because there's so much fighting. They're all going home quietly when all of a sudden this bomb explodes. The stupidity of human beings, and their violence and their horror towards one another, you must despair, you must despair — I almost said I defy you not to despair — when you see that. Or the stupidity of President Reagan trying to force the Nicaraguans into loving him, and just making things so much worse and worse and worse. I'm using perfectly obvious examples from what you see in the newspapers any given day. You must in effect despair at the logic or the sense that it makes any rhyme or reason. On the other hand . . . well — human mystery . . .

INTERVIEWER
In your work you have consistently shown an awareness of the nuclear arms situation we are in, including an eloquent depiction of the twentieth century's United Republics of Total Death and prospects for its enlargement in "On Death and Writing." In that talk you move away from the United Republics after contemplating the futility of writing as we face annihilation. Is it not possible for the writer to deal with the prospect? Is it right to ignore it? Does it affect you as a writer?

WIEBE
Oh yes. Part of an answer to your question is in what Maskepetoon talks about: it's not the white man's guns that kill you, it's the words. And in the long run, I think that's what it is. The guns come only after the language has disappeared. To a large extent that is always the case when people destroy each other. The guns are just the simple solution and, of course, they're no solution at all. They're the solution we reach for when there's no more talking left.

Bob Beal and I are working now on a picture book called *War in the West, Voices in the 1885 Rebellion.* Accompanying the pictures are texts of the people who actually participated in the rebellion, and were involved in it — the memoirs, the letters, the news reports, the diaries. When there's nothing to say anymore, when language breaks down, that's when you reach for guns; you go for those solutions, and then you blast everyone out of existence. Of course in 1885 it was simple, because there was an overwhelming force on one side and after you've shot enough of the rebels and you've put them on trial, they aren't heard of for the next fifty years. The Indian and the Métis people of Western Canada were absolutely destroyed. They were rolled over and no one even heard of them again until after World War II—in the thirties it started, and then after World War II—when a lot of them who had been soldiers again found they could deal with war just as well, and perhaps even better, than a lot of white men. They came back with a certain self-consciousness. But, for at least fifty years they just disappeared out of Canadian life. People have the tendency always to reach for those simple, stupid solutions.

The problems that the Indians and the Métis faced in 1885 have not gone away. As a matter of fact, when they were debating this matter on the constitution a year or so ago, somebody phoned me up and said, "Rudy, are you watching television?" I said no. He said, "Look, there's Bill Wilson from B.C. and David Aheneikew of Saskatchewan and they're talking just like Big Bear." Exactly the same problem—exactly the same issue—is facing their people. The problem hasn't gone away at all, but they're talking about it now. Then, they just got shooting about it.

In a very simple analogy that's what I'm trying to get across in that article, although it may not come across very clearly. The telling of stories and creating our world with words is still the only thing that there is. Once you stop, there's nothing left but to shoot. Once the U.S. and the Soviet Union stop talking, there'll be nothing left to do but to drop bombs on each other. It's the same thing.

INTERVIEWER

Samuel U. Reimer, in *The Blue Mountains of China,* hears a call and tries to do something about the Vietnam war. He comes off very sympathetically, but tragically. Is that a statement about protest, the futility of protest?

WIEBE

A lot of logical people, a lot of Christian people who read that book think he's just gone nuts, which I find totally incredible. That Christians, of all people, would think that Sam Reimer has gone crazy, I find totally disconcerting. I couldn't believe it when they told me; and they do: they just think he's gone crazy. More sensitive readers can't say that. I mean, he hasn't gone crazy. It's just that he's seeing something, he's experiencing part of the mystery which others don't know, and he just seems to be crazy because there's no explanation for it, no possible explanation. The minister is trying to figure out where it all came from; he's trying to psychoanalyse him, I suppose. And probably he's right: somewhere along there is where it came from. Sam isn't aware of it. That's what I'm trying to get at: he's tragic, but not, in another sense. The tragedy is that he didn't go and do it. The tragedy is not that he's misled or something, but that he had the experience and didn't respond.

INTERVIEWER
If one tries to do something about such an immense problem as the nuclear arms race, many people say you're crazy. So you're just reflecting that reaction in *The Blue Mountains of China?*

WIEBE
Well, sure. That's what I hear my friends saying all the time: "It doesn't help anyway. What's the use?" I hear people saying that to someone who has travelled in the Third World and has realized how terrible the nutritional problems are in the Third World, and they come back to Canada and they refuse to eat anything but vegetables and grains. And people keep saying to them, "What's the point of it? You're not helping anybody in the Third World." That's not the question that's being raised, or the answer that's being given. I think it's a different matter. There's one point to trying to change your society, and I think you have to try to do that, and I think a lot of people try to change their society, especially the way they're looking at the enemy at the moment, and that has to be done. But the first thing is that you do it with yourself. And then, if you feel called to that, you do it in a larger way. It's always most difficult to do it with yourself anyway. None of us is facing Gorbachev or anybody; none of us is facing the Russians with nuclear bombs in their hands; we're just facing those relatives that we can't stand. You start right there.

INTERVIEWER
When you plan your novels, do you concern yourself with literary theory?

WIEBE
I don't think in those terms when I'm working on them. Anyway—I shouldn't say this; I said it just the other day. The bane of my novelistic

life is that I've probably had more than my share of dull, plodding critics. I don't suppose one should say that, should one? I can't tell anybody what they should write about or what they should do. But occasionally one reads an article that is getting at something that I think is really important. But most of the time it's rather dull and thematic and plodding.

INTERVIEWER

Is Tolstoi in *My Lovely Enemy* a comment on critical posturing?

WIEBE

He's a dog! I don't know what you can make of Tolstoi. The last thing he does, at night, he's chained down to the camper.

INTERVIEWER

Besides the epic voices that W. J. Keith has described, I've always found a real lyric impulse in your writing. Gillian's poem in *My Lovely Enemy* is one of the first lyrics that appears as a poem in your work. Are you heading more in that direction?

WIEBE

It's possible. A lot of my prose is lyric in a lot of ways, the way the language is dealt with. Part of that is probably because I read a lot out loud. Some sections I like to read—I find interesting to read—again and again partly because of the way the language is used, not only the ideas and the pictures or the narrative that's involved. I wouldn't make that much distinction between the prose and the lyric. I think well-written language has that lyricism, that music, in it anyway, especially if you work on it hard the way I do. I work on it a long time to get those expressions right. In *My Lovely Enemy* the language clearly is very important, not only because of all the echoes of poetry that Dyck has running wild through his head—sometimes quite inappropriately—but because of the way a man whose mind was like that would be influenced in his normal thinking. The whole thing does take place inside Dyck's head, so you have to keep that always in mind when it's happening.

INTERVIEWER

In *Peace Shall Destroy Many* you mention Madeline Moosomin, the great-granddaughter of Big Bear. How far back does your interest in Big Bear go?

WIEBE

I didn't know anything about him when I was growing up. It was when I came to university—it must have been '58, '59, well, '57—when I discovered Cameron's *Blood Red The Sun*. That's where that awareness came from. It was not something that I found out when I was living in that world, in that country. I had to come far away from it. I was twenty years old or older before I was ever aware. I knew the Indians that lived around there; I'd seen them. I didn't know them individually. I'd seen them, but I wasn't aware that this major leader important in the history of his people had been there. That was totally unknown to me because there was nothing there to give that to me. I didn't know the Indian people: the white people didn't have anything much to do with them; they certainly weren't there in the school curriculum; the history of Western Canada wasn't taught that way then; it wasn't something that you would ever know about.

INTERVIEWER

You've said that the Indian must become the central figure for Canadians. Do you mean the heroic image of the Indian? What would be the implications of such a shift in perspective? It's certainly not the case now.

WIEBE

The classic Canadian position in the world is that we're not a particularly important nation as the world goes. At the same time, we are important because we're a rich nation and we're North America . . . perhaps that's too complicated an analogy . . . think about it the other way: the denial of our roots and of what was really here before the white man came. That's where you begin and in that sense the Indian has to become central—as a place of beginnings, as someone you must do something with; and not only a beginning, but a world that continues to be with us. It's part of our world. In every one of our big cities—not only Regina, Calgary and Edmonton, Saskatoon and Winnipeg, but also Vancouver and Montréal and Toronto—there's a large subterranean Indian world, often very poor, desperately poor. It's the kind of thing that's happening everywhere in the world where the poor and the people with very few possibilities flock to the cities. It happens in São Paolo, it happens in Lima, it happens in Mexico City, it happens everywhere. This is part of the phenomenon of our modern world too. The fact that it's relatively small here—it's not huge like São Paolo or Lima—means that we can ignore it. But it is becoming impossible to ignore in downtown Edmonton or downtown Winnipeg—if you go there. But most of us live in the suburbs and we can still ignore it. It is a very vital part of contemporary Canadian life, even though most people don't see it.

With one or two major exceptions, I still have never seen a really good novel, or even sociological study of that kind of thing happening in Canadian cities. Yet I think it's a pivotal thing; it's really vital in terms of what's going to happen in our country. These stories have to be told more, but it seems so small now that we can ignore it. When we go downtown and we see desperately poor Canadians there, we ignore them; the fact that a very high percentage of them are native people we ignore even more. Those stories have to be told too. A novel like *A Search for April Rain Tree* is the beginning of that story being told. That's a Métis girl telling a story about her own particular world and growing up, the foster homes she went through in Winnipeg. It's a very moving book.

INTERVIEWER

I had been thinking more of the heroic aspect of the Indian.

WIEBE

I don't know whether that heroic world has much to tell us anymore, the heroic world of the nineteenth-century Indian. As a matter of fact, that particular kind of traditional story is probably of less use now than almost any. The heroic tradition of testing yourself against your enemies, and always knowing who your enemy is, and there's an absolute difference between yourselves, who are the People, and your enemies, who are not the People. I don't think that's possible in the world anymore. And I think that tradition of Indian history doesn't have much to tell us anymore. The Indian people themselves nowadays never emphasize that part of their tradition, which was certainly there, and was a major part of what was breaking down in the nineteenth century.

It had to break down because it was exactly that tradition that the white man used to pit one group of Indians against the other, the more readily to destroy them so they wouldn't bother the whites. It began right when Champlain sides with the Hurons and the English automatically side with the Iroquois. One of the major reasons why the English could defeat the French in North America was because the French sided with the less warlike of the two major groups, the Algonkian-speaking people being weaker than the Iroquian-speaking people. That starts as soon as the white man encounters North America, and it reaches all the way across the continent.

That tradition isn't very useful, and I don't think the Indian people

92

think of it anymore either. Those traditions are of no use to us. The world has had enough of heroism in that just-try-to-knock-me-down sense. The heroes of our world are the Norman Bethunes of the world. The Indians have a tradition of those kinds of heroes too. Big Bear's one of them — one of the people of words, the people of feeling, the people of vision, the people of understanding who bridge gaps rather than stand up and say, this is Me and if you're not like me, I'll kill you. The world's too small for that. It's that other Indian tradition that's important now, not the warlike heroic one.

INTERVIEWER

The story "Did Jesus Ever Laugh?," like *The Mad Trapper,* has a central character who is insane. Do you have a particular interest in insanity?

WIEBE

I don't know if I'm terribly interested in insanity. I don't know any insane people, really. In a short story you deal with people driven to the margin of their existence, of their possibilities as human beings, one way or another. This kind of religious fanaticism is something I've had a lot of experience with — not as drastic as that, of course . . . well, almost — people who would shoot people if they denied their way of looking at God. That kind of incredible fanaticism is there in the Bible and there are people who imitate it. In that sense I'm talking about something I've experienced. The short story can do that: drive people to the edges of possible behaviour and thought. That's what fiction is for! To show you pictures of that. It's a lot better to encounter it in a story than to have to experience it physically.

INTERVIEWER

For your 1982 selection of stories, what criteria did you use in choosing them?

WIEBE

When you put a collection together you think of all kinds of things. The first time I put a collection together I was distressed by noticing that in practically every one of them somebody gets killed or dies or some damn thing like that, which annoys me.

INTERVIEWER

Your "temptation to violence"?

93

WIEBE

Well, yeah. But I'm always harping on this in my writing class: most of us have very little experience with death, so for heaven's sake, let's not choose the easiest way out of ending a story by killing everybody off. And yet, I see it in myself. It's an ending you can't argue with: people are dead, and that's it. So, one of the things I looked at was, can I avoid all these death stories? It wasn't really that important a principle, but it obviously must have been one. I'm not sure, except that I think that most of these stories are the better ones I've written.

I write short stories very slowly. I haven't written that many stories in my life, and I haven't written that many lately, so the selection was basically what was around at the time that I thought was useful to keep, although the other ones are around too. The reason for omitting "Scrapbook," the first story that I ever had published, is that it's very much a young writer's story and it's all right for when you're twenty-one or twenty-two . . .

INTERVIEWER

I like reading the ones where I recognize an incident from one of your novels, where you're coming at a situation from a different point of view—"The Naming of Albert Johnson" and "Where is the Voice Coming From?" for instance.

WIEBE

Those are probably the most anthologized stories I've written. But that's invidious too, because editors look at other editors' collections and they pick up the same stories. A lot of the time editors who put collections together don't read anymore. They see this story in seven different anthologies, so they'll use it too because obviously people think it's a good story.

INTERVIEWER

The Scorched-Wood People coincides in time with your interest in extra-literary forms such as the Riel television series and your play. Is the emphasis on vision, rather than voice so much, in *The Scorched-Wood People*—Riel's vision and Macdonald's vision—a part of this interest?

WIEBE

No. That's strictly the kind of thing the story gave me. I don't think that's anything but suitable to the story itself. It is a story of clashes of different ways of seeing what's basically an enormous empty land and what you can do with it. Sir John had one idea and Riel and the Métis people had quite a different one. It's just that Macdonald's rolled over the other one.

But you realize that historically that's an incredible moment: of actually thinking of the enormous interior of this land and what you do with it—empty of all people, as far as they were concerned, and the Métis and the Indians yelling, no, it's not empty of all people; there are some of us out here! And Macdonald was saying, in effect, well, there are a few of you, but you don't really matter. Historically that's an interesting moment because, at least in the Northern Hemisphere, it was the last of the possibilities of settlement like that. Australia was experiencing the same thing and parts of South America experienced it a little later. That was an amazing possibility for humanity at that time—almost the last; there hasn't been any land like that left in the world for a long time. What Riel's vision of that was is very strange and still, I think, exciting. It hasn't been seriously talked about much. It just seems like the ravings of a madman, another stupid man.

INTERVIEWER

And the other side seems so lacking in imagination, lacking in hope.

WIEBE

There's William Butler riding across this country: it is an extraordinary thing for an Englishman—it shames him!—to see so much undeveloped land. "Here's a beautiful lake. Let's develop it." It's the first thing they think of! This is Duddy Kravitz, looking for a lake he can buy, and then he can develop it.

INTERVIEWER

Were you happy with the way *Far As the Eye Can See* turned out?

WIEBE

It was great fun. Theatrically it worked tremendously well when it was staged. It was a great company to work with: the actors were very good, especially the strong central characters of Aberhart, old Antoine, and Betty. The actors were tremendous; the young engineer, Eric Peterson, who went on to play Billy Bishop.

INTERVIEWER

Would you try playwriting again?

Paul Thompson and I have talked a number of times. Paul is interested in what he calls Epic Theatre. You begin at three o'clock in the afternoon and you go to six, and you have a two-hour evening break, and then you go from eight to eleven. He went on a trip around the world to study other forms of theatre and some of the epic theatre traditions, not only in England, but particularly in Brazil. I don't know what's become of that. But we used to talk about doing some things like that. But interests change.

I met Thompson and got to know him while on the Arts advisory panel of the Canada Council. He was on that too and we used to talk about things. Then he brought his company west and we did a couple of things together. It gave me a much stronger sense of dramatic form for use in the novel. I liked it very much.

But the frenetic pace at which theatre people work, and the way you have to work together with a group, is different. On the other hand, you get instant response. It's a terrifying thing to sit in the audience. You've written it, you've acted it and you've practised it, and then you put it on and right there the audience responds. Right there! It's not like waiting for reviews, and years later somebody will come along and say something nice, or someone will come along and try to destroy the whole thing. But you're right there, sitting in the audience, and everyone around you is either getting the jokes, getting the story, responding the way you want them to, or they're not. It's instant; it's instant replay. It's terrifying! It's so different from what a novelist is used to. By the time a book comes out it's almost nine months or a year since you've written it. Then, by the time the response comes in—it's an individual response usually—you can say, well, it's a nitwit who reviewed it. But there, you've got an audience—two hundred people—and they like it or they're walking out. It's a totally different experience.

Is the story "An Indication of Burning," where the writing teacher falls in love with the would-be writer, an indication of *My Lovely Enemy?*

That's probably coincidental. It's an idea that came to me once, just driving through a town like that, and I saw a girl just like that and I realized that young women exactly that age were in my writing classes at the university. And how did they get here? How did these ones get here and that one didn't? Is there something inherent in their intellectual capacity, for example, or what is it? And what if she got caught? And what if you didn't have the perception and the first thing you did after you finished high school in a small town like that was get married and have children, which is what a lot of them do? And I do get housewives in their later thirties in my classes, perhaps when their children first start going to school and they have those first few hours of the day when they don't have children around. There's all kinds of complex variations. That's a story that comes out of my teaching, more than any story I've ever written.

INTERVIEWER

What are your aims as a teacher of creative writing?

WIEBE

The best thing you could aim for is for them to write a good story, to write a readable story. That's quite a big expectation really. But, it's amazing how often it does happen, considering that many of them haven't written very much before, and how much practice it takes to write consistently well. It's not that difficult, seemingly, for some people to write at least one good story; then they get hooked and then they find out how much hard work it is to be consistent at it. It's amazing how many people have one or two good stories in their system that they can actually write, perhaps because they already know a few good stories and the form is already inherent in what they're doing, so they don't have to struggle so much with the story but with the way of saying it. But bringing all those items together again and again is a very difficult thing. But a lot of people don't give themselves a chance at all. They give up, or they never try. Writing a good story isn't that hard, actually. My son's been playing organized hockey since he was six—ten years. If he had put all that time into writing stories, imagine how good he'd be! If you just think in those terms, of all that practice, there would be amazing storytellers. There's nothing inherently more difficult about writing good stories than there is in playing a piano piece by Bach, or playing a hockey game well. It's just the fact that you have more practice. As a matter of fact, I could argue that you use language more than you use skating abilities—in your daily life you're using language all the time—and that in itself provides a facility. It might be easier to write stories. It probably is.

INTERVIEWER

Women's issues come up often in *My Lovely Enemy*. Liv and Gillian, as well as Jesus, challenge James about his view of women. Are you beginning to see women the way many people do, as an oppressed group, similar, perhaps, to the Indian and the Métis people?

Certainly. Women have made us aware of that. If you set a story in the contemporary world, you have to face it. There's no way today that thoughtful people can avoid it. If you set your story in the 1980s, it has to be there somehow, if you're going to have any realistic range of human beings involved. If you're going to have perceptive women in the 1980s in your book you have to do something with that. I do it rather deliberately there. The time of your novel determines to some extent what you write about.

INTERVIEWER
Is James's fundamental problem epitomized by his wanting to, and not being able to enter the women's conversations on a credible level?

WIEBE
That's one of the big ones. He tries to do it sometimes by cracking a joke or by quoting an aphorism, by using language of getting into it, generally ironic or humorous. There seems to be a part of that women's world that he really does not understand, that he really can't get into. The women, partly because they just are women, seem to understand in ways that he, with the best of his intelligence, can't.

INTERVIEWER
That comes through strongly in "The Mine."

WIEBE
That's part of what's going on there, sure.

INTERVIEWER
How would you describe the relation between the Maskepetoon story and the other material in *My Lovely Enemy?*

WIEBE
This is one of the things that the reader has to come to grips with somehow. Where are those italicized stories coming from in terms of James's consciousness? They are not an historian's story. That's an interesting question actually. I won't talk about it; that's the kind of thing

the individual reader has to solve for himself. But, I think there's plenty of indication of how it could be working. I don't think I'm saying anything very profound here.

INTERVIEWER

In the light of *My Lovely Enemy,* do you still believe that "the morality of the world is built-in"?

WIEBE

I think I may have a bit of a larger idea now of what the morality of the world is than when I wrote *Peace Shall Destroy Many*. People change. Any good writer has to be a thinker, and at a certain point life teaches you that the ideas you held when you were younger need to be changed. If you still believe exactly the same thing and understand only what you understood when you were twenty-one, you're an impoverished human being. A person publishing a book when he's forty-eight or forty-nine should have different ideas about some things than he did when he was twenty-two or twenty-three. If he didn't, I'd pity him. It's quite true there could be contradictory things happening in *Peace Shall Destroy Many* and *My Lovely Enemy,* taking the widest possible range of books. That wouldn't surprise me in the least. As a matter of fact, I'd be sad if it didn't seem that way. *Peace Shall Destroy Many* is the Wapiti Mennonite community seen through the eyes of a young nineteen-year-old man, and in *My Lovely Enemy* it's a forty-two-year-old intellectual living in a completely different, very urban, world. You'd expect it to be different.

INTERVIEWER

Do you see your work as a whole, then, one big novel?

WIEBE

No. That would be a very odd way of seeing it. Eventually, if you look back, you would see a larger thing there. Some books have obvious connections: *The Scorched-Wood People* and *Big Bear* are pictures of somewhat the same time. There are a couple of other novels in that time too that I've thought of writing. I might yet. *Peace Shall Destroy Many* and *The Blue Mountains of China* are alternative stories about somewhat the same people. No, I wouldn't see my life's work as one big book. They're very much pieces that were found and written at the time they needed to be found.

INTERVIEWER

What's your favourite book?

WIEBE

I would shift among any of the three novels that I wrote in the seventies. Maybe some day I'll like *My Lovely Enemy* as much as I do those others.

INTERVIEWER

Do you have any fictional work coming up?

WIEBE

I'm working—I have been working for quite a number of years—on a novel. I hope during my sabbatical next half-year I'll be able to knock it on the head. *Deo volente.*

Interview by Thomas Gerry

Photo by ben soo

PETER VAN TOORN

Peter Van Toorn was born in a bunker near The Hague, Holland, in 1944 and moved to Montreal in 1954 where he later studied at McGill University. His poetry is a blend of all cultures: through free-style translations he has brought together poets as diverse as Basho and St. Denis Garneau in his most recent book Mountain Tea & Other Poems *(1984), which was short-listed for the Governor General's Award. It includes recent original work and work from his two previous books,* Leeway Grass *(Delta Canada, 1970), which Raymond Souster called "the best first book of poems I've read in years," and* In Guildenstern County *(Delta Can, 1973), said by Northrop Frye to be "the product of an unusually intelligent mind." He also edited* Lakeshore Poets *(1981), and coedited, with Ken Norris,* Cross/cut: Contemporary English Quebec Poetry *and* The Insecurity of Art *(both 1982).*

Anne McLean states that "Van Toorn's tongue is a match for the most jammed CB radio. His speech is an odd marriage of tough talk and eccentricity, accident and erudition, scholarliness and mystic sensibility." Here, for example, is a snippet of "Mountain Boogie":

> *O bronze leaf hopping a highway of mint & toffee headlights!*
> *O cigarette paper rolled by fog tongue!*
> *O crumpled copper onionwrap!*
> *O perfume of the stars around the moon!*
> *O barnstraw blond!*
> *O lollipop lick of streaming tangerine air!*

This interview took place on the afternoon of 23 February 1984 in Peter's office at John Abbott College in Ste. Anne de Bellevue, a suburb of Montreal, where he has taught poetry and creative writing for more than ten years. Outside his large office window can be seen a clear winter sky and the old library with its red clay-tiled roofs.

103

VAN TOORN

Well, well, here we are on a lofty afternoon.

INTERVIEWER

It's a beautiful sky.

VAN TOORN

Before, in my Canadian poetry class, the light was coming through from outside. I always feel that if I'm teaching in a bright room with a lot of windows, like this one, and I can see the trees outside and the cars in the snow and the sun shining through, it's going to be a good course.

Somehow, it's a Canadian skier's afternoon. Skiing in Canada is a very important thing to poetry. I used to do a lot of skiing when I was young. Once, I got a pair of old skis from the Sally Ann, slapped on my old boots to them and went through the woods all day long. I also remember making a pair of snowshoes. My first experience with snowshoes was when I got stuck in the woods. I was snowed in in a cabin. The drifts were so deep I couldn't get home. I was a little panicked. I cut two little moosewood trees . . .

INTERVIEWER

Moosewood?

VAN TOORN

. . . small ones, saplings. They were wet and shiny. I put them near the fire and heated them up and bent them around; thawed them out a little bit, they were stiff and frozen. And I actually wound out of them a primitive form of snowshoes. And the moosewood itself being shiny and so on, and the ice-coating on it like wax, so I walked home. But it isn't really like wax, 'cause some snow clung to it. But at least I managed to get home. It took me hours on top of deep drifts. Otherwise, I never would have got home.

INTERVIEWER

Where was that?

VAN TOORN

In the woods between Cartierville and Senneville. It used to be in those days—no suburbs—one long stretch of farm and woods, all the way along the north river here. So it was twenty miles of woods. Some communities were more developed than others, and pressing in. Like

104

Saraguay, still a small town in a way. Ste. Geneviève was developed, and now there's Roxboro, Dollard des Ormeaux, Pierrefonds, all those places didn't exist—it was all woods. I used to walk there. It's part of my poetic destiny that I ended up working nearby. I used to walk. Now I drive! It's only twenty-five years later. I used to walk it looking for poetry, you know.

INTERVIEWER

How do you go about looking for poetry?

VAN TOORN

I like to be in the woods. I used to spend long hours there. When you get up early in the morning and come home late at night, all day walking through snow, woods and trees, you've gotta take a leak in that time, maybe take a shit. And it's cold. There's no little oak tree, neatly perched there, which is warmed up and says: "Here." You have to make a fire at some point to toast your sandwiches and make them warm. You get out your thermos and have a little tea. You fill your pipe and you see some things. Certain trees that you knew well, that you thought were sturdy and beautiful and have now fallen in the wake of an ice storm, or have cracked. And you're surprised. Not that tree! What? Some little spot in the woods, you know, anywhere in twenty miles. You get to know the woods by little places, by the way light falls in certain ways, in certain different conditions, like early in the morning, when the light starts coming down and everything starts to dry.

There are certain feelings about certain places. Certain animals come on the scene. Fox, or racoon, or partridge. You know, in the winter, where partridge go. They always go sledding uphill to the low spruce bushes. You can tell right away because some of the stuff from the spruce bushes has dropped on the coating of ice and if it's crusty then the fox will be looking for them. A fox will burrow underneath the thin coating of ice to where partridge are sleeping, suddenly surprise them in the middle of a cold winter's day. You were walking along for hours and you didn't hear a thing, just wind. You hear nothing. You see nothing. It's frozen and looks like the terror that Northrop Frye speaks of in Canadian poetry. You know, that if right now, you didn't have a thermos in your pack, or bread, or if you didn't have matches, you could freeze. You'd lose your way and never get home. Or, if you stepped through some ice that's under the snow, then suddenly: Bbbvvwwwrrgh! This drumming, rustling sound, and the partridge goes pshrooh! right by you.

105

INTERVIEWER

It sounds like a helicopter . . .

VAN TOORN

You know, one of my favorite animals is the cow. I love cows. They give us an immense amount. Thanks to civilization and cows we have milk, yoghurt, cheese—I used to think eggs too. Cows patiently chew away. Maybe they're more in touch with reincarnation, or something like that. They realize what a long grind it is to get out of this long, vicious cycle of lives. So they chew away and do their bit. Just pure white milk.

INTERVIEWER

But try to get them back in the barn in fall.

VAN TOORN

They go in naturally, don't they? Put a little grain or alfalfa in front of them in the trough and they do it naturally. As long as they know you're not sneaking up with any bull behind them. Slam! Boom!

There was one instance when this bull, two-thousand pounds, heavy, reared up to mount a calf, who couldn't tolerate that weight; too young to be pregnant, too. Her legs might have snapped like toothpicks under the weight of this bull. The cows sensed it immediately and kept bugging the bull by getting too close or making sounds, and irritating him somehow, so he'd dismount to chase them off. At one point they decoyed him while others stayed behind and pushed the calf to the ground, on its belly, where the bull couldn't mount it. The hormone they must secrete when in heat couldn't reach him at this level. He just forgot about it. Interesting to watch the way these mother cows protected the little one. Not that the bull was mean, or anything like that. He was just doing his job. That's what bulls are meant to do.

INTERVIEWER

Do you do any bird watching?

VAN TOORN

When you're inside you're always doing little things. It's almost ritualistic. So often you're before a window, and if you're meditative about these things you *do* want to look outside at the trees and the things of nature. It's nice to see birds moving in it, representing a kind of freedom, perhaps. At the kitchen window, where I live now, the branches press against the window and I often see a fat winter sparrow. He survives, not lean and hungry, but fat and fluffy. He sits there on the branch and bounces around in the wind. A fat little thing. He only weighs about an ounce. If he's one-tenth of an ounce overweight for take-off, he takes a shit to lose it. He's such a fat little bugger, you know, he's fat and he's happy. All his feathers are fluffed up to keep him warm. It's fifty below out there and you don't want to go out, so you have a shot of bourbon and watch him bounce around and it's nice. It's damn nice. I prefer that to having something else to look out over.

INTERVIEWER

What is it that makes so many Canadian poets go to the country? Even the ones who worked as clerks, like Archibald Lampman, often went on canoe trips in northern Ontario.

VAN TOORN

It's a very old thing that, eh?

INTERVIEWER

It seems common in our literature.

VAN TOORN

I know the question. Everybody seems to formulate that. Somehow Canadian poets seem to be inspired—oh! I was reading MacMechan . . . *The Headwaters of Canadian Poetry* last night. He was writing at the same time that W. E. Collin wrote *The White Savannahs,* another book of Canadian criticism. These are beautiful books. Written by the old-timers. He says that the note of Canadian poetry has always been one of spiritual purity. That's not the only startling critical point he makes. He makes one other point too, and that is, that Canadian poets seem to do best in their first books. Then they dwindle. It seems to be always the first book that is strong and of great promise. He makes these two points throughout a scattered 300 pages. Nice. He talks about spiritual purity being a Canadian note. Why do poets go to nature for reflection? Very primeval. We don't have the American Cowboy-Indian-Saga-West. We don't populate it with that. We don't go out there with cameras to advertise Genessee beer. When going into the woods, if we were to have met Indians—this is my romanticism, maybe, I don't know—if we were to have met Indians, or the spirit of what the Indians were in touch with, or felt that spirit in ourselves, not the fearfulness of an arriving year—like,

107

maybe the first settlers were hungry, going through scurvy because there were no oranges or not enough firewood, or there were Indian battles; there is tremendous fearfulness in coming to a new country—but to experience that sense of the way the Indians looked around this countryside as belonging to God, to the animals and to themselves—they had a *whole* different vision of it—maybe that's what the poets were actually doing and secretly knew. That that existence somehow was an older religion than Christianity and Democracy. Maybe, like a Shintoist of Japan, poets have been always trying to get close to that vision of nature. Like Emily Carr in her paintings. And Tom Thomson. The ones who've succeeded are the painters more than the poets. That's why Canadian poets have an eye for painting, for the visual aspects of things. We're surrounded by so much of it. In Europe you don't just look out an office window, like this one here, and see a parking lot *that* huge. Look at all the open space there. See any people? No. Headlights. Cars. Buses.

INTERVIEWER

A spirit of solitude.

VAN TOORN

Yeah. Emptiness. And threat.

INTERVIEWER

Threat?

VAN TOORN

Yeah. If you get out of your car right now and it's cold out and it doesn't start, where do you go?

INTERVIEWER

To yourself? Poets in Canada seem to be very self-reflecting. Which is something you've tried to change. Lampman in his poetry is very self-reflective. He gets so intimidated by the outside. That's what did him in. The fear of otherworldliness.

VAN TOORN

Hmm.

INTERVIEWER

Would you say that you've chosen a slightly bohemian lifestyle?

VAN TOORN

I don't know if I'm *that* bohemian. I'm very middle-class in some ways. I believe in education. But the areas I've lived in would be characterized as bohemian, I suppose. The way I dress. Some of the external things.

INTERVIEWER

You've translated some poets with bohemian reputations, though.

VAN TOORN

You mean Rimbaud, for example. Baudelaire was an aristocrat. He lived an *expensive* bohemian life. Villon, *he* was a bohemian. A highwayman. He didn't drive a Mercury, as I do. That's very middle-class. I had a little incident before. I was parking and used the muscle of my car to get a space.

INTERVIEWER

What originally set you translating?

VAN TOORN

Huge areas of *Mountain Tea* that I had to go through. Every now and then it was a difficult piece of territory to navigate. Instead of venting my frustrations or cursing my luck, I would turn to a mode of sensibility sanctioned or enshrined in perfect expression by another culture. So if I came to a deep gorge with no way of getting across it, I'd think of Basho, you know, and bend a big piece of bamboo and land on the other side. Why repeat things that have been done better in the past? It's more like a transition. You learn something by travelling to the land of Basho or Baudelaire. The next poem you get to is easier.

The sky's getting darker.

INTERVIEWER

Yeah. Notice the tiles on the roof.

VAN TOORN

I love that roof! I once started writing a poem about the red roofs of John Abbott College and it turned out to be useful. I never liked that poem. It started off on a negative note. About how I was slouching home and these red roofs . . . Later on the image of the red roof tiles turned

109

up in a little sonnet called "Mountain Leaf" and then it turned up in "Mountain Easter" too. Somehow the roof was like a place to put your foot while you make a long jump. Sometimes things are like that; they're of no immediate use, they make no finished product, but they're like a note when you hold it in the air.

INTERVIEWER

More about the Mountain poems. What other things would lead to poems?

VAN TOORN

There were many times when the only reward I could give myself when I couldn't see anything getting into print or my book getting out, nothing happening in the way of reward (I don't even think my girlfriend understood what I was doing at the time), the only thing I could do was to find in my readings some beautiful statement or line that I could now, on every new draft that I worked on, put after my title. I'd say, "Mountain da-dum" and then something by Lao Tzu or Einstein. That gave me a meditative peace that made me feel good. I'd put it there and I'd look at it. And it made me reflect on the poem a little bit. Like a little bell I used to ring before starting again. Agh, draft number 200! I'm never going to finish this book. It's never going to be done. I know I'll never get through this particular technical problem, etc.

Every time I broke the thing down again, like a piece of jazz, I'd try to find a new way of doing it. The only pleasure I have, really, when writing, is breaking things up into the smallest parts possible. As Confucius used to say: "The rice can not be chopped fine enough." To chop the language into the smallest units possible so they lose all their abstraction: that means empirically building a hedge, trying to find the smallest, most common and yet uncommon, sparkling little bits of data to represent what otherwise would be abstract, and would require belief, or require certain other prejudices or preconceptions. This new language I aim at only requires the response of the very innocent soul, anyone responding in general to sense impressions in a fresh and innocent way. It requires a lot of labour to eliminate all the mechanical, undigested passages of inspired writing . . . oh well, never mind, it makes me tired to think about it. But that would be my pleasure anyway: to synthesize the poem, every poem. Always breaking it down and synthesizing anew again.

110

What do you cut it up from? What's the source of the language that gets dissected and pieced, fragmented and put back together again?

VAN TOORN

Just the everyday. Inspiration—plus clumsy everyday speech. It's the original line that's the momentum, the proud promise that the first line sometimes carries. Sometimes, if you're lucky, in a poem—or at least I feel this way—the first line will come sailing in like a ship, with all the fullness and promise and strength. Then the intuition gets lost. So you hold on to the first line, the sound of it, or the image, or the brightness of it, and you try to tune every other line, like the other strings on a guitar, to that first line (or string). That's at a very archetypal, unconscious, intuitive level. Not all poems come that proud and full. Sometimes little things that are banal or that I otherwise would throw out, that are part of everyday life, that are not really on the level of the poem at all, come into it because something in your life reflects at the same level of this full line. You know that somehow it could be made part of that if only you alter the note of it slightly. That's the poem. It's like in music, if you make a mistake, or somebody makes an off note, if you stretch it out a little longer and drop a few tones around it, suddenly the few tones around it will hold it and the wrong note becomes part of the whole thing. You make the mistake into something positive.

I know that with the poem "Mountain Kayak"—God—Oh, heavy duty! I was sitting at the Skala Restaurant and trying to write that thing. This beautiful waitress came out. She was a Métis woman, proud the way she walked. I like movement, you know. I had just a few lines, and to me they weren't very impressive and, in the last line the word "discombobulation" came up, and I had never used that word in my life. I never even knew what it meant. I must have heard it used, because it couldn't come out of me if I had never seen or heard it. To me words that I have not seen defined clearly, either in a use of a prose writer or poet or a dictionary, aren't used easily. I check them out first before I use them. Words have a way of losing their meaning very quickly, or being able to be reused in a new way. There it was at the end: discombobulation. I didn't know if it was like taking off a pair of wet boots or if it meant anything. But I felt somehow that that bit of irrationality stranded at the end of the poem was like a key to something, that this poem wanted something. I started trying to tune those lines to see what kind of sound I could make out of them and what was in them, so I'd be getting more strong images of a feeling of beauty. And then I really thought, oh God, this has already been done in the Bible, "The Song of Songs." And that's such an erotic beautiful thing—unlike Job, Job says I wish the gates to my mother's womb had been shut, he talks very negatively—and here you are, they talk about legs being like beams of cedar, and breasts that are like honey, with birds around them—that's something else, right? I thought, all this has been done already in "The Song of Songs," and it cannot be repeated. Especially in the twentieth century. Ezra Pound too, he has a song about an ideal woman, "Na Audiart," in which he says he would rather she had the bosom of so-and-so, the thighs and all the parts of the body. It seemed so like an assembly line; synthetic construction in the twentieth century made me feel it couldn't work. But I went along anyway. Then I got bizarrely obsessed at one point with this flooding image in the last line around the end of the poem. I had this personage, this archetype, of an Inuit in a kayak. And suddenly it was midnight and of course in the arctic the sun travels at different times on the horizon. Sometimes it's all dark; sometimes it's all light, and sometimes it's possible to have a sun at midnight like a red ball on the ice, like a pool of blood. I kept thinking of birth. I had this intuition about X (this lady I was zonked on at the time) giving birth. I wasn't sure what it was, or how to get the intuition into the poem somehow. Of course it ended up being proleptic—i.e., still to be lived out by me. At one point there *was* blood on the ice—I had a stroke (a sub-arachnoid hemmorhage). It could have been that too, because I was pushing myself too much physically. So slowly the image worked itself out.

INTERVIEWER

What about a poet's sense of maternal images for compensation?

VAN TOORN

I remember my mother. She was an immigrant. My mother was born of a merchant family, not used to hardship. She was a pretty classy lady.

INTERVIEWER

We replant ourselves in the Earth.

VAN TOORN

Canadian poets must be the people lucky enough to get a smooth ride in the womb. Like a mother who is very meditative and loving and is very aware of what she carried. Poets throughout that sea will provide semblances for small bits of it in reality, so that maybe our minds may ride more comfortably and may accommodate reality in a more profound and purposeful way. Oh, God! This sounds like a utilitarian argument for the social purpose of poetry. I could easily as a critic, say, well that poem is really about a guy, Peter Van Toorn, imagining this very exotic chick, I guess; he thinks he's an Inuit and he's met an Indian chick from down south. In fact, he's a northern person who's met somebody who comes from a warmer climate than himself. He's rejected and he's sitting in his kayak with a sore back, he has the beginnings of arthritis in his spine, he's wishing he's got her stove going, the wood "whimpering in her stove" and his "paddle in her shed" and he's having a good time. You could start looking at it psychologically. But I only feel the poem does that (i.e., project wish fulfilments and infantile fantasies) if it's weak. If it's strong, that's not what you see right away. That's certainly not what I was thinking of.

INTERVIEWER
About those little bits of language, the poem "In Guildenstern County" seems to be an improvisation, like jazz. Was your ear the main tool in that one?

VAN TOORN
Plus my keen sense of Canadian disappointment.

INTERVIEWER
And the wind comes in so often in that poem. Why?

VAN TOORN
Change. The times they are a' changing. It's an old image from Greek poetry. The idea that wind carries seeds. Unpredictable but musical, with a grace and inspiration. Something that comes over you.

INTERVIEWER
How did some of the other intuitions from the *Mountain Tea* book come to you? Many of the poems seem to have the wide, objective view that looking down from a mountain gives.

VAN TOORN
Cezanne was my constant guide and inspiration in all those years for *Mountain Tea*. I felt that he had gone, in impressionist painting, to directions beyond, in which I wanted to go in terms of poetry and imagism. His paintings are wonderful in themselves, as inspiration they're

113

beautiful. But in their method and what they're aiming for in terms of reality and what's behind it that's eternal. Cezanne was always looking for the permanent, the truth, the monumental, eternal truth that's behind structure and colour. He wanted to create not what he thought the impressionists were doing—he thought they were going nowhere—but something more solid, that would be durable and have a monumental quality to it (which he felt the great masterworks of the museums possessed). I felt I wanted that too. His method was to go about it by synthesizing his effect out of tiny little pieces everywhere. A tiny "shock" of colour in the corner here would alter something over there. And keep readjusting itself.

INTERVIEWER

The harmonies in opposition.

VAN TOORN

More and more harmonies. Ultimately reflecting a harmonious world view. The idea that there's unity in reality. A classical world picture, in which nature is assumed to be uniform and operating on vast inscrutable but scientifically valid principles.

INTERVIEWER

How about the title poem, "Mountain Tea" and its line, "Your head's off in your hands now"?

VAN TOORN

Cezanne at one point had a dream about decapitation. I was reading a biography of his in French or English—I can't remember—and I was startled because that was after I wrote the poem. So I looked back at my poem and I noticed that this too was about decapitation. For the rest I just worked in the dark. I had this line about your head being lost in your hands and—who knows? Maybe it's a puritanical fear of masturbation. God knows what it's about. I'm just guessing. But that poem in itself had its own little structure. Imagine the head off in the hands and this long haul and the smokiness in it like in those Japanese films where the Genji haunts this boy. Take *Kwaidan,* by Kobayashi—a blind musician, "Hoichi, the earless one," is haunted by demons. The priests get so worried at one point at night that before they go to sleep they cover his body with scriptural writings to protect him. The older priest says, "Okay, we're nearly finished, I'm going to go to sleep now. You finish off," to a younger priest. And the younger priest is not as meticulous

114

or cautious and he forgets to paint the writings on the ears. So the demons come at night when Hoichi is playing and they rip his ears off because they can see them. His ears aren't protected by the magic spell. In the poem "Mountain Tea" the image is that of mist floating down long corridors. It's an image of death. The whole idea of being in some indefinite stage of reality or level of reality, such as in an elevator in a building somewhere with fog floating in and you know suddenly you've arrived in another world. If you open the door it's going to be totally different. I know the pain in my own life that was behind it. It was my breakup with my wife. Such a wild emotion it was that it was literally planets deep. Somehow I turned it into a more philosophical quest.

I had been reading Lucretius at the time. *De Rarum Naturae (On the Nature of Things),* but not the David Suzuki version. That was at the end of the Roman Empire. All faith had been lost. Epicurianism, stoicism and many religions were felt to be failing people. Philosophy once again started to grow. The natural sciences were attacking bastions of human faith and/or superstition. There came a point when the intelligence of the sensitive mind no longer knew what one could do about death and decay and catastrophe. I remember thinking about his theory of the universe, about there being a steady rain of atoms that nothing could change. The Greek philosophers had this whole idea about how change came about. As Heraclitus says: "Well, everything is in change and motion, you can't step in the same river twice." But other philosophers actually thought that change was an impossibility, a mere human illusion. Lucretius had this steady rain of atoms. Change came about through a swerve or "clinamen." Notice the irrational creeping in. There was some original swerve. And he doesn't account for how it started. He doesn't put a God in his universe. But his assumption of change (i.e. the "clinamen") is an act of faith. How does a swerve come about in this uniform world where atoms rain in one direction? Suddenly there's a swerve and two atoms connect and something new happens. But he doesn't say that's the nature of love or of divine love. This assumption is irrational, an act of faith in itself. I thought that this was a very bleak world picture to have. Essentially one adopted by the scientists in the twentieth century—a lot, not all—especially when they insist that there is no classical paradigm, no unified field theory of the soul, nothing that goes beyond corporeal reality. I thought that this picture left a great gap. Any poet in the twentieth century operating on similar assumptions was at a tremendous loss, because it meant seeing reason and imagination not as God given, but as deistic apparatus.

Even the most skeptical of philosophers, like René Descartes, at some point put a God back into their world to help account for it more beautifully. In Descartes you could see a passage that went from Christianity to Buddhism, where he talks about the world being run by a demiurge who quickly places sensations in front of you, almost as in Bishop Berkeley, where everything's unreal and you can't trust anything. But he moves to something more familiar. He puts God back in. A lot of philosophers have tried to do away with Gods. In the twentieth century science has done away with the concept. Even the modern vogue has been B. F. Skinner and Behaviorism. As though we were born little blanks and programmed. The whole North American idea of freedom is bound up in that. It's no longer a Christian idea of freedom, where you're born with a soul and an innate capacity to choose between the good, the bad, and the ugly. Relativism and Behaviourism weaken everything in terms of ethics and put an axe through the imagination. I think it's a bit of false thinking, although I can see how we arrive at it. But I felt that a poet was at a tremendous disadvantage without a unified field theory of the soul. How the hell can he write? What do you do?

INTERVIEWER

What did *you* do? How do you stay in both the relativistic and Christian worlds at the same time?

VAN TOORN

What did I do? Well, for one thing, I stopped writing anything for a long time. I did find a few answers that were enough for me at the time in order to continue. I didn't put God into my poetry, or the soul of man, or anything, but I got them back in partly through someone I probably don't understand at all. Einstein. I don't really claim to have any more than the average Steinberg shopper's notion of what he's about. I can recognize his picture on the wall. I know he liked sailing. But it's not as if I understand his theories. But I do understand the implications of some of his thinking. Namely, I understand that, since the time he developed the theory of relativity, that it in some way got diluted and diluted until it meant that "everything's relative" in our society. This vague moral application weakened our faith from an absolute point of view. So that the cliché, "everything's relative" came into being, which took comfort or faith in the scientific position that Einstein had developed, but in fact is just a rationalization of a loss of faith. I guess in that way I'm very nineteenth-century. Somehow, for me, Einstein and Darwin destroyed nothing. In fact Einstein helped me find, in a poetic way, the new faith, by insisting as he did on the uniformity of nature. Take the

116

statement he made at the end of his life, "I shall never believe that God plays dice with the world," which contradicted the basic predilections and basic drift of most modern physicists and mathematicians who believed that there was only a kind of random order to the universe. They're the motivating force behind modern theological thinking. Anything theological coming out in the last twenty years has had to do with what physicists think about Genesis, about the origin of the world. Because religions naturally grow from thinking about the beginning of things. How did something get created and why? The moment you have a different picture of how or when, you have a different why. And a different idea of how to use it.

INTERVIEWER

Science becomes a myth in itself.

VAN TOORN

Of course that's what it does. But when you're so much a part of it, it's very hard to see that. Science just keeps adjusting its myth every century. That's how it comes up with new things. So Einstein is a big step over Newton. Even though Newton borrowed the apple too. He borrowed it from the old myth and imagery. The thing is, Einstein insisted on the uniformity of the universe. His metaphor for explaining his world was like the very ancient Hebraic and Biblical metaphor for the divine source—light. Light has always been an image in religious writing for godhead. The source. So when he insisted on a uniform speed of light, something absolute, so what if he didn't discover the most minute, subatomic particle, something scientists have been hounded by for centuries. He went to the other extreme, I guess. For me it was like saying, "When you're travelling that fast, you're travelling with God." It was like keeping God in, instead of keeping Him out. So for all the relativity about everything, there was still this Absolute. To me it didn't really change the world picture completely. I think that's why I have him in my little opening poem to the book, *Mountain Tea & Other Poems,* "Rune." There's a line in there about "If you dream it at the speed of light . . . it (rune) could break the skull's tiny glass."

INTERVIEWER

What is the skull's tiny glass?

VAN TOORN

A little fragile, I guess, a little fragile soul. Or the little cockpit for the soul. I don't know. Gee. The skull's a tiny glass because there's something very fragile in it that's essential to its being.

Can we get back to opposites? We seem to be talking about trying to deal with the spirit on one hand and numerical coherence on the other. In your work there's the dichotomy of objectivity and vision, of your art as artifact and creative splash.

I've always been very concerned I guess with producing a poem that's an artifact that's demonstrable in the same way, perhaps, that a scientific truth is, a model or a theorem that can be tested and verified by anyone at any time and therefore has a kind of universal validity to it. I feel that in the twentieth century the most important thing to us should be that validity, but in terms of faith. But I didn't want to ask of the potential reader, whom Joyce calls "the ideal insomniac," anything more than what science asks of him. When science gives you a light switch, you click it with your finger and the lights go on and you believe. It doesn't ask you more than that. Just as Philip Larkin in his poem, "Church Going," does not ask of the modern sensibility more than a certain neutral (agnostic) stance toward the Church. He kind of shuffles into church and has the average agnostic attitude to it. But he comes out perhaps feeling a little cleansed, feeling there's something to it after all. Larkin doesn't approach you from a religious position. He avoids corniness and cliché and all those pitfalls, while teaching you something along the way.

I felt at one point it was impossible to write if you did not have any ideal or *a priori* positions that you could assume, like a soul. How could you deal with what so many poems demand? Back in the sixties I thought, "If we're going to have a nuclear holocaust or something and all the libraries in the world get burned down to a crisp and there are no more books left, what's the point of writing if that tradition you're part of will no longer exist?" The answer to it came from a really non-rational approach. The question was rational. The answer actually wasn't. I remember living in this commune near McGill, in the ghetto. I remember a point of frustration with that attitude. One night before dinner, when my wife and some friends were there, I remember just saying, "Ah!" and feeling a little cheerful, a little inspiration. And thought about Baudelaire sitting on a hill doing a little fishing and made up this surrealist fantasy. The way I do in classes sometimes, just for the kids, when I talk about parking a Mercedes Benz on the ice of Lake St. Louis, opening

118

the door with the heater on to catch a little fish, and the Mercedes starts to sink through the ice and your windshield wipers are on; you're under water now and the fish are going by, you know. But it's just a surrealist fantasy. You're saying, what if? Like my Chinese friend in high school once said, and he was a physicist, he said to me, "What if all the molecules in this packet of cigarettes simultaneously moved in the same direction. There's one chance in ten zillion of that happening." They're constantly in motion, although this package seems inert and inanimate, all these molecules are moving according to modern physics. If they all moved in one direction the whole thing would levitate.

INTERVIEWER

But it never does happen. Isn't science, even for poets, just a model for how the world behaves?

VAN TOORN

Well, I remember reading a theologian on this. In the library at McGill they had this book by one modern theologian, I forget his name. He suggested—he was a philosopher too—that maybe in modern times, in terms of theological thinking, the ultimate model to use was not one of analogy but what he called an echo model. In other words, he talked about when scientists try to articulate phenomena in order to control or whatever, they try to make a model that expresses their understanding of its behaviour. This model, he said, somehow seems to echo the structure. The better it gets at receiving the phenomenon the better it echoes the phenomenon. So that we get to the mysterious. He thought that was a better way to describe the supernatural and to start thinking about man and his place in the world. The anagogical models are more on the level of myth, metaphor and poetic activity. So he was trying to update theology into the scientific world. I remember being really influenced by that idea, and thinking, ah so. And then Einstein in fact did that. I always was impressed by the fact that when he was young he dreamed of "riding a light beam." That's a very poetic perception. If you were to imagine, the whole idea of really riding a light beam or of what happens to matter, yourself, that's travelling faster and faster, do you expand or contract? It even struck me at one point—he must have thought this thought too—if you go that fast at one point you must become as ubiquitous as light itself. Maybe it contracts but at some time expands throughout the whole universe suddenly. Be everywhere at once like light. It impressed me as being a new metaphor, for the old monotheism, under the guise of modern relativity.

119

INTERVIEWER

Two things from Joyce come in again here. Echoland and quark. Now science is adopting poetic vocabulary. Are we moving away from precision into a world of analogy and echoes?

VAN TOORN

Hmm.

INTERVIEWER

Your poems. As a whole are they an echoland too? They've got so much in them. Planets, the universe, particulars, there's contour and shape. Have you developed a world of your own?

VAN TOORN

Not of my own in the sense that I think of it as a personal or private world. I always see it as larger somehow. More complete. Certainly more unified than *I,* the mundane PVT, am most of the time, if you've seen anything of me. But if you like, my poetry aspires to a state of consciousness that is unified. If you enter into that state that the poem, syllable for syllable, offers you, and you get into it right, I guess it tries to offer you a state of consciousness that is reaching for that, i.e., the poem dramatizes, in terms of vocal imagism, the celebration of the spirit, its being and destiny—Logos. That's what rhythm, or sacred intervals in space and time are about. "If it (poem) ain't got that swing, it don't mean a thing." Know what I mean?

INTERVIEWER

Even the words of the poems. You seem to mention planets and stars often.

VAN TOORN

I do? Yeah? That's true, ay. That's Cezanne again. Cezanne said the painter should try to see all of nature as the physicist, by the sphere, the circle and the cone.

INTERVIEWER

Which seems arbitrary again. Because geometry is human invention.

VAN TOORN

He's looking for, if you like, *a priori* shapes in nature, those shapes

120

corresponding to the eternal, immutable truths. Sphere, cone and circle. Platonic shapes that belong to the realm of the mind before incarnation into a body. To music, to math. Eternal shapes. He didn't want sunlight bouncing off a girl's dress on a certain day, he wanted something that was a permanent form. An expression of God's love for man or something like that. In the way that music and math are solid, and permanent expressions of man's and nature's spiritual origin and purpose.

INTERVIEWER

So the forms are not in what we see but in what we imagine?

VAN TOORN

God. I don't know if that can ever be answered. Why don't we adjourn for a beer in the village? Let's continue this over a game of Euclidean angles—pool. Snooker all right by you?

Interview by Stephen Brockwell

Photo by Denyse Coutu

NICOLE BROSSARD

«Ce qui caractérise les personnes qui ont un accent c'est qu'elles déforment les sons et que par conséquent elles risquent chaque fois qu'elles s'expriment en langue étrangère de créer des malentendus, des équivoques, voire même du non-sens. De plus, elles risquent de mettre l'accent c'est-à-dire d'amplifier là où, en principe, il n'y a pas lieu de le faire, là où ça ne se fait pas.»

(La lettre aérienne)

This is both a linguistic and a political metaphor. It is also a statement on the politics of linguistics which fuels the work of poet, novelist, and essayist Nicole Brossard. She is the author of fifteen books of poetry and seven of prose. Of those which have been translated into English the most recent include: These are Mothers *or:* The Disintegrating Chapter *(1983, translated by Barbara Godard),* French Kiss *(1986, translated by Patricia Claxton), and* Lovhers *(1986, translated by Barbara Godard). A collection of essays,* La lettre aérienne, *is forthcoming from The Women's Press.*

Brossard is very much a writer nursed by a Québécoise and a French literary tradition of the avant garde (in 1965 she founded the influential literary magazine La Barre du Jour *which has since evolved into* La Nouvelle Barre du Jour*), in which fiction is frequently seen as a form of theoretical praxis. Despite this French tradition, Brossard's nationalist sentiments are not for a geographic body of land but for a land of the body, one whose borderlines are written in ink.*

Brossard's literature speaks with an accent. Cognizant that it is subverting a language to which it has been denied access, it subverts the code of proper syntax and proper grammar. Initially this impropriety may be labelled as unladylike. Through the persistent repetition of the accent it becomes clear that a new definition of ladylike speech is being created.

A roundabout approach for a feminist reappropriation of language? Yes. In fact, the concept of the spiral and its movement through a space is integral to Nicole Brossard's literary politics. It is the spiral which ultimately explores the text without penetrating it. For Brossard this is a symbolic shift in methodology and one that she promotes and encourages. It is intrinsically linked to a feminist vision, which today is the sole focus of her linguistic political explorations.

Out of deference to Nicole Brossard, who agreed to participate in an interview conducted in a language other than the one in which she works, the following exchange, which occurred in August 1987, was conducted in both English and French. For the duration of our two-hour conversation I spoke in French, a language in which I undoubtedly speak with my own accent. Ms. Brossard spoke in English. This process allayed my apprehension regarding translation. To translate the words of another without leaving the mark of mediation is a delicate art. Concurrently, the act of articulating my questions in French, of translating myself into another language, illuminated how language can either reveal personality or, indeed, suppress individual expression.

INTERVIEWER

What do you see as the difference between Québécoise feminist writers and English-Canadian feminists?

BROSSARD

I think what is happening now in Canada among Anglo women writers is new. Before, there was a big difference, when I used to go to Toronto or Vancouver. But during the last five years—I'd say with the writing of Daphne Marlatt, Gail Scott and Betsy Warland—I believe that things have started to change. It's now possible for women writers to integrate their feminist consciousness into their writing and to integrate it in such a way that it deals in a radical way with language.

INTERVIEWER

What happened five years ago?

BROSSARD

I think that the Women and Words Conference which took place in 1984 was a turning point. It was an incredible occasion for women from Canada and from Quebec to talk about their work, to compare their approaches, to question feminism in their own work, how it works, how a feminist vision could transform their writing. A great deal of work and continuity is also achieved at the Westword School of Writing for women. Before Women and Words, it seemed that in Canada women could be either feminists or writers, as if no real connection could be made out of those consciousnesses. And as for relations between Quebec literature and Canadian literature made by women, it seemed that the only connections were being made through academics and translators who, in a way, made it possible for writers from both communities to get to know each other's works.

INTERVIEWER

Do you feel that critical theory played a particular role in this change, in this shift in the writing of English feminists?

BROSSARD

Of course, but that is hard to evaluate. Obviously, Cixous and Kristeva, who by the way are interested in the feminine but are not necessarily feminists, have been read. Theory is important, but living among the living is as important for transformation. By that I mean personal exchanges, validation by your peers. Mutual projects, affinities, are for women a great source of change, a great stimulation for transgression and consciousness.

125

Do you feel an affinity with Black and Afro-American writers who also frequently subvert the language of the master, the colonizer?

BROSSARD

I think all colonized people have some patterns in their response to oppression. In their writings we find a quest for identity, complaints, aggressive images against the oppressor, validation of their difference and tradition. If analogies can be made it is only up to a certain point, and I believe it would be a great mistake to think for a second that what women are trying to subvert in language can be compared to what colonized men have done in their search for identity. There is a lot of room in language for a man to express his anger, his revolt, his solidarity, his need of freedom, etc., but there is no space in language for a woman to express these same emotions in a patriarchal language where she, as subject, does not exist. In fact, we women are foreigners in our mother tongue, in language. In the patriarchal language we don't exist as individual, as person, we only exist as long as we are related to a man, as wife, mother or *femme fatale*. A woman relating to women is not welcome in language. This makes all the *difference*.

INTERVIEWER

What are your views on the Quebec writer as *White Nigger of America*, that is, the writer as cultural representative of an oppressed people? I'm thinking of the ideas of Franz Fanon and I'm thinking of what was happening in this province fifteen, twenty years ago.

BROSSARD

There are two ways in which a writer can play a cultural representation for her or his people. One is by being an intellectual and therefore being in a position to study, to understand and explain the situation. The other, which for me is more pertinent, is by being so personally involved, feeling the distress, the anger, the humiliation, the need for change, that the *I* and the *we* will be so much interconnected in the poem or the text that other people will be able to relate and identify with the speaking, screaming, longing, subversive voice of the writer. In Quebec's literature, writers like Paul Chamberland, Gaston Miron, Jacques Brault and Michèle Lalonde in her "Speak White" did it. But I have to say that in order for the *I* and the *we* to meet in a writer's voice there must be a convergence of political, cultural and social changes in the environment.

126

It happened twenty years ago in Quebec. It happened twenty years ago in the feminist movement and it is still happening in contemporary feminism.

INTERVIEWER
You're no longer involved with party politics?

BROSSARD
I was very much involved in the *indépendantiste* movement. Yes, I was involved in what was happening in Quebec, mainly between 1963 and 1974. I still care very strongly about what will become of Quebec, but mainly all my energy goes to my writing and to feminism because for me that's my *politique*: it is feminism. Also, I know that for all kinds of struggles in society there will always be men fighting for their cause and, as history has shown us, their cause is not necessarily our cause. So I concentrate on what I believe is most vital for me.

INTERVIEWER
How will Bill C-54 (the federal anti-pornography Bill) affect you? It could cause problems for writers whose work deals not only with lesbian and gay themes but also with erotica, read as pornography.

BROSSARD
Again this is a double bind position. On one hand, I don't want to see for example, *Sous la langue/Under tongue*, which is an erotic text that I recently published, to be censored, nor do I want women and lesbians to be silenced again about their sexuality. I feel that a lot of documents or testimonies on rape, incest and prostitution could be censored. This cannot be. On the other hand, we cannot go along with the madness of men in their sexual fantasies because those fantasies fragment and disintegrate women and children. Why can't sexuality do without hatred, violence or spite? Sexuality is energy. Why does that energy have to be used to dominate and humiliate women?

INTERVIEWER
Do you see yourself directly implicated in a fight against this bill?

BROSSARD
First I thought no. But yes I might. Though I would rather concentrate on my writing, exploring more about feminist consciousness, feminist and lesbian politics and ethics.

INTERVIEWER

In your collection of essays, *La lettre aérienne*, you say: "On a l'imagination de son siècle, de sa culture, de sa génération, d'une classe sociale, d'une décade, de ses lectures, mais on a surtout l'imagination de son corps et du sexe qui l'habite." Do you think that one's identification with one's class can be stronger than with one's sex? I'm thinking of feminists who align themselves with others who are not women, but who are of the same class, before they will allow themselves to communicate with other women who happen to be from a "lower" class.

BROSSARD

I would say this is a key problem. We live in a system in which for women to identify with women is the most difficult thing to do because women are disqualified as individuals and as a group. Men bond together or fight each other through traditions, mythologies, power and oppression. But women usually bond to their men within a culture, a class, a race. So we could say that as long as women's relations to language, to culture, to reality will be mediated by the abstract Manhood and the concrete men (father, son, brother, husband) who they have affection for, their first choice will be their first cultural belongings.

So this I'd say is the most crucial point or difficulty in having feminism spread as other social and philosophical theories have spread, because men stick together in their fight against oppression . . .

INTERVIEWER

Across the classes . . .

BROSSARD

Yes, somehow men stick together because the world belongs to them. For example, a revolutionary can always expect to change "le rapport de pouvoir," can expect one day to be in charge. Challenging the system or getting along with it, a man can expect a piece of the cake. A revolutionary can expect to be rewarded for what he did for his people. Dead or alive. The same thing does not apply to women fighting for women because in order to reward or value those women's actions, you have to approve of their aims. No one, except feminists, approves of feminism's perspective of social, economical, political and cultural changes because those changes would mean that women are not *just females* but beings. And this challenges the imagination, the mythologies we've been trained to live with.

INTERVIEWER

Is a part of the problem that all connections between women are cut by the patriarchal order, that is, that as women we are alone, we are put in a position where we are surrounded by men and we cannot rejoin/reach other women? Also, we have no place where we can go, which is a place for women only, a place where we can regenerate our energy.

BROSSARD

Exactly. We've been isolated from each other in our homes, each with our children and our husbands and so on. That's one thing, a real physical isolation. But another problem is that women, when reacting to oppression, will fight for equality (what does that mean?) and demand justice, forgetting that there will never be equality or justice as long as each woman is considered inferior. Male being valued as superior to women by millennia of traditions, religions and culture is the question at the heart of the problem. In order to change this mental imagery, women have to dig deep in the symbolic field, to *figure* out the image they want of themselves and to connect with other women in order to do so. No fundamental change can happen if women don't provide for themselves the appropriate environment where they will be in a position to take risks, to remember, to create, to invent their heroines. We have so few women heroes that we can identify with. History has left us orphans of women's figures which we can identify with to regenerate ourselves.

INTERVIEWER

Because we don't have a mythology, we don't have archetypes to which we can look for a role model . . . Because our idea of heroism is just that, the hero and we don't have heroine-ism . . .

BROSSARD

An inspiring role. Not a domestic role, a doll role, not a victim role. It is so strange to think that each little man can identify himself with God or with Man (capital M). And in fact each little man benefits from the fact that he belongs to Manhood, benefits from a wide range of images of heroes, of saints, of geniuses. As for us, we inherit just a few images hidden in the backyard of history. Because we have no scope of positive, challenging, stimulating images, we have to invent those images by projecting on other women the best in each of us. So without cultural heritage backing her up, every woman has to make proof that she is a person, an individual, a being, and even though she succeeds in proving that, in order to survive, she will eventually need the seal of approval of men.

And if she gains this position in Mankind this necessitates the negation of herself as woman . . .

BROSSARD
Absolutely. Either she neutralizes herself or she becomes *like* a man.

INTERVIEWER
It's like your definition of woman: woman is man, woman is me, woman is woman. The first two are often used by women who are politically motivated but who are not radically political. How, through your texts, do you approach a woman who's a feminist but not a radical feminist?

BROSSARD
Well, for me it is not a matter of approach. In my theoretical work I mainly try to understand how the patriarchal system functions. How it hyponotizes and tames women. How it sucks their soul out of their body. How do you become a "real woman"? How do you become a radical feminist? What makes it possible for some women to understand how much women have been cheated and abused throughout history? I try to understand how we have been colonized through very tricky ways like double binding, ambivalence, half lies, half truth. I try in my answers to go beyond dualism, positive/negative. I try to escape thinking in linear terms.

How would I relate with a woman who would want just a little bit of feminism so she can be a little more assertive with her man? What can I say? I write what I write and out of it women take whatever they can deal with.

INTERVIEWER
It's clear from your work that you don't have the time to speak to women like this. Your texts speak to women who are open to the possibility . . .

BROSSARD

I think in a certain way all women are open to that possibility. But can they take the risk to open themselves to being radical feminists? Because there is a risk, this risk being to change your style of life, your perspective on reality, your relation not only with people but also with literature, history, science, etc. A lot of women believe that they will be losing something if they become radical feminists.

INTERVIEWER

But do your texts call to women to take this risk? Maybe your work draws the beauty or the reward which exists if we take it, but it does not follow us, chase after us . . .

BROSSARD

Yes. I try to open a path or make space, in fact, for a new perspective on reality, a new vision on reality, on fiction, on language.

As a writer I see myself as an explorer. I want to discover for myself that which, I hope, can be shared with other women. Yes, it is really to explore, to understand. As long as I believe in what I'm doing, my energy tends towards a certain beauty, a positive energy. I believe a lot can be achieved when the energy is positive and when there is a challenging project. I want to know who I am as a contemporary subject living the end of industrialization and the beginning of technology. First, I'd say I do that for myself but I hope that what I feel and think can have a resonance in others.

INTERVIEWER

Can one be a radical feminist without being lesbian? And is the spiral necessarily or exclusively linked to a lesbian literary aesthetics?

BROSSARD

I think you can be a radical feminist without being a lesbian because in order to be a radical feminist you have to understand the system, how it works and you have to define yourself within that system. I believe that some women who are radical feminists have made a very special space in their own private lives for a man and that must be really hard to do. But they seem to manage it. On the other hand, I would say that being a lesbian binds you to women in a much more integral way. Also, being a lesbian gives you much more freedom to express the essential in you because you are not restrained by sexual or spiritual bondage to

131

men. This gives you an enormous space to explore, analyze and dare statements that otherwise you would feel guilty about.

As for the spiral, it is a metaphor used to talk about the type of position we as women, not only lesbians, are placed at in the world. I don't think that we can confront logically what I call the thick wall of lies of patriarchy. We would be hurting ourselves unnecessarily. So I think that we have to curve reality, re-mind, re-call our energy, go forth, move in such a way that our thoughts make a spiral. I like the metaphor of the spiral because it means energy, because it is a dynamic shape and it is also a shape that you find at the bottom of the seas and in the cosmos. For me it is a *moving* metaphor. I think that we women invent, curve after curve, our destiny.

INTERVIEWER
And it is something which is non-linear and anti-dualistic.

BROSSARD
Yes, I would hope so, because dualism is a thinking pattern closed on itself. It defeats itself. It doesn't permit extraterritorial elements. It narrows the thought. That is why I believe in curved sentences which while you craft them develop new materials to go beyond "les sentiers battus de la pensée." In the spiral you unfurl all kinds of possibilities.

When I talk about the spiral it's not only due to the fact that I want that metaphor to be there but because I feel that it is a necessary metaphor, a wise metaphor. But I have to say that my rapport to the spiral changes. It changed from *Le sens apparent* to *Amantes* to *Picture theory*. It transforms itself from one book to another.

INTERVIEWER
It is curious that you're interested in the spiral and the hologram, because the hologram is something that is born of technology and the spiral is more mystical, natural. Generally, technology is something associated with the great patriarchal machine. We also think of technology as something very urban.

BROSSARD
But it can be geometrical, too. Mathematics through spirals. The hologram for me is important. I was very much impressed the first time I saw a hologram. You look at an object which looks real, you want to touch it, to take it in your hands but you know it is fiction. You wonder about fiction and reality. Also reading about holography I found a very

exciting vocabulary. In *Picture Theory* I wanted to create a woman that would be real, a woman that would be from fiction but also a woman that would have a symbolic efficiency. She would not be the mother but she would be the one through whom everything would happen: the metaphor of the hologram was total inspiration.

Industrialization has provided us with tools prolonging our limbs, heart, senses. Technology is now providing us with tools for prolonging our brain. Computers and holograms are two of those tools which can now be added to a very ancient one, which is writing.

INTERVIEWER

Holography is also another language. Similar to, but not exactly comparable to film, it's a language not composed of words. Through semiotic analysis we can read something which is not constructed with words, not a literary language.

BROSSARD

It is vibration, it is waves, it is perception. It is very sensual in a certain way because it is waves that we read through our eyes while we are reading the image. I think that it is also waves that our body registers somehow.

INTERVIEWER

So is there a way to interpret holograms that uses the mind in another way or doesn't interpret through the mind but through the body, too?

BROSSARD

Well, the hologram for me is the mental physics of dream. I see it, I want to touch it, I move towards it. It challenges my mind, it defies my sight, my eyes, it challenges my relation to reality. It does inspire me to synchronize body, mind and soul in language.

INTERVIEWER

Your work is very different from that of Jovette Marchessault, who I imagine shares many of the same ideological beliefs as you. There is a big difference in how you work with language. In *Comme une enfant de la terre* there is a passage where Marchessault writes: "Les mots m'apparaissent comme des escaliers en spirale qui aboutissent à une porte. Qui s'ouvre." For you, I would think that that door does not open. Or maybe words "appear as a spiral staircase which leads to a door" but that spiral staircase breaks down the door, ploughs through it.

BROSSARD

Door and staircase are not images which are pertinent in my universe. I would more spontaneously use images of threshold, edge or border. For me the theme of the door doesn't fit into my network of metaphors, which mostly deal with an open space to explore, discover or transgress. I don't open doors, I trespass limits. At my own risk, of course.

INTERVIEWER

Do you feel that one of the causes of this difference is your different geographic environments? I know that you use the theme of the City or the Town as well as the idea of "les urbaines radicales."

BROSSARD

Well, I am a very urban person. I like to be in combat with the city because everything happens in the city, because the *library* is in the city. Civilization is in the city. What is also interesting about the city is that you can observe at the same time the utmost performance of a civilization, its most developed high technology and its most desolated signs of decadence.

I feel good in the city. Cities like Montreal or San Francisco give me great pleasure. For me nature (country doesn't mean anything) means the sea or the desert. It means a place where I can be but also a place from which I can have a *view*. It has a lot to do with the eyes. I like a huge expanse of nature where I can both be in it and look at it. The notion of the horizon is very important in my rapport to nature. I'd feel claustrophobic in a forest.

INTERVIEWER

But the horizon hits the eye in a linear manner.

BROSSARD

The horizon means open your eyes on the unknown. It connects earth and sky, sea and sky. It reminds you of your real height and dimension. The horizon is invitation.

INTERVIEWER

Do you have a particular theoretical project which you're presently working on in your writing?

134

I just finished a novel which is very different from anything that I have written before.

Formally or in content?

The shapes of the sentences are more traditional but the structure of the narrative is not. I believe that it is the first time that I have experienced so much the notion of time, patience and discipline needed to construct a novel. Usually, because of the way I write, which is in the present, present tense, present tension, I have an immediate gratification for what I do. But this time I had to postpone that gratification until the end of the book. I learned a lot writing this novel but I don't know how this knowledge will affect my future texts.

I find your more recent writings seem less deconstructed on a semantic level than your earlier works, those written in the early seventies that have since been translated into English. The more recent writings seem almost to be traditionally surrealist at times, less fragmented.

One thing you can be sure of is that the word surrealist is not part of my vocabulary or my intention. With every book I write, not only do I try to explore more, but at the same time I try to respect my needs, my moods, my feelings. In a book, I try to satisfy my needs and try to orient my desire.

The way I write now—I don't know how I'll be writing the next novel, if there will be another one . . . We've been speaking of the spiral and the spiral made this novel possible in a certain way. The spiral permitted something in my imagination to develop, not only in the imagination but also in the sentence. So then comes this novel *Le désert mauve* which is really very special and I'm the first to be amazed by that book. I'll even say that I had the temptation to publish it under a pseudonym.

I like to see myself as a scientist trying to discover, to explore, to experiment, and in this book I saw myself really as a craftsperson, giving shape to a universe which was in my mind. In fact, giving shape to sentences and really crafting each sentence because nothing happens just by yourself or out of inspiration. Things happen in the language and my

135

closest friend, the dictionary, was around all the time.

INTERVIEWER

Would you say in this last book that the language is more accessible?

BROSSARD

Oh, yes. Absolutely.

INTERVIEWER

What does this mean for your readers? Do you think this will widen your readership?

BROSSARD

It might, yes. But that's not my problem whether it surprises my old readers or it pleases my new readers. I needed to write that book the way it was written and for me that's it.

I don't know what will be my next move but by now I know my cycle. I think that it's a poetry book and then a novel, then it is an essay and then it starts back. After the essay I go back to poetry and then I have the temptation for a novel . . . It is really a cycle, a rhythm which sometimes can be alterated through events that happen in your own life.

I believe that there are lots of things that we can control in our life but that there are some also that enter our lives like accidents, love, grief, death. These you cannot control and it can affect the rhythm of your writing and your questions about the meaning of life and death.

About this, one might ask where do we draw the line between the individual's life, the fiction and the writing. I personally think that whatever happens in your life, the most vital thing to do, if you are a writer, is to have the creative person in you take over from the biographical one. Because thousands of people go through the same emotions every day. It is how you combine in language the strongest feelings and emotions that makes literature. So, though personal events can transform my writing, it is not the story of my life but the story of the creative process which is interesting.

INTERVIEWER

So we can ask, as you did in *Journal intime*, "une vie d'auteur est-elle une vie privée? Où et quand se termine la biographie?" It is as though the person, Nicole Brossard, no longer exists and all that exists is the Author, or The Author, Nicole Brossard. So what has happened to you? Maybe we can say the author's life is not private but very public. When we put our lives on paper it is no longer our life . . .

BROSSARD

It's more than our private life, but I would make a distinction between private life and intimate life. Private life is a personal story, as intimate life is a personal way that each of us has to process reality in order to make space for our fictions, our certitudes. It is through our intimate life that we make literature, not through our private life.

INTERVIEWER

So you discover another person when you write. It is still you . . .

BROSSARD

Well, it is the same person, but a more thoughtful person and therefore a person that is ahead of herself. Between the individual and the writer there is a free space, a mysterious landscape where one discovers and dares things that the individual cannot afford. It is in that space that I learn about myself and can transform myself.

INTERVIEWER

It is much like when we speak another language instead of our mother tongue, it forces us to look at words. How do you feel about the persistent myth of The Writer? The myth of Nicole Brossard?

BROSSARD

Myths about writers occur because literature is fascinating. It always makes you wonder about real life and fiction. Readers and writers become heroes through characters, meaning by that, that both invest characters with their emotions, identify strongly with them. That confusion is what Michael Rifaterre calls "l'illusion référentielle."

Also, I would say that if we are fascinated by writers, it can be that writing, even though most of the people can write in our society, is still a difficult activity, a difficult process. All writers will say that writing is an exigent activity because it is like walking through mirrors, mirages, and at the same time being able to find your own truth among all those illusions. Also, people mythify writers because writers are in a certain way magicians. They can make things appear and disappear in just one sentence. They make you cry. They make you high.

INTERVIEWER

Do you see implicit in mythologies a distancing which prevents the existence of individuals: neither us, who respect this mythology, nor you, Nicole Brossard, but allows only for the archetypes, the Devoted Reader and The Writer? Mythologies also allow for the act of romanticizing which is an act of fictionalizing which I see as possibly dangerous.

I don't think that fictionalizing can be avoided. We do that all the time when we meet a new person. I think that you've got to do what you have to do and for me it is to keep writing, hoping not to deceive my readers but mainly trying to stay faithful to what I believe. Since literature is an endless process to understand reality, language and fiction, I don't think that you can stop the fictionalization about it, about characters or about writers. And I as a writer do fantasize a lot about readers, especially women readers.

As for the people you say who look too much at the writer and forget themselves . . .

INTERVIEWER

It doesn't leave a place for them to exist . . .

BROSSARD

There is a lot of space to exist as a reader. All writers are readers and they make space for themselves. You can be inspired by a writer, you can be influenced by a writer. Both of them are rich in possibilities, in consequences. Admiration can also be a powerful source of inspiration. It would be a mistake to see that emotion as a passive response to a writer.

INTERVIEWER

How do you see the influence of literature compared to other more immediate mediums like film or video? Do you see literature as still a big influence on people, on ideas of history, on social mythology?

BROSSARD

For sure, literature has less influence than let's say thirty years ago. But I don't think that the competition comes from film. Its decrease of influence is much more a consequence of television. Literature is imagination in continuity. It deals with memory, thought. It tells about life with a complex frame of references. Television fragments reality, one minute you see corpses on the screen, the other minute, you see an ad for toilet paper. Television levels reality. It offers images with no

138

continuity. Free of context. It takes away your memory, your sense of criticism and even your capacity to experience emotion. Television is not competition for literature, it is competition for emotion.

I would like to add also that literature only influences those who read it and it is a fact that more and more people who read literature do it because they work in that field.

INTERVIEWER

So in this competition, literature is definitely marginalized. It's not at all a competition. The education of people is done by television. And reading and writing is on the one hand a privilege, and on the other hand a hobby, something that isn't part of people's lives.

BROSSARD

Yes, literature is marginalized. Even in bookstores literature is marginalized, Quebec and Canadian even more. People buy and read books but those books are mainly practical books, biographies, documentaries, etc.

INTERVIEWER

How do you define literature?

BROSSARD

I remember when I was a student at the University of Montreal wondering what was literature, what was that *thing* which gives us so much to feel and to think about. Literature seemed to be everything, psychology, history, sociology, philosophy, linguistics, but I could not come up with a specific answer, because literature being language, values and emotions, it is as complex as life is itself. Rhetoric, tricks and performance in language are easy to understand but the phenomena of literature, the motivation that engages us in such a process, is not. But now I could say that for me literature is memory, emotion, reflexed thoughts making their way into language and by doing so enlarging and transforming our knowledge, our consciousness, our version of reality and therefore our perception of reality.

INTERVIEWER

Is your writing a privileged one because of the language you use and the difficulty of its reading? Do you see it as appealing to an elite readership?

BROSSARD

I believe that a text tells subliminally how it wants to be read. Readers usually are able to determine if they want to go through a certain book or not, if they want to take a chance or not with a certain kind of writing. My books deal with desire and consciousness about language and about values: I would hope this is not only for an elite readership.

INTERVIEWER

What do you think of the film language used in *Les terribles vivantes* and *Some American Feminists*? Neither film used language in the sense that you use language, that is, experimentally.

BROSSARD

But those films are documentaries and so it is normal that they don't necessarily use the same language as I use in my writing. I think that this question could apply if I had made a fictional film. Then you could wonder why the film is so different from my writing.

INTERVIEWER

One can still use untraditional means to convey a statement when filming documentary as when writing theory.

BROSSARD

Yes, but you must not forget that I am not a filmmaker. I am a writer who wanted in *Some American Feminists* to give the floor to some women who could articulate a discourse on feminism. I had no specific aesthetic intention and had I had any I would have needed to learn more about film.

INTERVIEWER

But do you think a feminist filmmaker who wanted to make a film either fiction or documentary, could use the idea of the spiral, for example, in the form of her film?

BROSSARD

Oh, I think that if you are a filmmaker and you know what it means to make a film, you know the technique and so on, then it's up to you, to your imagination, to your talent, to your desire to do whatever you can do. Absolutely. I don't know anything about filmmaking but I guess I wouldn't lack good ideas.

INTERVIEWER

Does it interest you to write for film?

BROSSARD

Not to write for film but to make films. I used to say I'd like to make a film before I was forty. Now, it's three years too late but maybe one day . . . even though film is much more expensive than pencil and paper.

INTERVIEWER

You are interested in working in a multidisciplinary sense, your texts with images, as you've already done . . .

BROSSARD

I try to control the visual aspect of my books (typesetting, cover, pictures) as much as I can. I've worked with photographers Denyse Coutu and Richard-Max Tremblay, artists Francine Simonin and Irene Whittome. I used some comic strips in *French kiss* and I have worked closely with graphic artists for most of my books. It is challenging to understand another artist's universe and to share competence.

INTERVIEWER

Does collaboration change the nature of the act of writing for you? I get the impression that the act of writing is solitary and in a way very sad and difficult. In *Journal intime* you wrote: "je ne sors pas parce que je dois écrire et je n'aurai rien à écrire si je ne sors pas."

BROSSARD

Writing is difficult but not sad. I have written most of my books out of pleasure. But to answer your first question, it is hard to evaluate if the nature of the act of writing changes because you work in collaboration or because you are writing for another purpose than the book. If you write for the theatre, which was the case for *L'Écrivaine*, or for radio, which was the case for *Journal intime*, then you have to approach the text, its logic, its rhythm, differently because people have to be able to understand at first hearing. Theatre and radio are big challenges for me, because I have to write in a much more linear way. But I like to experiment and find out how I will behave in a different context than poetry, novel or *text*.

INTERVIEWER

In *La lettre aérienne*, in your discussion of what it takes to be a writer, you say that one must "ressentir une profonde insatisfaction devant le discours majoritaire." How does one continue to feel this dissatisfaction when, firstly, the struggle against this ruling discourse can be exhausting and, secondly, we often surround ourselves with like-minded people. It's not that we forget the bigger context of patriarchy but we can become . . .

BROSSARD

. . . more tolerant,

INTERVIEWER

. . . because in a sense, we forget what surrounds us.

BROSSARD

That can be true. But on the other hand it doesn't take much to bring you back to your dissatisfaction. All you've got to do is watch television, especially the news and then you are reminded about the real world, the standard values, who is in charge, who gets the goodies. Dissatisfaction, frustration, desire to change things are important motivations to write, to "recreate the world." But you also need to have other stimulations if you want to propose another version of reality. You need beauty, connivance, complicity in order to go beyond opposition and to be able to make new propositions on love, power, sexuality, work, etc.

INTERVIEWER

And if one maintains one's dissatisfaction it can become a violent anger or maybe it begins as a violent anger. In your theory and texts you speak about the reappropriation of the body and senses but you don't exactly speak of the reappropriation of anger. I get the impression that you suggest that violent anger is something that belongs to the patriarchal world.

BROSSARD

Anger is important. It is a powerful emotion that can propel you into action. We all have to keep our anger up-to-date. But anger with no words is dangerous, it can drive one to madness. Anger has to be filtered by language and transform itself in revolt, in subversion. You cannot be angry all your life. I do believe that beauty and desire can open many more things than anger, even though anger is something not to be forgotten. Personally, I've been working mainly through the energy of beauty, of desire, with the idea that out of your passion for life you can change something in the world.

Interview by Clea Notar

CHRISTOPHER DEWDNEY

Christopher Dewdney is one of the most complex and talented of the younger Canadian poets. Upon first reading, his poems sometimes appear merely arcane; burdened by a convoluted or alien intelligence. This strange intelligence is an essential component of the poems, but they are also distinguished by rich veins of humorous word-play and elemental digressions into religion, sex, the way the brain works, the way animals and words become fossilized, and the way light travels around the sky. Christopher was born in London, Ontario, in 1951 and currently lives in Toronto, where he teaches Coeval Literature at York University. He was steeped in the mysteries of science and art from an early age—his father, Selwyn Dewdney, is well-known as an anthropologist and novelist, and one of his brothers, A. K. Dewdney, writes for Scientific American.

This interview took place on 23 December 1984 at Christopher's home in the Italian section of Toronto, and was later revised and augmented by letter. A full plate of nachos and cup after cup of tea were consumed over the course of the interview. Shells, trilobite fossils, and concretions (one of them a foot and a half in diameter) rested on bookcases, endtables, and on the floor. After the interview we went upstairs to examine a copy of "Golders Green" and a booklet of words and drawings that Christopher produced at the age of nine. Like his later work, which includes Spring Trances in the Control Emerald Night *(1978),* Alter Sublime *(1980), and* Predators of the Adoration: Selected Poems 1972-82 *(1983), this early book deals with dinosaurs and missiles.*

Since this interview took place, Dewdney has published The Immaculate Perception *(1986), which deals with some of the scientific, theoretical, and linguistic scaffolding of his poems. This book includes short texts on the brain, pets, vice-grips, and love. As was the case with* Predators, The Immaculate Perception *was short-listed for the Governor General's Award.*

INTERVIEWER

I haven't read too many interviews with you.

DEWDNEY

There have been some on the radio—a nice one on CBC. And there's also one that Bruce Whiteman did a couple of years ago. It was in a publication of his, *Harvest*. There was also one in the *Globe*, sort of, with Judith Fitzgerald, and another one in *Shades* with Steve Venright.

INTERVIEWER

I've also been having trouble getting a copy of your chapbook "Golders Green." It's almost impossible to find.

DEWDNEY

Very hard to get. Nick has it on sale down at Letters on Queen Street, for $400, or something like that! I think he established that price on the basis of information I gave him attesting to its rarity. Incidentally, David McFadden is a good person to advise writers on these matters. The legend is that he used to run small editions, about 200 copies of a book, and let it go out of print and sell it for inflated prices—make money on his own work. In retrospect this could have been a similar strategy of mine in this case. I had seventy-five copies of "Golders Green" left over, but unfortunately they were thrown out by some workmen in London, Ontario, so there actually are only about seventy-five copies out there. Very rare.

INTERVIEWER

I've been taking a look at some of your father, Selwyn Dewdney's, books—not the novels so much as the anthropological books: *The Sacred Scrolls of the Southern Ojibway* and *Indian Rock Paintings of the Great Lakes*. It seems to me that these books would assist someone if they wanted to begin studying what was going on in your work. There's a lot of graphs, strange little drawings, pieces of maps . . . some remarkable bits of information which don't necessarily tie in with everything else but which seem to exist in their own right, like crystals. Do you see your work as feeding on that anthropological background?

DEWDNEY

Well actually it's interesting you should mention that . . . perceptive. My father was very important. I'm realizing now that the work he did on Amerindians . . . at that period of time, when I was six or seven or eight years old, he dragged me around every summer on these expeditions and he'd introduce me to shamans and we'd be documenting Indian rock paintings. So I was steeped in Amerindian lore. My father, I realize now, had actually converted from Anglicanism to Amerindianism. I think he believed something intrinsic about the Amerindian identity was one with his own set of beliefs. I don't think it was the romantic Grey Owl type of thing, but something more pragmatic, with perhaps a Faustian edge to it. Anyway, that was him. And this became my matrix.

That *was* really important for me because there were a number of assumptions made or that were, willy-nilly, made for me about the nature of the world, about the nature of magic, the nature of animism, spirits, a whole bunch of things. I'm just realizing now that I grew up without questioning this kind of Amerindian matrix, which was sort of our spiritual matrix as well as the very scientific thing. It was like a technological cocoon—we were surrounded by a cocoon of Amerindian psychic spiritualism, or something like that. It's kind of an interesting thing. I'm looking back now and realizing that this had a bigger effect than I thought.

INTERVIEWER

There's an interesting quote in *Indian Rock Paintings of the Great Lakes* where your father says: "Expect even the experts to disagree. All memories are fallible, and, not least, pictographs, like fish, are where you find them." It seems that a quote like that can help when looking at your work. There's a real strangeness to some of those pictographs, and one of the things I like about your father's books is that he doesn't negate that strangeness, that mystery.

DEWDNEY

That's very true. That's always been for us, in our family context, the sacred—the ability to maintain perspective on that which is not human, an inhuman perspective on that which is not human, and treasure the experience, and take it into humanity. To be able to embrace the non-human, or the truly alien, as the remarkable and that is something . . . It has something to do with anti-sentimentality, although it's not a negative definition. It's something intrinsic in my work I think. Good point.

INTERVIEWER

Let me push that a little farther. I was a bit shocked with something you were quoted as saying in the David McFadden article: that you were not interested in "mankind." It sounds quite negative.

It may be a McFadden quote there. He has a very precise slant on my work. You have to be careful with McFadden. Very careful!

Here's the quote: "I really have a profound hatred of mankind. I think that's one of my dominant themes." I was immediately inquisitive about that one. It sounds quite negative, but perhaps in relation to beast-kind or mystery-kind . . . are these things the opposite of mankind?

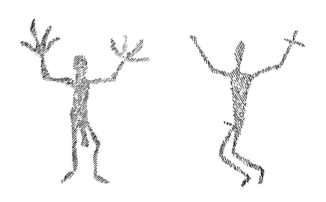

I think that what I meant . . . that's an emphatic statement for all those things which have been trampled or destroyed perhaps by West European industrial nations, or East European too. Perhaps it would be a proto-typical "direct action" kind of theme—sort of speaking for those that cannot speak for themselves. That's a sense of rage that comes from seeing some junior forest rangers trample a red squirrel to death, or who stone it from a tree and then kill it. Seeing incredible cruelty by people against living things. That statement in the McFadden piece comes out of that. It's not really fully articulated. It's not a blanket statement against humanity, but against a kind of violence and ignorance that really . . . well it still makes my blood boil when people kill bats or when they kill something out of ignorance. There's a part of me, of course, that is also drawn to this, which is what you're getting at. To truly exist in North America you really have to like these kinds of things too. A dark sense of humour helps, for sure. There was that mercenary conference in the States and the hottest selling T-shirt was that one with the muscle-man holding a smoking gun and there's an animal that has been blasted to pieces at his feet and the caption underneath says: "I don't know what the hell it was, but it's dead now!" A typical pre-Heisenbergian perspective—we destroy that which we see because we don't know what we're looking at!

INTERVIEWER

How was that intelligence that you got wandering around with your father transubstantiated or transmuted into what you're doing now? Is it slowly being lost, is it being integrated more, is it a childhood that you're trying to recapture?

DEWDNEY

Oh, no. It's a methodology. It's where I'm coming from. I've always been very careful not to exploit my childhood in that sense. I think it's possible for some people to use it up—if you just use your past as some kind of biographical sandpit or aggregate or something like that, where you just mine everything out. I think that the way I do it is sensitive to that. My father was always stressing, as the Amerindians do, leaving everything intact, of leaving no trace of your passage. If you turned a stone over, you turned it back the way you found it. It was to be very sensitive to the environment. For me, nature is the divine technology and I want to be sensitive to that. Also, there's the sense, of course, of dreams—of certain systems of magic and belief which entail almost anti-scientific understandings of the world to some extent, which co-exist in my mind with an extremely materialistic scientific praxis, so it's kind of a funny mix in a way. I sense no imbalance.

INTERVIEWER

With your father being both a novelist and a scientist, you must have been steeped in both the magical and the scientific, if boundaries between those two exist at all.

DEWDNEY

There was no contradiction between those two. There doesn't have to be any contradiction between those two systems of knowledge. For me, really, science is magic. There's an infinite mystery behind that. There's no need for anything to be more miraculous than it already is.

The household was always a hotbed of things going on and projects.

149

It was a creative environment that way.

To what extent does the "hermetic, religious, paramilitary" secret society that you describe in the *Harvest* interview exist?

DEWDNEY

The secret society, which at the time of writing *A Paleozoic Geology* and *Fovea Centralis* seemed very real, operated through dreams, to enact the designs of an ancient and genetically enmeshed organization which itself sought to repress particular books of poetry because they threatened its plane of existence. In some sense, this must be a metaphor, though I've never really gotten a handle on its analogical existence, so it would appear to be an actual reality that I stumbled upon. Every *real* poem enacts some sort of toll in this "secret society," which is itself used like an involuntary courier service to mediate the functions of memory, muse, dream, and poem. In a sense it is like a servant sworn by magic palindromes into service against its will, locked into service by hermetic incantations, and this is the inherent natural language itself, perhaps—that is to say, its deepest ability to shelter pure human spirit, abstracted past the manifestation of life as we know it.

INTERVIEWER

In the same interview you say that the past is completely determined. Do you mean the prehistoric past as well?

DEWDNEY

I was remarking in that interview about just how amazing that concept really was—if you sit down and consider for a while that the past is fixed, inalterable. It's amazing really, everything else is so flexible, malleable, so open to change. The past seems to be the exception. I suppose one could extrapolate this to include the prehistoric past as well, though perhaps there's some sort of relativistic effect that mutates the distant past—is there any reason to suppose so?

INTERVIEWER

Is the future determined?

DEWDNEY

I believe in free will.

The present?

The present is the only instance in which we are truly deterministic mechanisms in the epiphenominal sense. This is actually a good question to clarify my own views on this matter. We are totally, our entire beings, our thoughts, our actions, our emotions, determined by perturbations, neurological relations in our nervous system. Human consciousness is to the brain as the shadow is to the hand, to use the great epiphenomenalist metaphor, *at any one instant in time*. It is the temporal continuum, and this is my escape clause really, that denies total determinism in (the phenomenon of) human consciousness. Spirit could be said to exist in this continuum and therefore the whole corrupt and tedious discussion of the corporeal basis of the mind, which has wasted so much philosophical and scientific time, can now be discarded along with other dilemmas such as solar concentricism and the shape of the earth.

INTERVIEWER
There's a lot of religious talk in your poems—some very orthodox Christian allusions. The Immaculate Perception, for example, a marvelous pun on . . .

DEWDNEY
I know. It's weird. This stuff keeps coming up—the transubstantiation that came up in *Paleozoic Geology*. I frankly don't know what's going on. Maybe you can help me! It's true. I'm very caught up with the idea of the trinity as a kind of metaphorical handle for certain ideas that didn't seem to be approachable any other way. Now what's happened for me is that Christianity has set up a kind of armature on which—we'll exclude any talk of *The Great Code* at this point in our conversation, and at any future part—can be negotiated certain kinds of metaphors. And it just seemed appropriate armature for that.

My grandfather was the bishop of Keewatin, which at that point was a pie slice that went from Lake Superior, Kenora, right up to the North Pole. Now it's a smaller territory. Hence my older brother's name is Keewatin. That was my father's father—so my father is the son of a bish! That was one of his favorite puns. My father was also an inveterate punster. After his heart operation he sent out cards to people that had sent flowers and stuff that said "Aorta Thank You."

That punning is certainly evident in your work—"There be shall mutt natching of teat," etc.

DEWDNEY

I don't know—it's curious. It's really a funny thing. The metaphors are thrown up, and they can be useful. One more . . . I had this funny reading in England one time. Actually, Hay-on-Wye in Wales. I was reading at this old stone church . . . I don't know—overall my work can be perceived as Christian but there are certainly very dark areas. So I did this reading, and afterwards this woman came up with light in her face—I had been reading with two friends of mine, English poets, John Wilkinson and Geoffrey Ward—and she was looking askance at them and she said to me: "It's so wonderful to have a Christian poet." Her face was all lit up, and I thought, "Well, that's interesting!" Nobody has ever said that to me before. I think she had gotten that drift that maybe you are getting at, that there is something like that in the work.

INTERVIEWER

It's certainly there. Maybe it's the switch from the "altar sublime" in your earlier work to the "alter sublime" in your more recent work. What about Fragonard? He gets mentioned a couple of times. Does he represent a particular world-view for you?

DEWDNEY

Fragonard is mentioned *only*, I must emphasize *only*, because of his treatment of deciduous trees and hazy atmospheres. Otherwise . . . well.

INTERVIEWER

Where is Arkona?

DEWDNEY

Arkona is a small town in Southwestern Ontario which is north-west of London, about midway between Lake Huron and London. It is the town adjacent to Rock Glen, the memory capital of Canada.

INTERVIEWER

In "Golders Green" you talk about "some geometric defence/against the sun." I'm not sure what you're getting at there . . .

DEWDNEY

I believe that reference is to ice crystals and a slight anthropocentric metaphorization of their forms (a thin skin of ice on a puddle in the Arkona Gorge) as if they were marshalling some defence against the spring sun. Crystals are by nature geometric.

INTERVIEWER

How do *you* pronounce "theiyr"?

DEWDNEY

I pronounce "theiyr" as "their"—to do anything else would be too neoCeltic, too precious. The device is optical only.

INTERVIEWER

Are there any poems from the other books that you regret not seeing in *Predators*?

DEWDNEY

No. Everything in *Predators* is fine by me. It was, oddly, a fairly satisfying project. It was nice, for instance, to get the infra-books, like "Log Entries," under one cover, at least temporarily.

INTERVIEWER

What about what you're in the process of working on, what you're thinking about working on.

DEWDNEY

Well I'm working now on a book which is called *The Immaculate Perception*. I had titled it that and then I've been asking everyone: "This is a great sounding title but it sounds familiar to me. Have I actually thought of this title?" And apparently I have, but there actually have

153

been two—I found out there had been an "immaculate perception" in part of Nietzsche's *Thus Spake Zarathustra*. It is one of the parables. It really has nothing to do with my position on the "immaculate perception." And there is a Zen patriarch who talks about the "immaculate perception," which again is not close to what I mean when I use the term.

INTERVIEWER

Both of them, then, were in non-English, so the English translation could have been something else.

DEWDNEY

Yes, I'm still clear on that one. It took me years of research to find those two and they are somewhat arcane and recondite. This is a departure from my previous work because it is series of speculative, philosophical posits—criticism. A friend of mine, Derrick de Kerckhove, who is the associate director of the McLuhan Centre here, coined a term for what he perceived my thinking in these directions is as "neurocriticism," which seems like an okay appelation. It doesn't rest too uneasily. In a sense that is what this new book is—I'm talking about the nature of consciousness and its biological substratum, from what I know. I've learned an awful lot—not anywhere near as much as a neurologist should know—about the physiological substratum of thought. I'm really interested in that. And neurological mechanisms and the nature of consciousness and the nature of being—those kinds of questions. It's almost a frightening text. It does at certain points actually sort of turn into poetry. At certain points it seems to alter its structure and turn into poetic structure, although I have to admit that there's nothing about it that reminds me of pataphysics in any way. So I'd have to exclude that as a possibility. It's a very problematic text. It's very serious. There is some humour in it. There's some anthropological excursions in it. It's very strange.

INTERVIEWER

Can you elaborate on what you're showing or demonstrating in the book?

DEWDNEY

I give examples from ordinary experience that kind of substantiate the view that consciousness is an epiphenomenon of brain process. There are exercises in the text, the whole book is an exercise, whereby at the end you achieve almost an urban negative satori. By taking this highly materialistic view of the mind you can almost disappear, in a sense, or the mind can disappear. The illusion of self will disappear—which is both an illusion and the highest reality, a transcendental reality . . .

INTERVIEWER

. . . in an urban setting . . .

DEWDNEY

. . . well I'm working in an urban setting right now, not in the country. That's why there is that qualification. I always imagine reaching satori in a subway station. I think that's the ultimate way to go.

INTERVIEWER

In the womb of the city . . . What about all the work that's being done with the other parts of the body and how those parts are part "brain." How the fingertips, for example, have memory. Are you interested as well in the other parts of the body which have brain-like characteristics?

DEWDNEY

Well that's very interesting stuff although I guess I'm interested in that part of the body . . . well if you were being tortured and someone was cutting off various parts of your body—I'm interested in those other parts, but mostly in the last part that would be cut off. I think we'd probably end up with just our heads!

INTERVIEWER

There's a great scene in a Monty Python movie where the fellow keeps getting parts of his body cut off . . .

DEWDNEY

. . . he keeps fighting . . .

INTERVIEWER

. . . "Come back you chicken!" and then he's left with only a head, of course.

DEWDNEY

Conversely, I do believe that the body, brain, heart, and mind are one structure. You're obviously permeated with consciousness, and therefore as much as there is a representation of your body within your mind there is a representation of your mind in your body. I see the mind and the body as being one thing—there are pathological states of mind where there is a separation between the two and I believe that is an aberration. I think people unknowingly still make that split between the heart and the mind. The heart is *in* the mind, in a sense.

INTERVIEWER

This is that trinity coming back. Even the oil which appears in your work reminds me of "3-in-1 Oil." There are always a few things occurring simultaneously. What about the male brain? In "Parasite Maintenance" you talk about the distinctly male brain.

DEWDNEY

"Parasite Maintenance" was a very problematic thing. What's happening in this text now, *The Immaculate Perception*, is really what I've gone on to do after "Parasite Maintenance." I think I was qualifying that as the male brain simply because I felt I was a male talking about brains . . . we're getting into a very tricky area here . . . what would this be?—sort of neurological sexism, which I think probably does exist: it permeates everything every time you talk about the sexes. I think at that point I was saying "I am a male talking about male brains" and I think it was an excuse. It seemed easier to say "he" throughout the text than "he/she"—that was really one of the reasons I did that. I really felt I could not speak for the experience of being a woman. I think this text I'm working on now is more general perhaps. I'm getting less specific, relying less on very specific and recent neurological data which is changing all the time. I'm going to more general, arm-chair type assumptions, that anybody could make, although the metaphors have been discovered by neurologists.

Did you see yourself as a remote control agent when you were writing the section "Remote Control"? Do you see yourself as a remote control agent now that you're working on the brain?

DEWDNEY

Well—actually, yes to your first question and then no to your second. The remote control section was a metaphor for my own personal ability to lead a double life, not only to morally span the dichotomy involved, but to excel and enjoy the vigilance and paranoid critical structures (tantamount to espionage activity) which are the concomitants of double lives. This moral freedom, a licence of the poet perhaps, is purchased at great cost however—one burns thousands of gallons of ethical fuel a second just to stay in one place. One becomes the final repository of a truth which has the potential pain of two people inherent in it. It's the test of fire really. I'm not researching that particular mode of existence in the sense I was then, and my relationship to the brain is not in any way a subset of the "Remote Control" series.

INTERVIEWER

Do you think there is a difference between male and female writing?

DEWDNEY

I do. There is definitely a difference in consciousness, a difference in quality and nature of consciousness.

INTERVIEWER

Nadine Gordimer recently stated that "when it comes to their essential faculty as writers, all writers are androgynous beings."

DEWDNEY

I think that with poetry you'd find certain differences. Maybe I'm basing my assumption on older models. Gertrude Stein and Djuna Barnes have a kind of intrinsic nature that seems to me knowable and unknowable at the same time, and it seems to me, and maybe this again is not a "correct" view, but it seems they are fully spontaneous within a femality or an animus that is female. I don't know.

INTERVIEWER

Do you see yourself as being an androgynous writer?

DEWDNEY
I do, yes. I see my work as being more androgynous than male, or totally male.

INTERVIEWER
Do you see your writing as being animalistic, or non-human, as well as being androgynous?

DEWDNEY
I wonder . . .

INTERVIEWER
I guess I'm alluding to the Preface of *Predators* in which you say: "In a sense, then, this book is the voice of the land and the creatures themselves, speaking from the inviolate fortress of a primaeval history uncorrupted by humans. It is a codex of the plants and animals whose technology is truly miraculous, and for whom I am merely a scribe."

DEWDNEY
Oh yes, right. Now that was a curious thing to say! That comes from a very deep part of me, that statement. It comes again from what I was alluding to earlier, my alliance with creatures, with animals—which is a heartfelt alliance for me. And so it's hard to say, when the chips are down, which way I'd go: halfway between the animals on one side and the humans on the other.

INTERVIEWER
Did you see the Tarzan movie, *Greystoke*, because at the end of the movie he opts, of course, for the animals.

DEWDNEY
I have to see that—it sounds like my kind of film! It might solve my own ambiguity that way. It's a curious thing. I don't know, I really can't say. I may be able to talk about that later. It's an interesting point.

INTERVIEWER
For me one of the best attempts to talk about this was the twenty-three-year-old Samuel Beckett who said in a marvelous book entitled *Our Exagmination Round his Factification for Incamination of Work in Progress* that *Finnegans Wake*, which Joyce called *Work in Progress* before it was published, was "not about something; it is that something itself." So that

when Joyce is writing about smoke, the words smell like smoke; when he's writing about stones the words themselves feel like stones.

DEWDNEY
Almost like a kind of animistic objectivism.

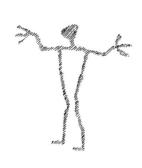

INTERVIEWER
Which is entirely subjective, of course, at the same time.

DEWDNEY
Well let's hope so. That's interesting. I like that point.

INTERVIEWER
The reason I bring that up is because in Steve McCaffery's pataphysics article on you he says that you're trying to dissociate the words from their meanings, and I'm not sure I agree with that.

DEWDNEY
Well at that time, that article was somewhat of a manifesto for Steve — his own point of view. He was hoping that my poetry would become a paradigm of his model of language as a fossil-bearing . . . His own metaphor flooded into that right away, like a fish in water. He immediately lost sight of any kind of referential qualities to my work, which you have to admit are there, and he wanted very much to marshall my work into his quadrant. I like his work, but I'm working with completely different matter and so he did make some assumptions which did not anticipate my direction. He's a very smart person, he's quite good, but

159

I don't think his piece is quite accurate, so that was good of you to pick that up. Although he did mention some important things: the lie, that's important, that's true about the ultimate lie. It's a lie which is a cosmically-aligned personal indulgence. It's a funny kind of thing, but it's true.

INTERVIEWER

In the last few poems of *Predators* you seem to talk a lot about lying.

DEWDNEY

There's a story, I think it's in one of the other interviews: at one point *A Paleozoic Geology* reached a geology professor at the University of Western Ontario and he sent me a memo saying he really enjoyed the book, but why did I have to lie so much? I thought that was beautiful. This was my favorite reaction to this text. Here's somebody who really got into it, but when he met with these twists . . . in a way I wish all readers would be as familiar as he was with what I was talking about.

INTERVIEWER

I think that's one of the problems—that's maybe the reason why there hasn't been much work done on you, and what has been written seems to appropriate you for purposes other than your own.

DEWDNEY

I think I came from such a rarified type of environment. My taxonomy, my lexicon, was not very similar to that of most other people, you see, and it dawned on me after the first few books—people were saying they were having trouble understanding me, and I could not figure that out until I realized, well it finally got drilled into me, that my vocabulary was very different from most people's vocabulary . . . sort of technical. I can't change my vocabulary but it's a strange sort of thing. Kind of interesting. I think people thought that I was trying to be elitist, you see, by having a vocabulary like that: "He's just trying to make it sound like he's really intelligent," which is not what I was trying at all, but some people got into that. Anyway.

INTERVIEWER

Do you see your poems as being "largely metalinguistic concerns" as McCaffery does?

DEWDNEY

Poems are a charmed net of words. They cannot, if they are truly poems, be much other than that. Even poetry in which referential intentionality is the major impetus must exist as a self-sustaining, holistic entity in its individual manifestation. I see the border between metaphor and referent as being reversible, that the poem is, to use Jean Cocteau's phrase, "a thinking jewel." In other words, a poem is a discrete entity which displays the ordered but recursive meanings in a meta-reading which is temporarily opaque (i.e., to the single reading) but which exists as a resonant structure over many readings. The words, the individual parts of the poem, are merely signposts indicating the direction and nature of the "intelligence" of the poem. The heart makes it true.

I am, however, in postmodern terms, somewhat bucking the flow, in that I'm actually very concerned with meaning, with actually saying something on the primary, apprehended level of the text.

INTERVIEWER

In the last poem in *Predators* the tornado stops moving toward you when you stop thinking about it or visualizing it in your mind. Is there any other world separate from the one that exists in the mind?

DEWDNEY

I think what I was getting at in that poem was the sense that seems to parallel a recent development in cosmological theory, that is to say the anthropocentric theory—that we create the universe by looking at it, to metaphrase Heisenberg if I may, that the universe exists so that we can study it. In this sense I was indicating a paranoid framework which gave the tornado both consciousness and telepathic powers. By looking at the tornado one formed a mental image of it in one's mind which the tornado homed in on almost narcissistically, a juggernaut of pure demonic annihilation of self consciousness, almost as if the tornado were a device for seeking out and destroying poetic or human consciousness by having in its mechanism, its mode of operation, a simple feedback circuit which would respond to recognition of its form within the consciousness of an onlooker who happened to be unfortunate enough to be looking at it, to happen to glance at it, thus starting an irreversible process inextricably linked to the very nature of human consciousness. It would make the experience of seeing a tornado much more exciting!

INTERVIEWER

I want to ask you about your article in *Vanguard* on Murray Favro, "Paradigm of Invention," and about that word "Oregionalism." As soon as that term came up in your article I thought it seemed appropriate for

161

you. Greg Curnoe may not like me asking you this, but do you see yourself as an Oregionalist?

DEWDNEY

Well, I guess so. I kind of see myself as a hyper-regionalist in a funny way, because there was this matrix and Greg and everyone else was coming over to our house and I had this funny sense of London, Ontario, as being the center of the world, and these guys were making art about it. So my sense of place was very much reinforced by these people's activities. I also had a very private attachment, which was happening anyway—my attachment to limestone, to certain kinds of ideas and sorts of feelings that were independent of the rest of this.

INTERVIEWER

How early do you mean?

DEWDNEY

Age three or four. My interest in limestone wasn't happening until I was six or seven. Somewhere in that would be the formative stages of whatever attachment or transformative relationships were happening.

INTERVIEWER

Do you mean seeing the myriad of directions that things could go—what you call in one poem the "vortex" of directions?

DEWDNEY

I can't say that there was any choice involved, in that sense. I'd have to say that it was just intrinsic in my nature and my place. Limestone probably would have happened wherever I happened to have been born. I probably would have at some point seen limestone and that would have added up for me in the right way.

INTERVIEWER

Because of the past, present and future which exist simultaneously in limestone?

DEWDNEY

I think those kinds of things come out of a feeling in the beginning and then some kind of affiliation of the texture of the stone and *then* a realization of what it is reinforces that. You put out an intuitive net first and then somehow that has a lot to do with the information that the intuition is based on, and it just adds up from there.

In the poem "Brain Pan" you say "even this/is out of context." Is everything out of context, which may be the same thing as asking, is everything *in* context?

DEWDNEY
Interesting you should talk about things being in or out of context. Karl Jirgens, the editor of *Rampike*, at the latest Pataphysics Conference in Toronto, constructed a device which supposedly enabled him to remove himself from any context. It looks like a shiny four-sided pyramid which he wears over his head.

INTERVIEWER
The concretions in your poems seem to be sort of eyes, geological eyes. Is that how you "see" them?

DEWDNEY
I did this very funny little postcard one time for an exhibition I had at the Forest City Gallery in London, Ontario. There's a shot I have in *Fovea Centralis* of a concretion imbedded in the bank of a little cliff—it's painted white, so I painted an eyeball on that and I put two of them side by side! It looks like a panicked Sphinx, one of those startled, Egyptian faces—frozen at the moment of being startled to death on speed or something very strange like that. These big bug-eyed concretions! There is a sense of concretions revolving within an oil lens, but I don't know if I see them as eyes so much as beings. Opal L. Nations came up with what I thought was a very appropriate perception. He called them

"imploded planets." And I thought that was excellent. That seems right in some ways.

INTERVIEWER

They're little nubs of stone, aren't they? I think of them as being like pearls. They start off as grains of sand and then slowly accrete.

DEWDNEY

They're pulsed crystal layers. They take dissolved minerals out of the rock around them. The minerals percolate through the rock constantly, through water action, and the dissolved minerals re-accrete, crystallize the concretions. So that's why they bulge the rock around them. Very strange things.

INTERVIEWER

I take it they can get very big.

DEWDNEY

Some of them at Kettle Point can get six feet across. They're all over the world. One time Lise and I were driving across the desert in New Mexico at night and we were very tired and we pulled into this pit stop, and as the headlights were sweeping over the desert I caught this very familiar shape. I stopped the car, stopped the revolution and went back through forty degrees and there where the headlights were was this concretion made out of this reddish sandstone, exactly the same as the ones here. And then I found out they're all over the world—New Zealand and everywhere. All waiting to be born. When I give the final command! Sort of "Village of the Damned" type of thing. That's part of my heritage too. Sort of Olaf Stapledon, Odd John. The idea of a group of people, aliens within the human species, who are sort of out of it. Anyway . . . that's part of my family mythology.

INTERVIEWER

Many people in Canada talk about inventing the world in their books. You seem to have bitten off a larger chunk. It seems you're trying to re-create the universe. You're involved not only with what you can hold on to but also with what you can't hold on to—what is beyond one's immediate grasp.

DEWDNEY

That's interesting. Is what you're talking about possible? Yes. For me, it's not an attempt as such, it's what I'm doing. I guess it is fairly big. I get the sense of it being big.

INTERVIEWER

What about black holes? Some of your work seems to get lost, the words disappear, as in the "Log Entries" section of *Predators*. You're creating something and then you're erasing it. Through that negation you create a multitude of possibilities. Everyone who reads those sections has different associations, different words that they fill in the spaces with.

DEWDNEY

You mean when the words cut in . . .

INTERVIEWER

. . . and then cut out in mid-sentence. One of the other scientific allusions in your work seems to be the quantum jump between words on the page. There's a big space between that chunk of words at the top of the page and "an octopus lying on the ice at half-time" at the bottom of the page. Do you see your work as dealing with these connections/disconnections between words?

DEWDNEY

I'm really interested in the idea that words have what you could call a "paradigmatic halo" around them, and that they have interference nodes. In other words, an interference syntax is set up between two discrete words on a page, two discrete entities, and that between them they'll set up standing waves of interference between their meanings. Conventional syntax is a net that we usually put between those words, but there are unconventional standing waves between those two discrete entities, and sometimes I'm interested in these other possibilities—the idea of an induced field of meaning. So that's true. I'm interested in what's in the holes, in trying to induce a hole by altering the text or making a mutation in the text which will induce this response that is not normally there. It's not visible—it has to be within the reader.

INTERVIEWER

That connects with some of the things your father says—how in the caves there will be one image, and then another about thirty or forty feet away. The two images seem separate, but they are in a strange, mystical way related. It's that space between them that creates the stories.

Like they are only the visible portion of a series that is much larger. That's something that is very close to me.

INTERVIEWER

In one of his books your father has a chart in which he attempts to categorize some of the cave designs that he was documenting, and fully one-half of the chart is taken up by unexplainable doodles and signs, and then there's a little cone of "hands" or "objects" or "animals" or other recognizable things. The unexplainable signs are as important as all the explainable signs put together. I think of your writing as spawning similar ideas.

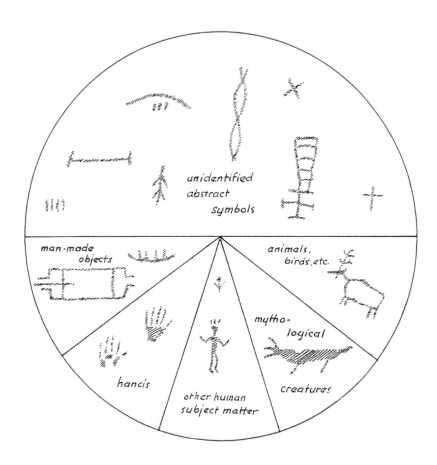

That's true. That's a very good point actually. That's congruent. He was dealing scientifically and pragmatically with vast quantities of the unknown. He was very careful not to speculate, not to project certain types of value assumptions into what he was perceiving were the relics, the products of another culture. He tried to perceive only those things that were obvious. That was a real gift that he had. Hopefully we are, in a sense, making some sort of progress—becoming less assumptive about these kinds of sociological knowledge.

INTERVIEWER

The brain, and your work that deals with the brain, is also important here. I was talking this morning with my sister Bridget, who lives in Guelph and who has recently been doing some work on the brain. We were talking about the synaptic space between neurons in the brain, and how information has to jump through a blank space in order to be transmitted. And also this researcher, Gary Lynch, and his work—he's been able to see a physical change at the spot where this jump occurs.

DEWDNEY

This is the synaptic spine theory?

INTERVIEWER

Yes. These holes between things—that's where things really get exciting.

DEWDNEY

That's true. I've always been very interested in gap phenomenon, or field phenomenon. I think that's the magic of the technology of our century—the invisible forces which operate with no tangible effect, but which are very "heavy." Radiation is the same sort of thing—you can't see it, but it's very "heavy." Our generation has been brought up with a fear of this invisible enemy, or at least knowing that things invisible can affect you very deeply. Which is not a fear that has been intrinsic to humans in the past.

INTERVIEWER

This seeing/not seeing has another twist, because in the Newtonian universe you could see whatever you wanted to see, whereas now, in our Heisenbergian universe, you really can't see what you most want to see. That fundamental uncertainty is essential to your work. I think the question for many people may still be: "What is that octopus doing on the ice at half-time anyway?" That image does have some basis in reality — I seem to remember it from the newspapers or something like that.

DEWDNEY
Well of course there is no half-time in hockey, but I couldn't really say "between periods" or something too wordy like that.

INTERVIEWER
That's right. I had forgotten that when I was reading that poem.

DEWDNEY
I'm glad. Anyone who really knows hockey would immediately say, "Hey, wait a minute, there's no half-time in hockey!"

INTERVIEWER
You're lying again!

DEWDNEY
Right, lying again! But that's not really important. It was a hockey image from my childhood. They used to throw octopi onto the ice at Maple Leaf Gardens. Here you are just seven years old and you're just piecing together reality, and the camera would pan the ice and there would be these flattened octopi, and I happen to have really liked octopi at this time, so I was intrigued by this conjunction. My brother screaming about hockey, the hockey game itself which was a very nebulous activity for me. I did know that octopi were somehow appropriate on the ice during hockey games. For me it wasn't an expression of anger or disgust, which it was, of course, for those people who threw them. It was just that octopi had a tendency to gravitate toward the ice at half-time! So that's a kind of steadfast or stubborn holding to those kind of primal perceptions.

INTERVIEWER
There's lots of other tidbits of information in your poems which it seems you want to jog people's memory with. "So flexible you can pick them up with a dime," which is a nice image from the TV ad of several years ago.

DEWDNEY
You're the first person who has caught that allusion to the advertise-

168

ment. Most people don't catch it. They still like the poem, which is curious. I don't know why that line came in at that particular time. There it was. Oh gawd! Oh well, I've seen stranger things!

INTERVIEWER

How do you write those poems? Do you rewrite a lot or . . .

DEWDNEY

That particular type of poetry, there's no rewriting at all. They just seem to sort of happen, I guess. It's hard to say. I don't really know much about that particular activity. I don't know if I can talk about that too much. Not that there's any trick involved, but it's just a funny area for me. Sometimes the poems come very fast, sometimes I would do them over a period of days. That poem it seems was always there.

INTERVIEWER

It seems there are bits of dreams, combined with real ephemeral information.

DEWDNEY

I'm usually careful to keep dreams out of poetry. I've always felt dreams were cheating, but occasionally dreams will be important to a poem. I don't think it's wrong to use dreams. You can tell sometimes when a writer is using exclusively dreams, relying heavily on dreams. It can be a real tricky crutch, if you're not careful.

INTERVIEWER

Are you interested in contemporary music—John Cage, Philip Glass, Laurie Anderson, people like that?

DEWDNEY

I'm very interested in contemporary music, in fact, contemporary culture of all sorts. Laurie Anderson's music bugs me for some reason, though I like her word and conceptual art. I liked Glassworks for its romanticism and I love John Cage's whole approach. I also listen to popular music: Shreickback, Cabaret Voltaire, Simple Minds, Men Without Hats, etc., as well as enjoying Rock Videos, and North American culture in general. I'm a real lover of North American culture, in the J. G. Ballardian sense of it.

I must admit that jazz seems to me the highest manifestation of music right now, the latest thing in the evolution of musical sophistication, though I'm not, oddly enough, listening to that much right now. I went through a big reggae phase in the mid seventies, Big Youth was a favourite, just the way I like Eek a Mouse now, UB-40, etc. I like dancing, so funky music has always stirred me. What's great about being North American is that we have this fantastic natural heritage of black music, black choreography superimposed in our nervous systems— wonderful feeling!

INTERVIEWER
Together with David Cronenberg, who are the film makers you keep your eye on?

DEWDNEY
My favourite film of all time is *The Enigma of Kaspar Hauser* by Werner Herzog, with *Eraserhead* and (oddly enough) *Blade Runner* very close behind. Actually, my second favourite movie of all time is *Once Upon a Time in the West* by Sergio Leone, then *Eraserhead*. David Lynch's soundman is my favourite soundman in the business, and I sat through *Dune* just to watch those two operate together. Lately I've enjoyed *The Man of Flowers, Cold Feet*, especially enjoyed *Repo Man* and *Stranger than Paradise*. Cocteau's films were great, *Orphée, The Blood of the Poet*, etc. — great stuff, I love films. With Cronenberg, *Scanners* is my favourite. I wish I'd seen that film when I was twelve.

INTERVIEWER
You titled your *Vanguard* piece on David Cronenberg "The Biological Imperative." Are you working from a neurological imperative? A geographic imperative? A geological imperative? All, or none, of the above?

170

DEWDNEY

I wouldn't say immediately that I was working out of any systematic or categorical imperative per se, in terms of my own work. I don't have an overriding aesthetic that determines my form and content, though I do have my own world view and my own philosophical/religious fusion which would be a more generalized imperative, in that it ramifies into my entire field of action. However, since this is I think the definition of an artist, or at least a professional artist, there is very little boundary definition between my work and my life, and my personal views must in some way exert some sort of at least nebulous influence on my work. I'm a total epiphenominal materialist. I believe spirit and heart are based neurologically, that self-consciousness is a transcendent paradox, in other words, consciousness effects its own neurological substratum. I also have a small disclaimer, an escape clause in my philosophical/religious fusion, which allows for the miraculous. The miraculous, I believe, extends to the everyday, and pervades all matter, in that matter itself and the existence of our universe, not to mention conscious entities like ourselves, are miracles obscured only by the functional temporality of our existence, the human dilemma.

INTERVIEWER

I do see a lot of humour in your work, but the violent images in your work seem to stick out a little more. In the Preface to *Predators* you talk about the seasons recapitulating evolution, and we're left now in the November of time. You've left us close to the "erasure of chronology," and I was wondering if this was some sort of Yeatsian apocalyptic vision, or am I reading too much into it.

DEWDNEY

Nuclear winter . . .

INTERVIEWER

Yes, something like that.

DEWDNEY

I hope not, I really hope not. It is a possibility . . . Fall is the human age. If you carry that metaphor any further you'd have to have a fifth season added on, eventually. But I think we can get by with the four we have. For me Fall is the age of mammals. It seems that all mammals burn brightly in the Fall, including humans. Squirrels have their nice Winter coats on, cats look good. All mammals look really good in the

Fall. They really pick up. That little chill but it's still sort of Summer.

INTERVIEWER
There's also a lot of pictures of explosions. What's the fascination here?

DEWDNEY
You're asking "Am I a violent guy, or what!" I love explosions. I've always been fascinated by explosions. I think it's a part of being North American and watching war movies. I just really like the beauty of explosions. Like Ripple Rock in B.C., the Fraser River. They had to blow up this rock which was a threat to navigation. It was the biggest man-made explosion since the nuclear bomb was invented.

INTERVIEWER
When was that?

DEWDNEY
It was on TV. It was in the late fifties or early sixties—something like that. It was an incredible explosion. I've always had this thing about explosions. It's something that is so overpowering, so huge that it's almost a universal phenomenon, and yet at the same time it has an unearthly beauty to it. I have a strange . . . I'm compelled by tornadoes too. I find them extremely attractive in a funny way. It's very strange.

INTERVIEWER
What about the pictures that you include? Are you working with different ideas than those that come out of the words, or are they complements to the words, or are the words complements to the pictures?

DEWDNEY
Some of them seem to be illustrations in a funny sense. Truly illustrative. Actually what they are is the poetry or the material in the poetry in a different mode. I follow an idea through whatever medium it will manifest itself—in words, or an image, or in a three-dimensional structure, like sculpture. Whichever seems to be the most integral medium—I'll try and facilitate it in its natural habitat. I just follow it wherever it happens to go. If it has to be in words then it has to be in words . . .

INTERVIEWER
There's also a lot of other stuff that I want to ask you about, even

172

about individual images. But for now I'll sift through this stuff. I haven't even asked you about the Governor and the Parasite.

DEWDNEY

I'm not using that metaphor as much right now, not that I'm discounting that particular essay. That was a very useful way of looking at a kind of transitional area that I was working in. The battle of Parasite and Governor is an ongoing process, neither being in an ultimately superior position, though hopefully with the Governor being deconstructed through the growth of negative capability. I'm less concerned now with that particular model, which is because I've simplified the issue in my recent work. I no longer speak about the Parasite or the Governor, which were metaphors useful for establishing a dialectic analogy. I now only speak of the house of the living language as a metaphor for the biological location of language in the brain. The Parasite has generalized into the more contextual restraints that language exerts on the consciousness of the language user. Now I'm more concerned, or I'm continuing my assumptions that language is a kind of intelligence unto itself, which we negotiate through our own meaning.

INTERVIEWER

What do you mean by meaning?

DEWDNEY

Well in other words, that language has a kind of involuntary structuring of our experience, that we are trying to negotiate through. It's a kind of narrow passage, that is more or less imposed on us, within which we believe we have absolute free will, but we have less perhaps than we think. But we're certainly not totally at its mercy either. I don't believe that language ultimately structures thought. I do believe that there can be thought independent of language, which I know is somewhat of a heresy, but . . . I'm sure it exists, somewhere!

Interview by Peter O'Brien

All drawings in the Christopher Dewdney interview are from *Indian Rock Paintings of the Great Lakes*, 2nd ed., by Selwyn Dewdney and Kenneth E. Kidd (Toronto: Univ. of Toronto Press, 1967) and are used by permission.

173

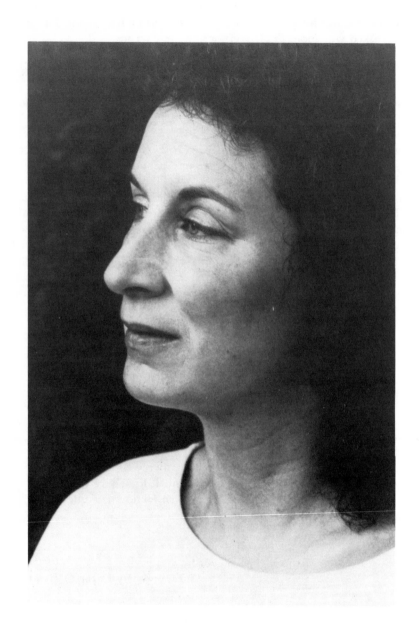

MARGARET ATWOOD

Margaret Atwood is perhaps Canada's best-known contemporary writer. Her first book of poems, Double Persephone, *appeared in 1961. Since then she has published eleven volumes of poetry, the most recent of which are* Interlunar *(1984) and* Selected Poems II *(1987), three collections of short stories, two volumes of criticism, two children's books, and six novels, the most recent of which is* The Handmaid's Tale *(1985). In addition, she has edited the* Oxford Book of Canadian Poetry in English *and is actively involved in both PEN (Poets and Playwrights; Editors and Essayists; Novelists) International and Amnesty International. A number of interviews with Atwood have focussed on her prolific literary output. In general, she avoids detailed technical discussion of her own work, which thus eliminates the possibility of taking her own criticism as the "final word." This openness and refusal to be pinned down is consistent with the form and content of most of Atwood's work, and is reflected in the difficulty critics have in labelling what she writes—novel? prose/poem? ghost story? romance? and so on. As a result, in this interview we chose to focus on the relationship between politics and literature. This sort of discussion seemed to offer more insight into Atwood's work than any particular discussion could, and furthermore, it did not subvert the implicit values which guide her writing.*

The interview took place on 19 November 1984 at the Ritz Carlton Hotel in Montreal and was later pruned and sharpened for publication. Atwood is reputedly a formidable interviewee, yet she was affable, friendly, and extremely accommodating, especially in light of the frequent interruptions from hotel staff and phone calls from people who wished to know where she was reading that night. At one point in the interview Atwood comments that Canadians do not allow their writers to become too arrogant or removed from the public, and Atwood's friendly telephone manner with strangers confirmed this statement. Obviously Atwood is adept at handling herself in such situations, as well as on the literary/political stage.

INTERVIEWERS

How about starting here: do you like doing interviews?

ATWOOD

I don't mind them as long as the people are reasonably polite. And have read the books.

INTERVIEWERS

I was reading through some of your reviews in *Second Words* and one review on Adrienne Rich's work seems to correspond quite closely to what you are doing yourself. The review I'm referring to is the one in which you talk about witnessing or seeing things with the third eye, recording and reporting disasters.

ATWOOD

Yeah, any writer does that—except some poets in North America who happen to think that writing shouldn't be political. This is the only area in the world where such a belief is held. It's not a general worldwide belief about writing; it's a specifically North American view of writing— that art should exist apart, above, beyond, not mixed in. It's not just me and Adrienne Rich, it's me and Charles Dickens and Neruda, on down the line.

INTERVIEWERS

Can you separate politics and art?

ATWOOD

Well, it depends what you mean by politics. Do you mean Mulroney and Trudeau? I can separate that very easily from art but . . .

INTERVIEWERS

No, I would assume a broader statement about politics. Is literature political writing about art or is literature art that's about politics? Or are the two, in fact, inextricable and essentially connected?

ATWOOD

Politics in the sense of who has power and how people behave. That's what politics is and that is also what novel writing is about. You could say that Jane Austen is a political novelist. And she is. She's talking about power and how you get it if you happen not to have any, namely if you're a woman in the early nineteenth century. How you get it is that you marry Mr. Darcy, and that's politics in the early nineteenth century

176

for middle-class women. You can go on from there and extend the term to coups, wars, elections and so on. But the separation of politics into boy's games and girl's games, politics being a boy's game—I don't buy that. Politics in the widest sense affects everybody. So writers write about human thought, behaviour, action, even when they're writing fantasy. Some of the most political writing in the 1950s was done by science fiction writers because people then didn't feel safe enough to do it openly. That's politics. *But* let's not confuse that with ideological mouthpiece writing, which is a different ball game.

INTERVIEWERS

Okay. Because in answer to that, some people may say everyone writes about that, therefore everyone is political.

ATWOOD

In a certain sense yes. But some do it with more awareness.

INTERVIEWERS

Can you think of any North American examples?

ATWOOD

Carolyn Forché. Just for starters. Do you know her work? Or E. L. Doctorow.

INTERVIEWERS

How about Canadians?

ATWOOD

Canadian writers do it a lot. Milton Acorn. Irving Layton, Al Purdy, John Newlove, myself, Michael Ondaatje, to a certain extent. That's poets. Novelists. *The Diviners* is a political novel. A lot of Maritime writing is political in that it examines the lives of the bottom layer in society. Quebec writing has been political for decades. I mean awarely political, obviously political. *Maria Chapdelaine* is a political novel.

INTERVIEWERS

Can I ask you then who is not political?

ATWOOD

Well, I would say Henry James, but even then you're dealing with the lives of the upper class in Europe at the end of the nineteenth century

177

and it's highly involved with money, and judgements are made, and the only ideal woman is an angel partly because she's so rich. *The Great Gatsby* is a political novel. But you know people get freaked by the word "political" because they think that it means propaganda. But it doesn't necessarily mean that at all. What we're *really* talking about is not being afraid to put in things that are there because somebody might think they're political. Now the issue that arises on this continent: some people are aware of "politics" but they deliberately leave out that area of life because they don't want to be called political. So instead they write about trees and nothing but trees, for example.

INTERVIEWERS

I don't want you to damn people but do you have any specific names?

ATWOOD

No. It tends to be a U.S. phenomenon rather than a Canadian one. Canadians wallow in politics of all kinds; on the local, national, and international levels. They are very interested in world news. For instance, whenever you go to the States for any length of time you start to feel very odd because you don't hear about what's happening in Madagascar, but you get the local politics. You don't get very much world news except in *The New York Times* or *The Washington Post*. You don't realize this until you are out of the country. The Canadians and the British too love world news. I just opened the *Gazette* and there's a section called "World."

INTERVIEWERS

As opposed to Montreal? Would you connect this political element in writing to witnessing with the third eye?

ATWOOD

You don't have to witness with a third eye. You can witness with the two that you've got.

INTERVIEWERS

Is the third eye going beyond what we consider to be normal vision?

ATWOOD

Well, I don't know what I said about it. What did I say? Can you quote?

Sure. In the review on Rich you write: "Trying to see clearly and to record what has been seen—the rapes, the wars, the murders, the various kinds of violation and mutilation—is half of the poet's effort; for this she requires a third eye, an eye that can see pain with 'clarity.'"

ATWOOD

Okay. That's a quote from one of her own poems. But she is not the first poet to use that figure.

INTERVIEWERS

You use it throughout your work too.

ATWOOD

Yes, but I would probably mean something different by it. She would probably mean that she doesn't have immediate access to those particular scenes because she is living in cushioned North America so she needs the third eye to see further. Now lots of other people would not need that because the stuff would be right there in front of them. By "a third eye" one tends to mean clairvoyance. Now that may be part of clairvoyance for her but what does clairvoyance mean? All it means is clear seeing.

INTERVIEWERS

You mention in *Second Words* that writing a novel forces you to imagine what it's like to be someone else. I've got two questions. One of them: do poems do that as well?

ATWOOD

No.

INTERVIEWERS

Okay, do poems force you to imagine what it's like to be yourself?

ATWOOD

I wouldn't put it that way, no. No, when you're talking about novels you're usually talking about creating a character, even if it's a very autobiographical novel. But with lyric poetry you're talking about the voice of the poem.

179

INTERVIEWERS

As opposed to the voice of the poet?

ATWOOD

Yes. Some people dramatize; that is, they have a speaking voice that is supposed to be Uncle Ned and if they are doing that then the same statement applies: they are imagining themselves as Uncle Ned or they are giving a voice to Uncle Ned. And sometimes poetry does do that, but it doesn't *necessarily* do that, whereas fiction writing *necessarily* does that. You can't be a fiction writer very long without doing that.

INTERVIEWERS

Okay, I guess I'm not sure then what you mean by the voice of the poem.

ATWOOD

Okay, what would *you* mean by that?

INTERVIEWERS

I guess we talk about style, syntax and so on; that is, words on the page, in a very physical sense . . .

ATWOOD

First of all, a poem is not words on a page. A poem is words in the air; or I should say words in the ear, because a poem is heard. And the words on a page are a notation like a musical score. We would not say that Beethoven was a bunch of black marks on a page; you would say that Beethoven is what we hear when we transcribe those black marks. And it's the same with a poem: when you are reading a poem the words are in your air.

INTERVIEWERS

Although the space is important on the page.

ATWOOD

So are sharps and flats and half notes and quarter notes. Not that I can read music. Not without great strain.

INTERVIEWERS

Is there a multiplicity of voices within the voice of the poem?

ATWOOD

Who can tell? I mean it would have to be the individual poem we're talking about; in a very derivative poem, yes. It might be John Keats and Shakespeare and numerous others. But a poem is not necessarily the voice of a single person, either the poet or anybody else, in the same way that music is not the music of "Mozart." In the same way Mozart, although recognizably Mozart, is not Mozart brushing his teeth in the morning. That's not what we mean. So the voice of the poet—do you mean the poet who has just spent a night in the Ritz Hotel, or do you mean the voice that comes when you are reading the poem to yourself; what you hear when you are reading the poem?

INTERVIEWERS

Well, presumably both.

ATWOOD

Only if I put the Ritz Hotel in the poem. Let me put it this way: was Shakespeare a girl and do you care? Or was he Francis Bacon? You know, I don't happen to believe that, but Shakespeare is a wonderful example because "he" is very thoroughly out of the language. We don't hear that much about "him" at all but we hear the words.

INTERVIEWERS

Yes. I don't necessarily want to connect the poet to the poem.

ATWOOD

Well, sometimes you can but I think such connections are helpful only when you come to a point in the poem where it doesn't make sense. Then you ask what happened to Coleridge at that point in the writing. We can tell by reading in his journal why this poem ends where it does and doesn't continue on. But, by and large, if the poem is finished and complete we ought to be hearing just what the poem has to say to us, and by what it has to say I don't mean single line messages.

INTERVIEWERS

Speaking about voice—much of your work seems to be going back to a time *before* language and I assume your aim is to rewrite from there? This movement corresponds to a lot of contemporary criticism, the feminist criticism, the nationalist criticism . . .

ATWOOD

I've given up reading criticism on my work. There's no point. There's too much of it; they are having a good time. Why should I want to interrupt?

INTERVIEWERS

A lot of the critics do look at this going back to the "beginning." Do you see yourself doing this? And if so, why do you see this "rewriting" as necessary?

ATWOOD

All writers work with language. Let me tell you a story. When I was in Wales getting this thing that I got, part of the festivities included a conference of women writers. And there were some of these wonderful British writers including Fay Weldon and Angela Carter and Beryl Bainbridge. It attracted all kinds of women—from women of nineteen who were saying that the women's movement has done all this so we don't want to particularly think about it anymore, we just want to write, to women of seventy who were living long before there was the current movement. And there was a workshop held called "Women and Language," and it attracted two kinds of people. One extreme was radical feminists whose stance was that language had been so corrupted by having been passed through the mouths of men that it was a hopeless affair and nobody ought to be able to write anything, and therefore anybody who had was some kind of gender traitor. The other extreme was the group for whom the word "language" meant "bad language," as in "I won't have that language in my house." And they were there to say that it was all very well for women to write, and they enjoyed reading books by women but why did they have to have so much language in them?

INTERVIEWERS

Where do you fall there?

ATWOOD

Well, I said to the person running this workshop: what happened? I mean what did you do? And she, who was a very optimistic woman, said: "Well, you know, it was very nice. They actually ended up speaking to one another." My point is that if you're a writer you cannot avoid using language in both senses of that word, because that's how people talk. But every writer is also locked in a battle with language because

182

language, when you work in it, as when you work with colour if you're a painter, always seems to be too limited for what you want to do. So the question is: how do you make what you want to make with a medium that you constantly find restrictive? So every writer has a love/hate relationship with the language and I think that women writers may have it a bit more because there aren't words for some of the things they would like to say, or words have taken on certain meanings and they would like them to have other meanings. Or words have been exhausted and you have to re-energize them by putting them in different contexts — contexts that we don't ordinarily put them in. And all of these are things that happen, I believe, with every serious writer. So if you're a genre writer you can go on using stock phrases, as it were, but if you're a serious writer you are constantly wrestling and battling and fighting the language; but in order to get something out of it, not in order to destroy it. The paradigm would be Jacob's encounter with the angel, rather than strangling something to death.

INTERVIEWERS

So you don't think that it is necessary to go back to the beginning?

ATWOOD

Well, the beginning of what?

INTERVIEWERS

That's the problem. How about animal language?

ATWOOD

Animals do have language. They do communicate with one another. They don't necessarily have grammar although they do have memory.

INTERVIEWERS

You seem to give them some grammar too though.

ATWOOD

They do have grammar in that they have memory. They have a past tense and they can remember things. We can't get them to put it into English or French.

INTERVIEWERS

I could show you a couple of passages where you seem to . . .

ATWOOD

But they do recognize people and what kind of animal it is; they remember things, they are not devoid. And it has recently been discovered that some animals can in fact lie. They practise deceptive behaviour in order to gain their own ends and this has been observed among certain birds. I mean animals are not stupid or just mechanisms as some would have it.

INTERVIEWERS

In the poem "Progressive Insanities of a Pioneer" you close with the whale and I've always wondered if you could interpret the whale as "wail."

ATWOOD

Well, it hasn't occurred to me but you could try it out in a critical article and see if it works. I think with any of those double meanings you have to see if they fit the poem.

INTERVIEWERS

I think it does.

ATWOOD

Well, maybe you are right. Who am I to say?

INTERVIEWERS

In Tony Tanner's introduction to *City of Words,* he says that one of the problems for the American writer is to create a freedom that is not a jelly and an order that is not a prison. It seems to me that you are dealing with the same sort of problem.

ATWOOD

Well, you could go right back to Milton's writing on freedom vs. license. Incidentally, we'll just throw this in to set the political stuff in context. I'm chairman of PEN International Canadian Centre, Anglophone, right now. Why did I take over this position? Because PEN wishes to focus on writers in prison. So it isn't just a question of what you write; it is also, to a certain extent, a question of what you do.

INTERVIEWERS

Can you give us some specific information on what PEN is doing?

PEN is regrouping itself. PEN was in Montreal for years and years and it split into francophone and anglophone sections. The anglophone section then quite rightly felt that the head office should be transferred to Toronto because there are more writers in Toronto and more publishers in Toronto. I looked at the membership list and there was nobody west of Toronto. So one thing PEN has to do is make itself a national organization. Another thing PEN has to do is become more actively involved in the writers in prison program, and another thing it has to do is start acting like a branch of PEN International; that is, it has to start going to the congresses in greater numbers, it has to start hosting visiting writers; it has to start functioning the way other PENs function. It is a respectable organization with an honourable past and Canada is now a world-class country whether we like it or not, and we have to start behaving like one. And that means taking on our share of the responsibility and action, as well as publishing abroad—which we are increasingly doing.

INTERVIEWERS

What about Amnesty International? It seems to have a little more success.

ATWOOD

Well, PEN International has had success with individual writers. It was PEN who got out Solzhenitsyn and so on. So they do function. You haven't heard much about PEN here because PEN had a very low profile for a while, but the new active PEN under the auspices of, partially, Greg Gatenby who runs Harbourfront, is going to be more visible. Touch wood. So Amnesty International is very good but they are not just dealing with writers. They are dealing with everybody. PEN has a somewhat more narrow focus, so for that reason they can concentrate more on writers. I'm not advocating either/or here. I don't see why one can't support both.

INTERVIEWERS

Can poems help that stuff as much as the actual physical work?

ATWOOD

Well, let us say that in North America words are cheap. By that I mean nobody is going to put you in jail for writing a poem. They may put you in jail for other things but not for that. So you can write a lot of stuff but it won't necessarily have any discernible immediate effect. I think one of the ways writing functions in North America is that it validates people to themselves. In other words, when Toni Morrison writes about black women, black women can read that and say, "Here is somebody similar to me and therefore I exist." Because this is a very media-conscious society; it's almost as if people think they are not important unless they are on television.

INTERVIEWERS

Do you think that is a good thing or a bad thing? It sounds as if you think it is a bad thing that the validation has to come from an external source.

ATWOOD

Well, yeah, but we're all like that to a certain extent. If your mother says to you, "You're a freak," you may not believe it but if she says it to you at a young enough age, you're going to internalize it and think, "Gee maybe I'm really a creep, maybe I'm not a valuable person." All communication in that sense has some effect. If we all say "boo on Trudeau" in the newspapers then everyone starts thinking "boo on Trudeau" and you elect Mulroney.

INTERVIEWERS

So the external validation is at least a start of things of a more political . . .
cal . . .

ATWOOD

Well, okay, let's get it really clear here. I don't believe that art exists just to do good works. Okay? When writing, the artist has to be allowed to do exactly what the artist wants to do and that may be writing about trees. Good on them. I write about trees. All this talk about political poetry and political writing might give you the impression that I think that people who don't do that are wrong. This is not so. Culture in which one could not write about one's relationship with a cloud but instead one was told one had to write about one's relationship with one's tractor is just as repressive as the other way around. So let's make that point.

INTERVIEWERS

Canadians do both.

Why not? They're both parts of human experience. Artists have trouble with ideologies. All artists have trouble with all ideologies. Feminist artists have trouble with feminist ideology because what ideology wants you to do is say what it wants to say, and maybe you want to say something else. So the artist is an unruly personage and so it should remain. As soon as you tell an artist that what you should be doing is writing about your relationship with the downtrodden masses, the artist will say, "But what I want to do is write about my relationship with a cloud." On the other hand, if you say that only poems about clouds are valid poems, the artist will wish to write about the downtrodden masses. And so it will continue. Let's make that clear. Now what were we saying?

I don't know what we were saying but I think you answered it. So would you say that you are against censorship?

This is another knotty problem. Censorship, yes. What censorship is, is the cutting off of a thing before it has been made public and I am against that with very, very few exceptions; and among the exceptions I would list film material involving children in sex. That is encouraging the use of children in that way and I just . . . Everybody draws arbitrary lines and that's one of mine. But in Russia they have real censorship; you have to submit a book of yours to a censorship board before it even gets released and they say whether or not it can be published and I find that really pernicious.

You, I take it, would be against any sort of censorship against a book by the Marquis de Sade, or any in that tradition?

Well I have to be. It's part of my position that I have to be. I think film material is something else. That involves real people. What this other stuff is is the writer and the page; no other person need be involved in that. I think that then people are free to *say* "boo" on the Marquis de Sade or take that book off the bottom shelf; or get it out of this bookstore; or whatever else they want to say. Other people are free to resist that. There must be debate. But to try to stop it before it's published—that's censorship. People can react to things once they're out there. All of those things. But to cut it off at source—that is so dangerous.

On a different subject: often when you represent movement in your writing you seem to say that a) movement is good, but, b) that it can just lead to running on the spot or running around in circles.

ATWOOD

What do you mean by movement? Do you mean change?

INTERVIEWERS

Yes, both change and movement strictly speaking—as opposed to staying still.

ATWOOD

You mean moving from A to B?

INTERVIEWERS

I'll give you a few examples of what I mean. In *Life Before Man* you have Elizabeth say, "I want to be moved. Move me," and Nate saying to his children, "Run Nancy, run Janet, or time will overtake you, you too will be caught and frozen." So these are precise references to movement. Other times you represent it differently.

ATWOOD

Yeah, well it's very, very hard to take those things away from the characters that they belong to in fiction. It's hard to turn them into a sermon, to take something which is part of a characterization and to say Margaret Atwood says movement is bad. It's not me that is saying that, it is the character in the book.

INTERVIEWERS

Absolutely. But I'm wondering—on the other hand, some of your characters say movement is good and they seem to give it a positive value rather than a negative value . . .

ATWOOD

North America is obsessed with movement. It's obsessed with the idea of change being good in itself, which isn't necessarily so. So when I'm doing North American characters they're obviously going to sometimes be thinking along those terms. "Where am I *going*?" How many people think in those terms? How many people say that to themselves? "Where is my life heading? What is my goal?" Now some cultures don't think in those terms at all.

Could you comment on the relationship between your poetry, prose and visual art?

My poetry, my prose, and my visual art . . . You mean I'm a failed painter! Well I am. I started out when I was ten or so to be a painter rather than a poet and so I turned into something else and the painting has remained pretty secondary. When I retire I'll do painting. What is the relationship? I don't really know.

Do you consider your visual art lyric or fictive?

It's lyric. Definitely. It does not narrate.

Do you do anything besides watercolour?

I draw. But it ain't social realism.

What about the cartoons you do for *This Magazine*, for example?

Yeah, they're fun but it's not great cartoon art. I'm a friend of Terry Mosher, [Aislin] and he's good. I'm just a kind of amateur in the cartoon world. In fact I haven't been doing them in a while. Maybe I should start again.

I know you don't read criticism on your own work but do you follow contemporary trends in criticism? Deconstruction, for example?

Deconstruction is on the way out, according to my sources. Big dressing, on the other hand, is in. Or as somebody said about semiotics, it's better than no otics at all.

INTERVIEWERS

Mimesis is your mesis.

ATWOOD

I'm not a modo, I'm only a quasimodo . . . So, I'm sure it's very interesting. Getting too interested in that kind of thing can be seriously inhibiting to a writer. Or, let me put it another way: I started out in Philosophy and English, not English Literature, when I was in college. I switched because I realized that continuing in philosophy would be too much of a one-armed game. You would develop only one side of your brain to a considerable extent, ending up with symbolic logic, and that can really do things to the other part of your brain which is used for composing poetry. So I think we leave the semiotics to the semioticians and long may they enjoy it. I think that it is an interesting and valid study; I just can't get too concerned about it when I am trying to create a character in a book.

INTERVIEWERS

Are there any other writers you would now add to the Oxford anthology since you made the original selection?

ATWOOD

Yeah, there's a new crop of female poets who have blossomed forth in a couple of anthologies which just came out this fall. I'm thinking of possibly Erin Mouré, Bronwen Wallace, some people like that who had either not published or not published very much when I was making the selection. I got some of those. I got Roo Borson but some of the others had not emerged.

INTERVIEWERS

I don't know whether you got Mary di Michele but she's certainly one of the people.

ATWOOD

Yes I did. I was actually doing the selection in '80, '81 and it's now a few years later. Things move fast.

In your Introduction you talk about the Canadian cautiousness and dislike of hyperbole. Is that a statement more about Canada as a country or is it about the writers of Canada?

ATWOOD

I think it's a statement about style: interpersonal style, rhetorical style. Canadians will say, "That's not bad at all," when Americans will say, "That's stupendous, that's the most wonderful thing I've ever come across." And you notice it when you go to the States. I've just come back from the States and I gave a speech at Wheaton. It was a pretty good speech but it wasn't the Bible or anything like that, and you get: oh, faint with pleasure. And you know it's a way of responding and it's genuine and so forth but from Canadians you get a much more understated thing: "You done well."

INTERVIEWERS

Is there any political or sociological reason for that?

ATWOOD

I think Canada got the Scots and the States got the Irish during waves of immigration. America is also very big on success and very scornful of failure. Canadians accept you know, medium failure. In fact, Canada is a country in which if you're neglected long enough someone is sure to come along and say, "This person has been neglected; let us pay some attention to him/her." So there are plusses with that. Also, big success in the States can absolutely ruin writers. There have been books written on that. Canadians make sure that their successful people don't get feeling too smug. Cut them down, keep them the right size. "We knew you when you were just plain old Bob." "Who do you think you are?" You'll notice that the title of one of Alice Munro's books is *Who Do You Think You Are?* which was changed in the United States to *The Beggar Maid.* Because, "Who do you think you are?" is not so characteristic of the States. Got it? Keep some humility; if you're not going to keep humility then we're going to make sure you do.

INTERVIEWERS

Do you feel that that's changing at all now?

191

ATWOOD

Why should it? It's not terrible. It can have terrible manifestations. But so can the American success thing. I think that it has something to do with the indigenous style of both the poetry and the novels. We don't tend to produce Walt Whitman; we produce something else instead which isn't bad. To each his or her own, as the case may be.

INTERVIEWERS

In the *Room of One's Own* interview you talked about the possibility of doing a women's anthology.

ATWOOD

I think other people are doing that. I don't see any point in doing things if other people are doing them. I did the Oxford book because it would get international sales and attention for Canadian poetry elsewhere. And that happened, but other than that there are people doing women's anthologies.

INTERVIEWERS

Do you think that the women's anthologies are a good thing?

ATWOOD

Poetry has been a male-dominated area in the sense of who runs the magazines and who does the editing, and to redress the balance I think certainly so.

INTERVIEWERS

They're not so much right now though.

ATWOOD

Look around. It's different from the way it used to be but . . . it's partly who takes the trouble, who takes the time. It's not that anybody says you can't do this because you're a girl; it's a question of how ambitious you are and how you want to manifest that ambition.

INTERVIEWERS

Do you have a favourite book or poem?

No, none are my favourites. If I had a favourite I would probably stop writing.

Interview by Barbara Leckie and Peter O'Brien

JACK HODGINS

Jack Hodgins was born on 3 October 1938 in the Comox Valley on Vancouver Island. He grew up on a stump ranch and started writing at an early age: "My first book was a murder mystery which my baby sister typed up for me; my second was a catalogue of everything in the house, which I offered to sell cheaply to a cousin who'd left the district." Since 1976 he has published five books. His first book, a collection of short stories called Spit Delaney's Island *was nominated for the Governor General's Award and won the Eaton's Award as the best book by a British Columbia author. His novel* The Invention of the World *was published in 1977 and has been praised by writers and critics from across the country. In 1979 he won the Governor General's Award for his novel* The Resurrection of Joseph Bourne *and in 1981 he published the novel* The Barclay Family Theatre. *His most recent book,* The Honorary Patron, *appeared in 1987, and is perhaps Hodgins' most realistic novel. In a relatively short time, Jack Hodgins has attracted considerable attention. His uses of history, legend and myth explore both the invention and the un-invention of the world. As J. R. (Tim) Struthers states, Hodgins "revitalizes our imagination through inventiveness and fantasy." He is currently teaching creative writing at the University of Victoria.*

This interview took place on 11 January 1983, in Hodgins' barren office on the University of Ottawa campus, where he was writer-in-residence. He does his writing at home, and apart from two dozen anthologies and a few posters tacked up, there had been little done to personalize the office. The one touch of character in the office is a small wooden "statue" from the West Coast. There is a carved bathtub to which is glued a tiny ship's helm. In the middle of the helm is a colourful picture of what looks like a smiling pirate. At the bottom of the "statue" are the words: "Mayor Frank Ney, Nanaimo, B.C. His worship is the official starter of the annual, world famous 'International Bathtub Race' between Nanaimo and Vancouver, British Columbia."

INTERVIEWER

John Metcalf recently said that, if forced to make generalities, he would say that the strongest genre in Canada would be the short story, and the weakest the novel. As a writer of both short stories and novels, how would you respond to that statement? Do you see a strength or a weakness in these forms?

HODGINS

It's hard for me to separate my feelings about what's going on in Canada with what I'm trying to do myself. Certainly some of the most spectacular successes in Canadian literature have been within the short story form. I don't mean in total careers so much as in individual works. We undoubtedly have more masterful short stories than we have masterful novels. On the other hand, we have more people, it seems to me, attempting to do new things with the novel, or carry the novel in new directions than we have in the short story.

INTERVIEWER

Who are you thinking of?

HODGINS

Robert Kroetsch has done some new and different things with the novel. Rudy Wiebe has done some different things. Someone like Ray Smith in *Lord Nelson Tavern*. And other "experiments" if you want to put it that way — although I'm leery of the word "experiment" when I'm talking about fiction because as far as I'm concerned even the most traditional of novels or short stories is an experiment as far as the author is concerned, because he's trying to find out whether he can make it work or not. There are some interesting attempts being made to carry the novel in new directions.

INTERVIEWER

Do you prefer writing any specific length?

HODGINS

No. If somebody put a gun to my head and said, "You have to write only short stories or only novels," I'd feel crippled, or partially crippled, because I think it's the material itself that must decide whether it should be a short story or a novel. And there are some things I want to write about that just naturally fall into a short story form, and others that demand the novel. Very loosely speaking, the division tends to come

196

in whether my interest is in a single person going through a single significant turning point in his life or whether my interest is in a community. And because an exploration of a community will lead into all kinds of plots and discoveries then the novel form is more comfortable for me.

INTERVIEWER

It seems that sometimes you have one lead into another. Your story "In the Museum of Evil" it seems was transposed . . .

HODGINS

Yes, I've had the experience of a short story refusing to stay within the bounds of the short story. It's *not* that "In the Museum of Evil" became a part of *The Resurrection of Joseph Bourne* so much as a character refused to stay in the story but came back in the novel. Now the reverse has also happened of course, because after I finished *The Resurrection of Joseph Bourne* I felt I had finished with those people, yet discovered that the mayor, Jacob Weins, had stayed in my head and was demanding a chance to be explored again. What happens in that case was that I got the copies of the book hot off the press the same day I flew to Tokyo to do some speaking about Canadian literature, and took some copies with me. While I was in Tokyo I discovered that I was experiencing things as if I were Jacob Weins or as if I were Mabel Weins. They'd come along with me on this trip for some reason or another. Not just in the book but in my head. As I was sitting in a Kabuki theatre watching a play, thinking Mabel Weins would just love this and I'd start to feel excited the way she would, and then I'd suddenly realize that Jacob Weins is probably sitting right beside me, grumbling and snorting, and so I'd suddenly be Jacob Weins and I'd feel just really resentful thinking: "What am I doing watching this stupid thing? Listen to that, that's a *man* down there with that high squeaky voice. I can hardly wait to get outta here. I want to go see a Sumo wrestling match." Well, this was just sort of a private amusement until I got back to Canada and realized that Weins was telling me that he wasn't satisfied with the way he was treated in the novel. I guess I must have felt a little uncomfortable myself to have been so easily convinced. I had made him a figure of gentle satire. I'd given him characteristics I dislike in a lot of mayors and real estate promoters on Vancouver Island who are busy ruining the Island. And I laughed at him at every opportunity I could have throughout the whole novel and it wasn't until the very last section, against my will almost, that I suddenly felt sorry for him and almost liked him. I enjoyed him, but I was laughing *at* him as opposed to *with* him, as I had with the other characters. Then suddenly I realized that he didn't even understand what he was doing himself. How could I condemn him so definitely?

INTERVIEWER
So "The Sumo Revisions" came out of that . . .

HODGINS
. . . feeling that *he* felt I hadn't treated him fairly. It was as if he'd said, "Why don't you take the time to look inside?" The nature of that novel did not encourage me to look too deeply into a person like Jacob Weins. He was out there, he was part of the landscape. I looked inside three or four characters but he was just out there. Well, he got his turn and his turn at first grew to about 150 pages, but then I realized a lot of it was very slow, very self-indulgent. I did a lot of trimming and I brought it down to about 90 or 100 pages.

INTERVIEWER
One of the things that I'm interested in is that there do seem to be characters and places that reappear in several of the books. Well, I guess there are connections in all four of the books.

HODGINS
This was not planned. I won't pretend that I had a vision from the beginning of all the stories I was ever going to write and then it's just a matter of sitting down and writing them one after another. Although I did have a very strong sense from the beginning of a place I was going to write about and a kind of collection of people.

INTERVIEWER
Do you look at them as distinct bits, or as one developing story?

HODGINS
I see them as pieces fitting together to make up some whole that I haven't even grasped yet and maybe never will. First there is the inescapable fact that when you're writing about people who live on an island it is not exaggeration to assume that they will wander in and out of each other's lives, that the main character of this story could be a secondary character in the next story. You're working with a world whose boundaries are very definite. So I feel totally comfortable about the notion of people being in each other's stories, that doesn't bother me

a bit. But I didn't realize that a lot of them were actually related to one another until I got as far as the fourth book, where I discovered that Mabel Weins was one of the Barclay sisters. I knew from way back that Maggie Kyle was a Barclay grandchild, but I was halfway through writing the stories about the Barclays before I remembered that. So, it's not something I've looked for, something I've forced or something I've tried to impose on my work. It seems to me a perfectly natural part of the world I'm writing about, the people I'm writing about. I've even had a request from another Vancouver Island author for permission to have one of my characters wander through *her* next novel, without saying anything, and that too is perfectly logical as far as I'm concerned. Again, we're writing about the same world.

INTERVIEWER

Rosencrantz and Guildenstern are *not* dead?

HODGINS

The thing is, even to talk about it or think about it becomes dangerous because it's not something I think I should be too conscious of, in case I'm tempted to start imposing a pattern. When the character appears and demands to be there *that* is the natural time. Though my short stories, for instance, tend to be a little more close-ended than a lot of contemporary stories, they still leave a lot unsaid. So that I have no doubt that characters have left a story and are wandering around the world and could easily walk into another story. I swear sometimes I meet my own characters. I thought I'd invented them and there they are. It can even be almost frightening, except that it is entertaining. First there are people who claim, *boldly*, that they *are* somebody I wrote about. There's a woman who says, "I know you're not going to admit this, Hodgins, but I am Maggie Kyle, and you know it, don't ya?" And, well, *no*, but *yes*. And there are other disguises. I remember after I had started writing *The Resurrection of Joseph Bourne* going back up to the north end of the Island to see if I was getting some of the flavour of the little towns, checking into a hotel. About three days was about all that I could stay there without people asking questions. I'd go out and listen in on conversations, come back to the motel and write notes, not to copy what I was hearing, but to see if I was getting the flavour of my guesses about why people were there and what kind of people were there. And I discovered, after having already written the first hundred pages that the guys in the beer parlour that I thought I'd invented, were actually in the beer parlour talking about the things I thought they'd be talking about. But I think the part that really shocked me was sitting one day by the window of a motel bar and Jenny Chambers walked past. I had already invented her, with her pink hair, and her plastic raincoat and her sort of dumpy figure, tromping home through the rain. That's about as far as I had got with her. And there she was! Except she'd gone me one better and put a plastic bread bag over her head! For a split second there was that feeling: I didn't know what's real and what's not real. What have I invented and what have I not invented? So that, on one hand, there's a feeling that I wanted to go to the window and yell out, "Jenny!" just to see what would happen, and on the other hand I was scared to death that if she turned around and said, "Jack" what would I do? It wouldn't be inconsistent with some of my other experiences. It's fun, actually. All I take it for is a little signal that I'm telling the truth, I guess, about some things. That I think I'm inventing people and situations, and then I found out later that I didn't invent them at all. They're already there, I've picked them up out of the air. Or just from having lived all of my life in that atmosphere I knew by instinct that they existed.

It seems sometimes that what's going on is not only an invention, but an un-invention. You take bits of legends, bits of myth, bits of stories, and overlap them, string them together, juggle them, sometimes denying them, sometimes accepting them. It's interesting what you do with inventing and un-inventing.

I suppose that's because all of the examples you gave are different forms of storytelling. Basically, my primary instinct, I guess, is to tell an interesting story, and all of these are available for me if I want them. But then, on the other hand, I'm also wanting not just to tell stories that are entertaining, but tell stories that somehow glimpse what maybe you might be tempted to call "truth," and in order to do that some tales and legends must be seen through, and others must be supported. So all I'm doing is using whatever narrative device I can get my hands on that best serves the purpose the work happens to have before it at the time.

Presumably there are several purposes in that. One of them would probably be to entertain an audience. Another one would probably be to entertain *you* as a reader or as a writer. Do they sometimes get in the way, do you sometimes see yourself writing more for yourself than an audience, or more for the audience than yourself, or . . .

I don't think I can distinguish. I think I very early decided that whatever audience I found, what I would have to assume would be that they would be people who like to read the kind of thing that I like to read — whether there's only ten of them, or a hundred of them, or ten thousand of them, that's all I can do. I won't deliberately go out of my way to try and find other readers, because one of the most important guides I have to know whether something is working is whether it makes me feel I would really have enjoyed and appreciated and admired this if somebody else had written it for me to read. I think I've become increasingly aware and appreciative of the power the writer has to control the way people are responding to his characters, what he's putting them through. I think at the beginning I just assumed that if I sat down and told you a story you'd believe every word I told you. I'm becoming increasingly aware of the degrees of belief, the techniques I will have to employ if I want to make sure you believe *this* and make sure you can see through *that*. All of that, of course, makes writing much more difficult, but it makes it that much more exciting as well.

INTERVIEWER

Do you mind mentioning what you're working on now, or would you rather not?

HODGINS

Well, I don't mind mentioning it. I don't want to talk about it very much because in my experience if I talk about things they tend to disappear, or whatever need I have to write it will be lessened because I've already told it to somebody. Briefly — I'm writing a novel which is set in Ottawa, Vancouver Island, and New Orleans. The narrator is a one-legged faller from the Vancouver Island logging camps named Topolski who, in the opening scene, arrives in Ottawa having driven his rebuilt '37 White logging truck across the country in the middle of winter just in time for the Winterlude celebrations on the canal. The main concern of the novel is with the way people fight to preserve what they have and the way people learn, I guess, to find other things that are important. It's a love story. A middle-aged love story being told by this one-legged logger who fancies himself a servant of love.

INTERVIEWER

You've written before of a city being closed down, and then one of those people beginning again. I'm thinking of *The Invention of the World*, how at the end of the novel the town slips into the ocean. You've also used love before as in *The Resurrection of Joseph Bourne*, the Peruvian sailor. Love as a . . .

HODGINS

. . . healer, among other things. But to talk about it would be to anticipate what I haven't even done yet. I'm just exploring my way through it. I've already been surprised several times so I wouldn't presume to demand certain things further down the line. I know I'm having fun with it. I know I'm taking advantage, I hope, of some of the things I've learned about the relationship between the reader and the material and myself.

INTERVIEWER

What about your writing schedule?

HODGINS

I currently have quite a nice setup. In fact, about all you can hope for maybe. As a half-time member of the English Department here I'm free for half of the week at least to do my own writing and I do it at home rather than on campus so that the two lives don't interlap. I teach a fiction-writing workshop two evenings a week, so, relatively speaking, I have quite a bit of time for my writing. It's never enough, but there's no such thing as having enough time to write. But when I'm home, I start after breakfast is finished and work right through the morning and into the early afternoon without interruption. I discovered that if I work through the morning and take a lunch break and then go back to it, the going back to is virtually wasted. So I'll work until I've done what I wanted to do this day or I give up in frustration or whatever, and that might be 1:30 in the afternoon, it might be 4:30 in the afternoon, or it might be, well, it's not likely to be longer. There was a day when it would have been longer. When I was writing *The Invention of the World* I'd start at 8:30 in the morning and sometimes would have to be dragged out of the room in the evening, the sweat pouring off me and my hands shaking because it was just coming so fast, almost as if I was possessed by the material. But I find now that I'm able to stop when I've accomplished a certain thing and be fairly confident that I can come back to it the next day and continue it or rework it or whatever. Something is lost, something is gained. I don't have quite the feeling I used to have that I've got to get this down before it disappears.

INTERVIEWER
Do you write every day? The days that you're teaching included?

HODGINS
Actually, the days when I'm not able to write can be good for me because that gives time for new ideas to come up. What I do is make notes on those days. I'm doing whatever other things I'm doing but I'm never very far from a note pad. I can be reading a student's work, I can be talking to somebody else, and suddenly I would get an insight into what I was struggling with yesterday or will be facing next Wednesday. And so when I start the week's writing I quite often have a set of notes, things I can hardly wait to get at, not just the novel or the vision of the novel or the next part of the story I wanted to tell, but specific things I wanted to say. I may even have sentences and paragraphs scribbled out. It's nice to have something concrete like that to begin with because starting cold is *the* worst part of writing. The sight of blank paper, the feeling that I may never be able to write anything again, just to have a few notes ready to go. That's more or less my pattern. I used to write everything in longhand and not type it up until I'd written the whole story or whatever. And now I discover that I'm writing a paragraph or a page and will type it up right away to see what it looks like and then maybe do some revisions on that before I go on to the next page.

INTERVIEWER
No fancy I.B.M. computer or anything like that?

HODGINS
No fancy computers. I just have a little electric portable which for me is quite an advance because I hate typing, I have never felt comfortable with typewriters. And I despise the sound of electric typewriters humming away. It's like a vacuum cleaner. It makes me want to scream and rip the wall down. So, I was converted to an electric typewriter only when I discovered one that was almost noiseless. The hum is perhaps below my ear's ability to pick it up or something — or above. *But,* if I had a screen where the thing was coming up in front of me as I am doing it. Ah, I tell you, teaching here in Ottawa has opened my eyes to the gimmics and equipment other people have. Almost all of my students bring me manuscripts that are so beautiful, I'm afraid to write on them.

The things I type for *them* to read, instructions or suggestions, every letter has a different darkness, there are all kinds of mistakes. It's the typing of a rank amateur. And theirs come in so beautiful, all typed up on the latest equipment. One student has a machine in his home where he can type up a story at night and the next morning he goes to work at the far end of Ottawa and he pushes a button and the story comes up in the machine there all beautifully typed up. And, to me that is magic.

INTERVIEWER
That's really "magic realism."

HODGINS
That's "magic realism," believe me. And then they will be very apologetic if the manuscript has all the little holes in it along the two sides and they'll say, "I'll take it back to the secretary this afternoon and have her type it up properly." I'm sure there is no other city in the country or on the continent where people have access to so much fancy equipment — makes me think I'm using rock carvings in comparison. The way I write is like writing in the sand with sticks or something. They all work for the government, I suppose. I don't know. I don't ask too many questions about these things. It's a treat, though, because all too often you can find student writers who didn't realize that it's *not* okay to hand in something in handwriting. You have to explain to a lot of people that you're not going to look at it. And I haven't got the time to try to decipher it. And here, oh my goodness!

INTERVIEWER
I would like to ask you a few questions about some of the general "themes." I don't really like that word, but . . .

HODGINS
. . . Neither do I . . .

INTERVIEWER
. . . some of the things that I see you talking about in each of the books. I think there are some connections, some stylistic and thematic connections in some of the books.

HODGINS
With the understanding that you're probably more likely to be aware of them than I am. These things grow, I like to think, naturally as I'm

working. And it's only afterwards that I see some patterns or repetitions or themes. To me the theme of the book is something I'm exploring, not something I set out to teach. These things, sometimes I understand them, sometimes I don't. When I was writing *The Invention of the World*, I had just for my own pleasure sort of mapped out on a big chart on the wall seven different levels at which you could read the novel, and that was quite exciting for me. The old English teacher in me came to the surface. It was almost as if I was looking at it from the point of view of the teacher. One of the weaknesses, the only weakness in the novel that I will admit to is, I suspect, that all of those so-called seven levels will seem separate from one another unless somebody clues into a kind of allegorical element that unites the whole work. If you didn't pick that up, it will seem fragmentary, or it will seem to one person that this is a geographical novel, or to another person that it is a historical novel, or to somebody else . . .

INTERVIEWER

Eveyone seems to latch onto one or possibly two, to the negation of the rest.

HODGINS

That's okay. What it's done, I suppose, is opened the novel up to students and teachers who get some kind of kick out of it . . . in other words, it has found readers for reasons I hadn't anticipated. A professor gets an insight into it and goes to town teaching it from his angle, but then he will read an article which doesn't even touch on what he said and it's a whole new area. But for me that's all part of the fun, I suppose, though it hasn't got much to do with what I'm doing at the time, because meanwhile I'm onto something else.

INTERVIEWER

I would like to talk a little bit about that fun. It seems that some of the really fun parts in the books are the names. I still chuckle when I say the name Fat Annie Fartenburg or the characters, the three brothers Percy, Bysshe, and Shelley.

HODGINS

Well, the name of the character is a *very* important aspect of his character. I don't feel I can write about him, or write about him honestly, until I know what his name is, until I know his name is exactly the right name for him . . . sometimes for reasons I don't understand. For instance,

I picked the name Topolski because I liked the sound. Then I learned later he wore a peg leg, then I learned later that he wore a wooden leg rather than a fancy modern machined plastic leg. He made a lifetime supply of wooden legs out of the tree that fell on him and took his leg in the first place, as a kind of sense of justice. Then I began to discover that he was a man of the woods, he was not only a logger. He had come from the bush, he identified with the trees, and it wasn't until last month when I was having a conversation at a lunch with somebody who *happened* to have a Polish background and I just *happened* to mention that I had given my narrator a Polish name, "And what was it," he said, and I said "Topolski," and he said, "Oh, that's 'poplar' in Polish." I said, "Poplar?" He said, "Yah, the tree." That's the kind of thing that makes me go cold all over. And I realize, of course, and then I saw all the reasons why that *had* to be his name. Not only because it was a tree, but it was the kind of tree that on the West Coast would be out of place. It's the kind of tree that people plant for decoration or cut up for wood. When that kind of thing happens you just realize that's the only name he could have had. Even if I had never learned about the poplar stuff. There are times when the effect is a deliberate attempt to be . . . not satirical, or even comical so much as . . . evocative or maybe even provocative. There are times when I realize my instincts push me towards being Dickensian in my choice of names and I have to pull back. Some people think I don't pull back far enough. There's the odd name that appeals that you can't get away with. Then you turn around and you meet people with these names and even more ridiculous names. I don't know where the line is.

INTERVIEWER

I wanted to ask you who Kanikiluk is? The character in "Spit Delaney's Island?"

HODGINS

He is the god-like creature who transforms people into fish and fish into people, a legendary figure of the West Coast Indians.

INTERVIEWER

Do you mind saying a word or two on where Strabo Becker came from?

HODGINS

Strabo Becker. First the "Becker" was originaly "Belcher" which I changed for reasons I've just talked about. That was too much and I just moved back to "Becker" and it wasn't until the book was already published that somebody drew to my attention he was the one that beckons you onto the island. Well, that's lovely, but I never thought of it. Strabo came from a little bit of research that I was doing. One of my main motifs through the novel was the notion of counterfeit. There's probably not a page in the novel that does not have something counterfeit in it, or a synonym for counterfeit. A second kind of motif that runs through it has to do with maps as counterfeits of landscape. And once I started exploring maps then I started finding out about different kinds of maps and here's a case where my characters know more than I do because I've now forgotten while they remember. Strabo was the name of a map maker, a Greek map maker. And for the life of me I couldn't remember now what kind of map it was but at the time in my reading it I discovered that this was exactly what I needed for this novel.

INTERVIEWER

In *The Invention of the World* you have someone say, "Are there laws that say a map has to conform to reality?" That's another bit of fascination I see. You use places that seem to be just on the edge of maps, Japan, Vancouver Island, Ireland. Places that, as you said, are on the edge of the world or almost tend to be slipping off the edge of the world.

HODGINS

I think that's a state of mind I could hardly have avoided, given where I grew up and the kind of imagination that I have and the way I happen to look at the world anyway. I was very aware, as a child, that the mountains that seemed to grow up out of the backyard were the last things there were between us and Japan. And of course for a small child that was pretty significant because there was barbed wire along the beaches and there were rumours of shooting off the coast and this kind of thing. Every plane that went over the house at night I knew was going to bomb me. I was sure that we were going to be invaded any minute, so the presence of Japan as that other world way across that ocean was very important and that individual mountain was the edge of the world. Beyond it there was all that open space.

INTERVIEWER

. . . that "ragged green edge of the world."

HODGINS

I didn't put it into words at the time but I was very conscious of it. And only the adult could see that the child's way of looking at himself

207

would have been partly conditioned by the fact that there is only one side to his world. All the rest of the country that he was expected to identify with was on one side of him, as opposed to those who grow up in Ontario, for instance, and quite rightly feel themselves to be in the middle of things. The country of Canada is all around them. Or the prairies where the world goes on forever in every direction. That must really make a difference in the way you look at yourself and your position in the world. And without giving into a romantic desire to exaggerate that, I do feel very strongly that that's got to have had an effect on me and the way I feel about things. It's not even the island-ness so much as being on the edge of the continent, although the island-ness increases it because at the time we didn't think in terms of being part of a coastline that ran all the way down to the tip of South America. I was an adult before I made that kind of connection. Well, I was an adult before it meant anything to me. We were on the edge of the continent, the edge of the world, the edge of an island. Just us. Period. So I find something the same in Ireland, something the same in Newfoundland, looking in a different direction.

INTERVIEWER

Yes. Yes. I grew up in Vancouver and what we did as children of course was go to the beach often. And what adults would tell us was, "You know, if you go out into that water, the first thing you'll hit is Japan." You're on the edge of something. As you look out, in a sense, there's nothing, there's just possibilities.

HODGINS

I'm very much aware of that. I don't know whether children growing up on Vancouver Island or in Vancouver have quite as much sense of that now. I suspect they don't, because the coast has been drawn more into the swing of national events. And Japan is a lot closer than it was then. We have Japanese tourists pouring through. Hawaii is of course a place that everyone on the West Coast has to go and visit once a year.

INTERVIEWER

But still, Long Beach and the West Coast Trail for some reason still hold an attraction. Everybody I've ever talked to who has been out west has said, "You've got to go to Long Beach, to the West Coast Trail."

HODGINS

That's why it was no surprise to me to discover that to some of the

Indian cultures of the West Coast, the coastline itself was a place of magic, transformation. Where in legends creatures from the sea came up and turned people into fish and fish came up and turned into people. That mystic line there is very important.

INTERVIEWER
Doesn't Jacob Weins in "The Sumo Revisions" become a fish? He has the dream of diving into the water and holding on to the bottom. There's someone else who has a dream of being washed up onto the shore?

HODGINS
That's Spit Delaney. He's the one that goes out to Long Beach and sees this, gets the sense of the dividing line there. He feels beached, partly because his marriage has just broken up, he feels high and dry. That's all part of it, that wonderful borderline culture of society which I think probably might exist in another way along major rivers. There's an animal kingdom along the edges of rivers. I remember canoeing a very, very quiet shallow river in Saskatchewan for the first time and Saskatchewan was at the time very foreign to me. I'd see the birds that lived and flew from the top of different bushes along the sides, and little muskrats that lived on the edge of the river that would come swimming out and then they'd go zooming back. You knew there were eyes watching you as you went past. To me, there was a little kingdom along the edge of the river. I could see somebody who really felt close to the river capturing some of that.

INTERVIEWER
I think it's most acute for me when I can't see something *beyond* the water. On small lakes I feel I'm still in a bathtub or something. It's only when I can't see the other edge that I really feel the possibilities.

HODGINS
I think this also can be very disconcerting for people who are used to mountains all around them.

INTERVIEWER
I wonder if we could talk a little about Ireland. I'm fascinated by the fact that somebody would go after those myths, those traditions, those legends, as opposed to the Greek legends, which it seems we are all fed with as children. Why you went with the Irish Achilles as opposed to the Greek Achilles?

I suspect it had something to do with family background, that without ever being fed Irish stories, because after all it was five generations back that my family came from Ireland, I did pick up a certain amount of Irishness, references often to the Donnelly story and Lucan which is part of the family background. So that the island of Ireland to me always had a kind of romantic aura. The island-ness of it itself attracted me. Peasant culture for a country kid on Vancouver Island seemed somehow mysteriously attractive. It never even entered my head once to go to Greece or to explore Greek myths. If I had gone to Greece and worked with Greek myths and came home and started working on my novel I would know without a doubt this was manufactured, artificial, an artist at work borrowing foreign myths. I went to Ireland for Ireland. I went to Ireland for landscape and background to the characters I was working with. When I came home and started working with them it seemed the most natural thing in the world. I never felt for a second I was importing something or that I was artificially inventing something for the novel.

INTERVIEWER

It seems that as a country Ireland imports so little. The Romans never made it there, the Protestant Reformation never made it there, the Enlightenment never made it there. It is an incredibly insular country.

HODGINS

That is one of the things that interests me. The other thing was that, just as Ireland didn't import much, it exported *all*. And I, at some level that I never articulated or thought much about, was from the frontier that people came *to* while Ireland was very much the place that people left behind, left behind so desolated and so barren that when I was there I had the feeling that it was like being on another frontier that had yet to be discovered. I lived in a place that people had come to, not necessarily from Ireland, but almost everybody there had come from somewhere, most from Ontario or somewhere east. And when I was in Ireland I was aware that everybody that I met had somebody in the family who had gone. Villages that were empty, villages that were nothing but piles of stone or empty houses with no windows in them. They had gone away, they had gone off to Canada or to America and we were a perfect match as far as I was concerned.

210

Do you still keep in touch with the Cuchulain-Conchubar, Finn
MacCool stories now?

HODGINS

The interest is still there but the need is not as strong. One of the
things that happens when I'm writing is that I get something nailed down
or feel I've got something nailed down that I was afraid would escape.
Having got it nailed down, I don't feel much need to worry about it any
more. It's there. I don't ever read my own work, I don't go back and
read a book once it's published. Fragments perhaps for a reading
sometimes, but I've never sat down and read *The Invention of the World*
from beginning to end since it's been published. But I know that whatever
I discovered about Ireland and the connection between Ireland and
Vancouver Island is in there somewhere. If I need it I've got it.

INTERVIEWER

I'm fascinated by influences, especially for the Canadian writer. You
hear Irish writers, when asked to talk about their influences, well, it's
not impossible for them to give a list of four or five Irish writers. Or if
you ask somebody from the States, they can give you four or five
American writers who were important to them. In Canada, writers would
be very hard-pressed to say, "My main influences have been these five
Canadian writers."

HODGINS

Part of the answer is not just an inability to say that, but a reluctance
because you are almost inevitably talking about contemporaries. I can
say to you, the fact that Robert Kroetsch has written the novels he's
written is important to me, he's bound to have influenced me in some
way, not by his theories but by his presence. But you don't talk about
your contemporaries or your neighbours as influences. I discovered, after
the fact, that I am influenced to a certain extent I guess by individual
works rather than individual writers. And individual works that I admire.

INTERVIEWER

Would you care to name a couple?

HODGINS

I could point to individual Alice Munro short stories, or I could point
to a Bob Kroetsch novel like *Badlands* if I want to stay in Canada. But

I'd have to say a couple of Wright Morris novels have been important to me. In America, some of John Gardner's work, or I could go beyond that and say that one or two of Mario Vargas Llosa's novels out of Peru have been important to me. Strange that there seems to be a feeling in Canada that it's okay to admit to being influenced by British writers or to a certain extent by American writers. Beyond that, there's something suspect. My attachment to South American writers has been exaggerated perhaps because about the same time suddenly people were getting enthusiastic about South American writers. And then that caused some to feel there was something perverse in this, that Canadian writers have no business being influenced by South American writers.

INTERVIEWER
I think everybody mentions Marquez these days.

HODGINS
I'm not influenced by everything Marquez does, but I was undoubtedly influenced by *One Hundred Years of Solitude*. I was undoubtedly influenced by Mario Vargas Llosa's *The Green House*. Those are individual works that excited me, excited me even more when I realized that those people cheerfully claim to have been influenced by Faulkner, who was and is my great hero. So there's not an artificial thing, and yet, you know, recently I went to a poetry reading by a British-born poet. When he was asked if he ever thought of writing in the lesser forms, such as novels, I'm quoting, he said, "Yes, I'd like to write a novel sometime, but I can tell you right now that if I ever did—and I know I'm going to give offense to someone in this audience," he looked straight at me and all twelve heads turned and looked at me, he said, "I can tell you right now it won't be one of these ridiculous South American *things* that Canadian writers are writing." Then he went on to denounce such influences. At first I was very uncomfortable but I was also quite curious. He went on to suggest that the models we should be looking to are the Thomas Hardys and the Jane Austens. And I wanted to scream out that if you had grown up in Canada, perhaps you'd realize that Jane Austen is every bit as foreign as Marquez. And if you had grown up on the West Coast, you'd realize that all literatures were equally foreign. That South American literature is not one bit more foreign to me than British literature or American literature, or, almost, Ontario literature. And that's not something I've had to rationalize, that's perfectly natural. Here we go back to our coastline again. That coastline that goes past Vancouver and past my house goes right down past Fuentes' Mexico and Vargas

Llosa's Peru and Marquez's Colombia, and I don't want to make too much of it but there is that connection which is as tangible as the CPR lines across Canada, as far as literature is concerned. All literatures are foreign literatures and, as I think I've said somewhere else, you're faced with the choice of being influenced by nothing, and writing in a vacuum, by pretending that the West Coast native culture is your own, or by deciding that all literature in the worlds is yours equally, and to be touched—if that's what influence means—to be touched by any work that excites you no matter where it comes from.

INTERVIEWER

It doesn't seem that would *have* to even be rationalized.

HODGINS

I wouldn't think so. For one thing, when I'm writing I'm not the slightest bit conscious of what anybody else has written and I'm certainly not thinking of South American writers or trying to write a South American novel. I am trying to write a thing that is true to the personal vision I have and to the world I've come from, which happens to be a world not too many people have written about. So I have to find new forms to do it.

INTERVIEWER

I wonder if you could talk a little bit about some other influences. I don't just mean literary influences but maybe visual arts or jazz or classical music or whatever. Or are these things unconscious influences?

HODGINS

Having a growing family makes a person more aware of these things. For instance, my appreciation for art has developed recently because one of our teenage sons is headed for a career in art. My appreciation for drama has increased—partly because our other son is seriously involved in acting. And with three young people in the house how could I be more aware than ever before of music?

INTERVIEWER

Do you see those things as being absorbed into your writing or are they more external to the process and the resulting stories?

HODGINS

Probably external, although I've noticed that in the thing I'm working

213

on now, the characters seem to be more aware of music and art than any of my characters have ever been before. Perhaps it is because I'm working with a different environment. The people seem to be singing snatches of songs and of course there's the music that's pouring out of the loud speakers of the canal all the way through this whole section. There's one character, the character that the narrator has come to find, who is singing snatches from *Sweeney Todd* but the next day his daughter, in defiance of something that he's brought up, slaps down a stereo record player recording from *The Rocky Horror Picture Show* where he is singing "I'm a sweet transsexual." And the snatch that the fellow is singing on the canal happens to be about eating people, because it's from *Sweeney Todd*, which is about turning people into meat pies. My children tell me that there is cannibalism in *The Rocky Horror Picture Show*. So all these things are connected and I'm having to uncover the connection myself as I go along. So music in that sense is sneaking in, is helping me along the way.

INTERVIEWER

Do you find yourself using silence in your present writing? The reason I ask is because in the novel *The Resurrection of Joseph Bourne* you do make mention of silence quite a bit.

HODGINS

Do you mean the silence of the landscape around?

INTERVIEWER

Yes. Things slipping into silence. It's just that I see the word "silence" mentioned quite a few times. Well, I think it's natural for any writer to resist silence or to suspend silence.

HODGINS

Since it follows our conversation about music, perhaps the reason I've never settled on one particular kind of music that I like consistently is that I basically prefer silence. I love quiet, although I do more than my share of spoiling the silence. I need a certain amount of it every day.

INTERVIEWER

Is it silence that is filled up with voices in your head? I'm interested in your definition of silence. Can it ever be silent, or is it externally silent but internally vibrant or . . . ?

Yeah. Yeah. Silence is an opportunity to be alone with thoughts or plans.

The rumble inside?

The rumble inside I suppose. No question about that. But also it's freedom from performance. Silence is a rest, a withdrawal, a recharging, gathering forces I suppose or whatever. I think it's very important and of course silence is the opportunity to read, to write. I don't have music going on in my room when I'm writing or reading—well sometimes when I'm reading. This may be something as simple as the fact I don't have very good screening out devices. Maybe because I'm so nosey. I've made a lifestyle out of being nosey. You have to I guess to be a fiction writer, to do the kind of thing you want to do, but I cannot have a conversation with you, for example, while another conversation is going on in the same room. I can't screen out that other conversation. Even if I didn't want to hear it, even if I decided it was boring and it wasn't going to ever be something that would come in handy for me—in other words if the writer in me didn't want to hear it—I would still be as conscious of what was being said there as of what we were saying. Which means that my attention is distracted, which means I'm not fully involved in this conversation.

A fascinating part of *The Resurrection of Joseph Bourne* is this overlapping of voices. It seems that legends or myths, always in the process of becoming, tend to elbow each other out of the way, so that you talk of the legend of Joseph Bourne, but you cut that off and start talking about Fat Annie Fartenburg and her legend, then you cut that off and you're talking about Mr. Manku's swimming, you cut that off and talk about Jenny Flambé. So in a sense there are things that do seem to be clashing, and then you tie them together.

This happens, I guess, because I'm concerned with a community rather than an individual, and each member of that community has his own story. They're all existing at the same time. It takes either a work of art, or a disaster, for the connection to be made that a number of these

215

characters are all longing for the same thing, all looking back on similar things. It also reflects the fact that legends are constantly being re-written, re-seen, re-invented and the very life that's being lived while remembering a legend is itself becoming part of the story. So that Mr. Manku's grandchildren will perhaps sit around and tell about the summer in which he learned to swim—or rather he learned to put his face underwater. That will become part of the family storytelling, subordinate perhaps to sitting around and telling about the time the town fell into the ocean. That's just the *thing* they had in common. That was the thing underlying the insecurities they all had to start with, the people clinging to the most insecure life rafts. But it will be the summer grandpa Manku put his face in the water, the summer that Fat Annie Fartenburg came down, or the summer that . . . the summer that Larry Bowman finally fell in love with a *real* girl.

INTERVIEWER

I think in the same book you have the image of postcards coming into the town and each of the postcards has a little bit of the story.

HODGINS

That's right.

INTERVIEWER

I think that's an interesting notion because there is simultaneously a connection and a disconnection to the story.

HODGINS

I don't remember thinking that at the time, but now that you've brought it to my attention I'm pleased with it. In fact, what else is a new novel or a new short story but another postcard. Here's another little bit of the story, which is where we came in to this conversation.

INTERVIEWER

The other example that I was thinking about is Strabo's Book in *The Invention of the World*. There are voices in there, each with their own legend or bit of legend which seem to clash with each other, negate each other, build up each other, support each other. And at the end of that section you have someone say something like, "You're going to get mixed up if you try to sort this stuff out too much. Just let it be." The work vibrates with its own energy. Things always in the process of invention and un-invention.

Part of that as you say comes from the fact that they're speaking with individual voices and part of it also comes from the fact that they're side-by-side. They're lined up there telling their different stories, so they play off one another, at least in the reader's mind.

INTERVIEWER

I think in another interview you mentioned that *that* section came to you *very* quickly and I thought that was an interesting comment on the writing process, how there is a tumult of voices.

HODGINS

That was the way much of that novel presented itself. The Irish "mock-legend," for lack of a better term, just poured out the way you read it. That was virtually untouched afterwards. I was scared to touch it for one thing. I thought I might wreck it. I just had to sit down each day and call it up, if you will. And the scrapbook in the same way. I said, "Who am I going to interview today" and I'd imagine somebody and then see what they'd say. Part of that spontaneity came from a sense of freedom, that individually they weren't contributing that much to a story line that I was tied to. It was their group effort that made something. So I was free to let them speak whatever they wanted to say and I was willing to listen. And I didn't throw very many voices away. I kept almost everything that I wrote and didn't touch them afterwards.

INTERVIEWER

Another thing that's relating to this question is the idea of obsessions. It seems that your characters are obsessed, but they aren't your average obsessions. I think immediately of the Japanese fellow riding around in that circle in "The Sumo Revisions." There are many other obsessions. The dressing-up mayor in *The Invention of the World*.

HODGINS

I find that the obsession *defines* the character without overwhelming him. It's the constancy that allows me the freedom to explore other subtler aspects of his character without losing the overall picture. And of course from a storyteller's point of view the obsessed character is, not easier to work with necessarily, but more . . . The obsessed character lends himself more naturally to some of the demands of narrative. Part of the nature of the plot, for instance, if you were going out to invent a plot deliberately, would be to give a character a goal, and then invent a way of trying to stop him from getting it. Well, to have a character who is obsessed in a minor or major way is to make that *artificial* thing unnecessary. The obsessed character has an overwhelming goal and you don't have to invent obstacles either because the whole world is a natural obstacle to anybody who is so single-minded about something.

INTERVIEWER

It does seem that some of your characters argue with their own physical existence, they resist certain aspects of it in an attempt, maybe not even to explain things, but just to deal with their own restrictions. And there are a number of restrictions—physical restrictions, I don't want to use the word "philosophical," but perhaps "mind" restrictions. The characters fight a little bit against those things.

HODGINS

Well, it's not even just a little bit. This is an extension of the obsession business. If I find characters who are obsessed interesting to work with, I find most interesting those who are determined not to be restricted by limitations imposed from outside. Those just happen to be the people I'm most interested in following along. If I'm gonna have to spend two or three years with a character, that's somebody who I can admire or be intrigued by.

INTERVIEWER

Religion is talked about in all of the books. Although maybe it's my Catholic Irish upbringing seeing this!

HODGINS

Well, I don't think it matters where you're coming from to relate to this, so much as the very issues that we've talked about already: the business of fighting against material restrictions, the business of being single-minded or obsessed, the business of this mysterious dividing line between the real and the unreal, the business of living on the edge of the world, the edge of nothingness. All of these things are what somebody would call "religious" matters, or "metaphysical" matters, or "spiritual" matters. And there's no question that one of the things I'm exploring, of course, is different notions which . . . Actually, I guess I'm not just exploring them, I'm testing them out and I'm seeing if they work. Putting to work, if you wish, matters of a spiritual nature or religious nature. So the characters themselves are not identified as religious characters. I don't think I've ever created a character who is in any traditional sense tied to a religious viewpoint, but the ones that I end up following most intimately tend to be the ones who, through some instinct, like Maggie Kyle, are relating to matters of a metaphysical nature. Well, I think it ties in with just about everything we've been saying up to this point. It's natural, it seems like a natural part of the landscape on Vancouver Island to have a church that nobody uses as a church, to have a lot of the people who live right around the church being concerned with some of the traditional religious questions, without ever necessarily connecting them with the church. It's not something I lay out ahead of time, it just happens to reflect my own interests, I guess, and those of the people that I'm interested in working with.

INTERVIEWER

Stylistically, just speaking about words and sentences, your most recent two books and your first book, *Spit Delaney's Island*, are fairly conventional. *The Invention of the World*, by contrast, seems to be more pushy, muscular, or fragmented. I guess this goes back to the question of experimentation. It seems that experimentation must be a natural part of the whole process.

HODGINS

If I'm not doing something I've never done before or if I'm not taking huge risks I'm not much interested. What I'm doing, again, is responding to the demands of the material. When I was writing the stories for *Spit Delaney's Island* I was learning how to write stories and I was taking apart stories that I admired and seeing how they ticked, and then I was writing short stories about the kind of people I knew. But when I came to write *The Invention of the World* the issues that I was concerned with, the people I was dealing with, the time element that I was dealing with, all demanded a shape that I had no right to believe that I could pull off or that could be called a novel. And I resisted it. And I tried to think of ways that would be more traditional, and it wouldn't work. It just wouldn't work. Reading Rudy Wiebe's *Blue Mountains of China* I was reminded that there were many different shapes possible for a novel. I read *Lord Nelson Tavern* about that time, and I read a number of other novels where obviously the novelist was not concerned with what other people decided the novels should look like. And I thought, "Okay, it's impossible but I'm gonna do it anyway" and I just let 'er rip. I saw the novel in the shape of this huge "X" I guess where we've got two stories going at the same time, and one of them is about a person who comes

219

from the sky, if you wish, and ends up burying himself in the earth. The other person who begins life playing in the dirt underneath the cabin ends up sailing off into greater possibilities. I saw two stories that were totally opposite, crossing, and I went back and forth between the two. That's not all that radical but it did cause a few eyebrows to be raised. Some people were a little worried that it might be really a story collection. One very friendly reviewer did end up suggesting that the day would probably come when I would wish that I could rewrite the novel because of this very thing. The implication being I hadn't found yet a way of making all these ends come together. Well, okay, that's neither here nor there, but the thing is that the novel that got written was as close as I could come to the demands of the material and the people in the story. But when I came to *The Resurrection of Joseph Bourne* I knew that I had to find almost an opposite direction. That this group of people demanded almost a seamless narrative. Where I had only two major characters before, I suddenly had a whole collection of characters, which meant that I had to learn devices of coherence and unity, transition, that I hadn't needed to learn before, so the most traditional of the works was in fact the most experimental for me, in writing. Then the fourth book was another matter altogether because I thought of it at one and the same time as individual short stories which have their own traditional form, and a novel which was anything but traditional, so it was some kind of combination.

INTERVIEWER

Even the table of contents clues the reader into some of those things. The book has one title, and at the same time numbered chapters.

HODGINS

It wasn't that I was trying to say that the book was this or that, it's just that in my mind it was both at the same time. Any one of those stories can stand alone. But when you put them together in a certain order they were in unity. And that's not invention. And again, having to discover a new form for the material I'm working with now, which is leading me into some dangerous waters. But that's what increases the pleasure for me. The novel I'm working on now is changing form in front of my eyes, as it must, because its location changes and the reader's depth of understanding of what's going on here changes as the novel goes on. So the language will have to reflect that change and I have yet to discover how it will be. I've been surprised often to discover how important rhythm is to me, it wasn't something I went looking for, but

I've discovered that I can't get my hands on something I'm trying to write until I have re-written and re-written the opening passage until I have created a kind of rhythm that carries me forward almost despite myself. So that the book takes on its own life and moves forward. The opening pages of *The Resurrection of Joseph Bourne* must have been re-written fifty, seventy-five times before I began to feel that it had taken on a life of its own and that there was a narrative voice here that wasn't at all mine, however this was, and away it went. I couldn't have written the novel until I found that.

INTERVIEWER

Clark Blaise says that if a story begins one sentence too early or one sentence too late the whole energy is diffused.

HODGINS

That's very important. I don't know how many times I've discovered, later, that is in later drafts, that the first three of four pages must be thrown away. In a sense they were revving up the motor. You bring the reader in when the gears are engaged or whatever, and away you go with your story. But it's hard to throw something away. I threw away seventy-five pages of the new novel last week and that hurt, because I think that was some of the best writing I've ever done but it wasn't serving *this* novel and there it went.

INTERVIEWER

Do you really throw it away or do you save it for something else?

HODGINS

Oh yeah, I put it aside. My experience is that I will discover a few things will need to have been in the story but at a different time. So that I may discover that what I'm looking for down the line I've already done, but it just didn't work before. But it's tough to throw stuff away, especially to throw away stuff near the beginning because that's where you're setting up a relationship with the reader. If you set it up wrong you're in trouble. I was still re-writing the beginning of *The Invention of the World* after it had come from the printers. It was at the galley proof stage and I realized that it was going to take a more patient reader than myself to put up with a lot of what I was expecting to go through to get to the action. So chop chop chop. That was more a matter of paring than just throwing chunks away. So timing is very important, seducing the reader into your story is so important. The more I learn about writing the more I wonder how I ever had the nerve to publish anything I've ever written. Well it's exciting to be that involved but it's also humbling because you realize how little you knew before and how little you still know compared to what you hope you'll learn someday.

Do you read other people's criticism of your work or do you find that important?

HODGINS

I don't go out of my way to find it and as a result I don't see half of it. I hear about some of it from people that report things to me. I have a kind of ambivalent feeling about it. One is an excitement that somebody takes what I've done seriously enough to study it and probe it and try to understand it. On the other hand, I feel my interest is so totally with the next thing I'm doing that to become too interested in what somebody thinks of what I've already done is not only distracting, it's perhaps irrelevant. When I read it, I read it in a sense as I might read one of my children's report cards. It's about the *book*, it's not about *me*. The book is out there, it has its own life and I take real pleasure in the fact it's being paid attention to, that it's doing well or whatever. But it's about that book which is a part of my past . . . I don't want to carry this parallel too far. Perhaps the reason that I don't go out of my way to find it is that, despite the very strong feelings I have that the book has its own life, the book has to go out and earn its own way, and it's not the book I'm writing now and what has it got to do with me anyway. *Part of me is going to feel that the criticism is not about the book but about the book I haven't even written. In fact, I don't know whether this is typical of critics everywhere or just in Canada or just some of the ones I've bumped into, but there does seem to be a tone sometimes that implies these words are not just about the book they're talking about but about the person's entire career which as far as I'm concerned has only just begun. And again, and this is consistent I think with what I write and apparently what I like to write about, I refuse to believe that what I have done up to now defines the limits of what I'm going to do. So I want to use this as an opportunity to say that I am still nosey and curious.

INTERVIEWER

I remember you saying in one interview that you don't want any labels slapped on for another hundred years or so.

222

HODGINS

The notion of labels immediately brings my back up and makes some small part of me want almost deliberately to work against the label. I have to resist that, I think it's an immature reaction, and it's silly and I have to remind myself that these labels have got nothing to do with me, they've got nothing to do with what I'm writing now. It's just somebody attempting to define what I've already done and that's great, that's fine.

INTERVIEWER

I'd like to push this a little farther. Robert Lecker said that you undercut through parody and burlesque the belief expressed by Morag Gunn in *The Diviners* that "The myths are my reality." Do you see yourself resisting that Morag Gunn statement?

HODGINS

I don't think *The Invention of the World* is saying all myths are wrong. I think the implication is you better watch out which myths you latch on to, and that leaves room I think for Morag Gunn's myths. I hesitate even to talk about this because it's beginning to make the book sound didactic.

INTERVIEWER

I like when you say it leaves room.

HODGINS

I think it's got to. No, *The Invention of the World* uses all the devices he mentions, but I think Maggie Kyle's instincts are attached to something else larger than any of them, which could be *labeled* another larger myth, which is not lampooned or undercut or anything. If the real versus the counterfeit is a motif that runs through the novel then the lampooning or whatever it is is a way of trying to sort out which ones should be listened to and which ones should not be listened to. It's not saying that they're all equal. No, I'll stand by what I said, it leaves room for Morag Gunn's myth.

INTERVIEWER

I think of you as putting places on the map, or creating a map. Waterville, Port Annie, places like that which in a sense exist and which in a sense do not exist. Even places like Medicine Hat, Swift Current, aren't on any *literary* map.

HODGINS

We're not used to seeing them in books. The other part of the quotation that I'm not too sure we are addressing had something to do with the establishment?

INTERVIEWER

I think what Hugo was reacting to was the eastern establishment in the States. New York, Boston, all those other places. His comment talks about a potential Western establishment, formed out of loneliness.

HODGINS

There's two thoughts that come to me when I hear that. One is that it seems to me a contradiction in terms for an establishment to come out of the West. The very nature of the West and the nature of Western writers seem to me to contradict the creation of a new establishment. On the other hand, there's no question that, because of matters of space, because of numbers of writers and because of the distance between the West and Toronto, the literary centre of the country, there is perhaps a gnawing need to get together once in a while. Being not only in the West but on the Island where there weren't other writers at the time that I knew of, fed that isolation fairly keenly at first. The first time that I noticed a sense of this camaraderie was when I was invited to a conference in Banff of Western writers of Canada and the United States. It was a very important conference, I think, of Western writers. I was invited as a token coaster. They don't include the coast as part of the West at all. I was from farther west than anybody else at the conference and yet I was *not* a part of the theme of the conference. I was not a Westerner. There were people from the Canadian prairies and then right down through the Midwest, the part that's not the western states. A very very strong sense of comradeship amongst writers from both sides of the border with common interests. People meeting and supporting one another and talking "writing" talk, recognizing one another, catching up on old times. It was difficult to go back actually after that. I sort of had the feeling that all this was going on without me. But of course when the national magazine was invited to cover the conference, the answer is reported to have been, "No, we're not going to bother to send anybody because there's nobody of enough importance there." The list of writers, may I hasten to mention, included Rudy Wiebe and Bob Kroetsch and W. O. Mitchell, and also Wallace Stegner, William Stafford and Manfred Alford.

224

Are you excited by any young writers today?

Yes, there are a number of them in the country who really excite me. And I've bumped into a few in different parts of the country from working a number of summers in a row in Saskatchewan at the summer school in the Qu'appelle Valley. I've met a number of young writers there who seem to me to be creating an energy that will lead to something quite important in the country's literature eventually. And already one of their number has burst onto the national literary scene with a first collection of short stories, a young woman by the name of Edna Alford, who has an original vision and a considerable talent. Guy Vanderhaeghe, another Saskatchewan writer, has written a terrific book of stories.

INTERVIEWER
In your review of Edna Alford in *Books in Canada* you mention that you keep in touch with what's going on in small journals.

HODGINS
Part of this is curiosity, part of it is real interest in good writing, part of it is keeping an eye on what's coming, but a large part of it is also a sense of appreciation of the important part these journals play, especially in the life of a writer who is new, fresh. To be published in a journal that is read mainly by other writers and real lovers of short fiction is an exciting opportunity for a writer who hasn't published much before. The fact that most of them are read by a very limited number of people means, along with that great privilege and pleasure, you also have the opportunity to learn writing and get this exposure without being exposed to a huge audience prematurely. I don't know whether I'm saying what I really mean here. Yeah, out of twenty short stories published in magazines, only ten I felt deserved to be in my first collection of stories. The other ten have disappeared and I hope nobody ever finds them. I keep running into people who find some of them! But that's great, it gives me an opportunity to find out what my work is doing from people who really care without going too far . . .

INTERVIEWER
There's a certain objectification of the work. You see it out there . . .

I can hear that somebody read it, somebody liked it, somebody might even write something about it. On the other hand, if it's good enough to be published, but not good enough to be read by a lot of people, it will disappear without doing all that much damage, whereas if you published it in a book and it was given national coverage, you may want to go around buying up all those books and burning them later. So I think those journals are very important. As a teacher of creative writing, or whatever you are when you are conducting a writing workshop, I'm aware of the number of people who are interested in writing, the number of people who are quite good, who are very good, and who are aware that the chances of getting published are pretty slim right now. The competition for space for short fiction is pretty tough which means that first little bit of positive feedback is longer in coming and is harder to get. Maybe this is just personal experience talking but I happen to think that there is no great tragedy if it takes a long time to get your first stories published, which is certainly my case. And I am grateful that people did not accept the first things I sent out, which includes five novels. And I never would have believed at the time that I would say "thank you" for not publishing these five novels that I spent years and years on. But how awful to have them out there now. What if I had hit on an editor who said, "Let's go with these." I would now be sorry. Anyway, I don't know, but I don't ever make a big deal about early publication with my students. I don't even talk about publication until they pressure me into it. I don't consider that in a workshop that's what they are aiming for. You're aiming to make your stories and your writing as good as you can, or at least better than it is now. Publication comes way down the line somewhere.

INTERVIEWER

I want to talk a little bit more about history. Three words that I associate when I think of you are history, memory, and imagination, and I'm wondering if there's a difference among those three things?

HODGINS

In my background, history and memory are very closely related because the history is what people remember, like my parents' generation remembering their parents' generation living through the depression and the stories about making a farm out of the wilderness, and cutting the trees and picking the rocks, and the story when a forest fire swept down and just about wiped them all out. Things like that are memory and local history.

Can I throw the word imagination in there too?

Imagination is brought to it.

Is that creative imagination?

It feeds it. Let's take my father's parents' experience with building a farm in the middle of this forest and having a forest fire swoop down off the mountains and totally surround them. They're in their house, a family of a mother and father and about a dozen children, including the barn. The history is of that happening. Everybody in the community remembers it happening, some of the people are lost. My grandparents' family survived by getting the whole family involved in beating out sparks on the roof of the house, and having somebody down at the well carrying up gunny sacks of water and all that kind of stuff. Then the wind changed direction in the night, and the next morning all the animals were dead. That's all history. Then it gets transformed somehow when my father's brothers get together at some wedding or funeral or family reunion of some kind and they start feeding each other memories which inevitably lead to feelings they had about their father, this man who made them work like thirty-year-olds when they were ten, picking rocks, and the hard work they had to do, and the educations they didn't get, and all these things. It's that kind of memory I'm thinking of. But there's this little kid sitting in the middle of them and listening to these adults spinning these tales. The image in my mind of the whole family on the roof of the house, in the dark, with flame surrounding them totally, smoke, some members down in the well, some huddling in the well, is something that haunts me, and it's something that has tried to get into story after story. A lot of the rejected novels had a house burning down or a house almost burning down. It's the image, it's something I can't shake and it's not history any more, and it's not memory, it's not my memory, it's not even the memory of the people telling it. It's the image that those people's voices create in my mind that I can't shake. But it's something I don't know what to do with, because I don't understand it

227

yet. The fact that it happened about a mile away from my childhood home might be significant, I don't know, but it happened before I was born. And yet I lived in the remains of a farm where cows were out grazing in the pasture, they weren't out in the beautiful rolling field, they were wandering in and amongst stumps left behind by the early loggers and these stumps would be ten feet high and fifteen feet across and they'd be charred black from the forest fire that had gone through. In fact they had been gutted, so that our play places as children would be *inside* blackened ten foot high stumps of giant trees that had been burned, or at least the remains had been burned, by the passing fire that had almost wiped out my entire family before I even came along to record it. There's got to be a connection. Someday I'll find it.

Interview by Peter O'Brien

Photo by: Ken Mouré

ERIN MOURÉ

Erin Mouré has published four books: Empire, York Street, *which was runner-up for the Governor General's Award in 1980;* The Whiskey Vigil, *a "suite" of poems in 1981;* Wanted Alive *in 1983; and* Domestic Fuel *in 1985. Her books have received considerable critical attention and her poems regularly appear in a wide variety of Canadian magazines and anthologies. She worked on trains for many years and some of her poems deal with this work. In "VIA: Tourism," for example, she talks about women "beaten by their husbands / who bear the marks / as they bore their children, / without disgrace, / who bring their children away with them / across the country in coach seats or / jammed into one berth / drinking pepsi, eating aspirin / Locked in the motion of rails, of constant arrival." There is a desperate optimism in many of the poems—a desire to discover more about the strange functions of the heart. In a recent issue of* Arc *Christopher Levenson noted that Erin Mouré "is constantly taking risks with language and with feeling." Her recent work has become progressively more political, and more concerned with the ways in which language both liberates and limits the imagination: "An excess in the mouths of presidents / who talk of the nation's sanctity, the right to pray / of which there is none / We pray without right, as we must."*

This interview took place over the first few months of 1984. About half the interview was done through letters while Erin was living in Vancouver. Around the end of February she visited Montreal and the other half of the interview was taped. Erin now lives in Montreal. The written and taped portions of the interview have been liberally spliced together.

I wonder if you could provide some biographical information—when you first started writing, how long you've been working on the trains, interests outside of poetry . . .

MOURÉ

I was born on 17 April 1955 in Calgary and grew up in the same house in Altadore where my parents still live. In the late fifties, it was the edge of Calgary, or nearly; now it's almost downtown. A 3-bedroom bungalow, California-style stucco painted green, lilac bushes, Manitoba maples in the back.

I first started writing when I was 7 or 8; I always knew I was going to. My mother taught me how to read when I was 4; the first words I ever read, really read, myself were "Go go go. Go Sally go. Go go go." It took about 4 pages to unfold!

I've worked on passenger trains for 9 years. I'm interested in anything I can learn about. Sumps & drainage. Coffee. My neighbours. Everybody's opinions. Co-op housing.

INTERVIEWER

You've been involved in both ends of the writers' workshop—as a student of the Banff Centre School of Fine Arts and this summer you'll be teaching at the Upper Canada Writers' Workshop. Do you think any of that stuff does any good?

MOURÉ

Well, I get to visit my friends! As for the students, the only things you can *really* teach them are measurable things such as how to type: you can't teach them how to write a poem. And then you can teach people about convention, about philosophy, about what Descartes said, for example, what he wrote down—that's measurable too. Although poetry is a thing you'd like to be able to teach, it doesn't fit into any one of those categories. You can't teach it. People have to take it for themselves, and do it. Meeting other people who write is probably the best advantage of the workshop. At the initial stages of writing it can be good to know that others are thinking about what you've been thinking about. That kind of support is really important. And even if the people who take workshops never end up writing anything, they are part of the audience for poetry. The audience for poetry is part of what makes poetry go on. I don't write my poems to be a decoration—they don't match anybody's sofa; the poems are there because there's an audience on the

other side. Workshops are a good idea. I never discourage anybody who
has energy.

INTERVIEWER
Can you talk about what goes on in the Vancouver Industrial Writers'
Union, with which you've been involved?

MOURÉ
The Vancouver Industrial Writers' Union was formed in 1979 as a
support group for writing about work and the workplace. If people are
more sensitive to the work they do and how they do things, it humanizes
work *and* poetry. The Vancouver Industrial Writers' Union has organized
a reading series called "Work to Write," one of the most successful reading
series in Vancouver! We went down to San Francisco to read with the
San Francisco Waterfront Writers and we had members of that group
(defunct now) up to Vancouver. Part of our thing was not only to
promote the writers but also to bring that kind of writing to the
community, because most reading series are run at universities. Most
reading series don't reach out to the community. They have a more
narrow focus, I think, anyway. They bring a lot of interesting writers
to town of course. Our focus was to bring writers who have written
about the workplace, people who write about their ordinary lives, and
introduce them to a community that they wouldn't normally get to read
to. It's a way to increase the audience for poetry overall.

INTERVIEWER
Do you consider your poems as either biographical or antibiographical
or somewhere in the middle of those two?

MOURÉ
I don't consider them to be biographical although probably a large
part of the event comes from something that happened to me, or someone
told me a story about something that happened to them. I always consider
my poems to be public events, even if they originally had something to
do with me. When I write about them they become public events.

INTERVIEWER
Is it a private event that spawns a public event?

MOURÉ
And sometimes the reverse! I think that somehow in the middle of

233

whatever I'm doing, or if I'm remembering, all of a sudden it doesn't seem like my life I'm writing about. And it isn't, really. I absorb a lot of influences while I'm writing. The process has more dimensions than the page. I feel almost transparent when I'm writing well. I like that. The "I"s in the poem aren't the "I" that's talking to you now, you know.

INTERVIEWER

Who do you think of as influences on your poetry?

MOURÉ

"What," "where," "why" influence my poetry too! The women I know and don't know, dogs, my brothers, even big Jim Sheppard once, a sleeping car porter who told me about rye & pickerel. But I suppose you mean writers. Rilke. Because he said: "Ever newly begin the praise you cannot accomplish." I follow that! I believe that poetry is, above all, praise. And that line of Rilke says to take risks. Begin newly!

Vallejo, Seferis, Ritsos, Stein, Merton, Böll, James Wright, Audrey Thomas, Gail Scott, Newlove, Ondaatje, Lane, Camus, Marlatt, St. John of the Cross, Pogo, Kafka, and the poets I feel are currently writing in a world I share—Thesen, Don McKay, di Michele, Wallace . . . The beat goes on!

INTERVIEWER

Pablo Neruda seems present in some of the lines.

MOURÉ

That Pablo Neruda! He's supposed to be dead! If he's present in some of my lines, then I'm honoured he's visiting me.

INTERVIEWER

What about early influences?

MOURÉ

Rocky Mountains, southern Alberta accents, aspen parkland, the Budd Car Company's train cars. And together with those poets just mentioned should be Atwood, Purdy, whom I read when I was in high school. I bought *The Circle Game* for $1.95 in a Coles bookstore when I was in Grade 10, in 1970.

But I don't write like these people. They influenced my being and my relationship to the language, shook my young self up, woke me up . . . I was a kid once, you know!

234

INTERVIEWER

How do you see the newest batch of Canadian poets—Roo Borson, Christopher Dewdney, Mary di Michele, Pier Giorgio Di Cicco . . . ? Are there poets you are particularly interested in? Do you see yourself as part of this new wave?

MOURÉ

New wave? What about McKay, Scheier, Brand, Claire Harris, Lorna Crozier! The new work I see excites me more and more. *Alter Sublime* is my favourite Dewdney. His work intrigues me. I think that where it's coming from is totally wrong, and where he gets to is totally amazing!

Me? I just work and don't worry what wave I'm in.

INTERVIEWER

There is much mention of the past and the present in your work, but not much talk of the future. Could you talk about the reasons for this?

MOURÉ

We are making a future! What do I know about the future? It's just the present falling forward. And the present is given form by what we remember, don't you think? If I don't remember the noise "chair," "desk," "future," and you don't, can we have an interview?

INTERVIEWER

The memory which does exist in your work is often a disturbing kind of memory.

MOURÉ

That's true in more than one sense: sometimes the remembering itself is as disturbing as what is remembered. Memory never gives you what happened. What we remember didn't happen at all! We are always at the centre of our memories, and are we always at the centre of events? What event? Every event is a plural multiplied by the number of people present, multiplied again by the lapse in time and the number of times each person remembers. When we remember, the event is altered by our remembering. Who knows what really happened? Nothing happened. What anybody remembers is what happened. It's good enough for me. It's all I have!

Memories affect the present. I start to write a poem about how I can't describe my own feelings to my lover, and to give an example of how

235

I feel, I start to talk about fish and fishing and pulling the hooks out of their mouths. Pretty soon the example takes over and starts writing the poem! I'm dismayed, it's pushing all sorts of stuff about fish into the poem, I don't want to write about fish, and in the end an event emerges that is not straightforward, and it's immaterial that there's nothing about feelings or communication, because curiously the poem is still about that! It's what you *feel* at the end—how *hard* it is to feel and communicate personal/public/animate pain. The poem is about fish too! From the sound of words that mean "fish" we find out about the difficulty and inexpressible nature of pain. And how pain is not an end.

INTERVIEWER

You take on the personae of many people in your poems, for example in "Divergences." Are your poems the search for a collective memory?

MOURÉ

The personae acknowledge "community" rather than collective memory, I think. We have to begin to realize how our acts affect community; that we have collective responsibilities, that we're descended from the people we disagree with as well as the ones we agree with. That's "Divergences." It's an acknowledgement. A community *has* collective memory; I don't search for it but try carefully to uncover what is there.

INTERVIEWER

What about the differences between male and female sensibilities? It seems that many of your poems are written for women.

MOURÉ

My "community" is largely composed of women; I talk to them, write to and for them, share a sisterhood and a hope for change with them. But I write *for* an audience of human beings; even when a poem is ostensibly addressed to a woman, the address more or less acknowledges my debt. The fact that I publish it means that it is for everyone or anyone.

Regarding male and female sensibilities—I think male writers are at a disadvantage right now because they can take for granted a language that is already invented for *them*; it already *belongs* to them. The written history and literature of human beings has referred to "he" and "him"! Women writing feel the unease and strangeness in our language more readily because they are out of it. And in the last while, women are beginning to write a new language, their own language, using the common word-

236

signs of the old; women have to discover new correlatives of desire, or ways of expressing them. Thus you see people like Audrey Thomas, Gail Scott, Daphne Matlatt, Sharon Thesen breaking down the railway line of the phrase and paragraph, and Wallace and di Michele building it up again, trusting the words for the first time, and I find this very exciting. The clutter of the world has to be described all over again. There are men open to this too, to some extent, I suppose; Ondaatje and McKay for example, but mostly there's women.

INTERVIEWER

What do you mean by "women are beginning to write a new language, their own language, using the common word-signs of the old?"

MOURÉ

Using the words of the old but in a new way, but actually words too are just signs for something. Women are writing interesting things now, still writing in "English," but somehow the language is more exciting and they use words in different ways.

INTERVIEWER

Can you be more specific?

MOURÉ

Well, no. Have you ever read any of Daphne Marlatt's work? It's quite dense, and she takes words off in a direction of her own. Even Sharon Thesen. The words seem new. I think women come to words in a different way, because it's hard to make words say what we want to say. Because the way words are used is another convention, a convention that's come down to us, has been taught to us by *men*, because men had access to publishing systems. Well, men originally had access to education and women didn't. Things are beginning to change late in this century.

INTERVIEWER

Let me ask a harder question then. Would this exploration and appropriation of language be different than the kind of thing that Christopher Dewdney is doing?

MOURÉ

Yes. Yes, it is, definitely. That's why I don't agree with where he's coming from at all, though I like where he gets to.

237

INTERVIEWER

Where is he coming from?

MOURÉ

Where he comes from, to me, is this whole study that says, "We are men, we know what these rocks mean and what this brain is." But his work seems to pull past that kind of control and mastery, that sense that we can name everything and figure it all out. His language ends up being kind of technocratic in one sense, but the words pull away from that, and make something else. The exciting thing about Dewdney's work is when he enables you to see amazing things about the earth and human thought and words, that actually they are not controlled by human beings, there's something else, a kind of neural patterning that's in some senses "culturally" induced, from an early age. And that's what really excites me about reading his work. Of course he may read something entirely different in it.

INTERVIEWER

Let me ask you one more pushy question then. Are all male writers unavoidably locked into that male-dominated reverberation of history?

MOURÉ

I don't think you can say *all* "X"s or "Y"s do anything. *All* poets run the *risk*, even women can be affected by that, even women can write like that, and not think about the language. Given that, the answer to your question is probably *yes*. It's harder for a woman *not* to think about the language and that words and systems belong to someone else. Take for example Hemingway . . .

INTERVIEWER

That's a pretty extreme example . . .

MOURÉ

It's easier to explain an extreme example! Beautiful English sentences, but a totally obnoxious writer. And not just the way his characters treat women, but it's just the "he"ness of it all. There's all this "he" "he" "he" talk, and then bit parts for "women," who are not women as women see them, at all. Men can read and fall for that because there are male characters at the centre of that world. When women read that, there's a friction. Women can never read that and suspend their disbelief enough to put their world view into the story. I see the change that's occurring

238

as a gradual process. Right now I can hardly believe there was a time when I wrote poems that were biographical, where the protagonist would be a "he"! All of a sudden I woke up to the fact that these poems were written by this convention, and they weren't written by me at all! Women know what language means, but it doesn't refer to them. Knowing that makes you more careful with words, not just with the pronouns, but with approaches to syntax. You start to realize a lot of syntax is just convention. You don't just throw it out the window if it doesn't say what you want to say, if it's not saying how you feel—the whole convention of syntax has been built up by people who have had access historically and currently to printing and publishing systems—often the way I feel, well, English syntax does not work to express it, so you have to push the syntax forward until you can say what you want to say. You begin to realize that the words too are confined by the syntax, that the words don't mean to be there either. You're in this ecstatic state when you start to realize this.

Actually, the way language is worked out, the way syntax is worked out, doesn't speak to men any more either, it's just that it's easier for them, it's a hole that it's easy for them to fall into, because they have wordly "power" there. I think visible language is going to change because more women are published now by women. Everything people read influences them, I think. Even books people don't read influence them! The opening is going to be there for women and ultimately everyone not to be represented by these "he"s. I think this is a really exciting time to be writing, just because of all that. And then there's me—I'm pretty conventional as far as everything I've been talking about goes, but those are the kinds of things that really excite me. And it's good that women are getting together, for example at the Women and Words Conference last summer, and talking about language. Women and Words was incredible because all of a sudden there was a group of women who got together and said, "Well this is what I feel," and all of a sudden everybody realized they had all been feeling the same thing, and it just knocked everybody over! French and English, too.

INTERVIEWER

I guess the only thing I worry about is the idea of a secret society. I think that the secret society of female writers is as dangerous as the secret society of male writers. Granted, of course, the societies are pretty big.

MOURÉ

Well a secret society is a good name to give something you just decline

239

to know anything about. I can understand women being tired of centuries of male voices but I don't believe in dividing things into camps. That's not the answer. Yet there has to be a real polarization in order to get any kind of change, otherwise nothing will ever happen. I see things as a big process, and it's important that the polarization occurs because then something is going to move forward. Out of this something else is going to come, and it's going to come because language is this powerful, pure, beautiful thing. The words are so powerful they are going to win.

INTERVIEWER

Could you talk about the line "The angels of the apocalypse are housewives / after all, well-printed, dusting chairs" from the last poem in *Wanted Alive*?

MOURÉ

Well, the poem echoes many of Stanley Spencer's paintings (and the poem's dedication acknowledges my debt); he painted many pictures of ordinary men and women; one in particular I allude to here is called "Angels of the Apocalypse," and curiously the angels are women dressed in printed skirts like you imagine housewives (he has painted other "Domestic Scenes" which I'd confused in my mind when I was writing the poem—one called "Dusting Shelves"). Of the painting, Spencer wrote that he "did not like the idea of angels of the apocalypse as bringers of retribution, but wanted some measure of mercy." He hopes their vials were less poisonous than plagues. And so the lines you quote agree with him, and their gesture, instead of retributive, becomes that of dusting chairs. The apocalypse becomes an ordinary act that most of us have overlooked; it has been happening all this time; because we are waiting for some great event, we don't see it. It is the mercy and spirit of very few seemingly ordinary people that protect the world, I think. Thomas Merton wrote that too. The little people, who do not know themselves, keep the world from being annihilated.

INTERVIEWER

Is the poet different from these "little people"?

MOURÉ

I think the poet is just a focal point for these little people, their feelings, thoughts, or whatever. The big people are not people, they're IBM, Canadian Pacific, ITT, United Fruit—those are the big people. I think international corporatism is one of the most dehumanizing things

240

happening to us right now. Corporations have become nations in themselves. And most of them are American-based, so that's what gives America such a pervasive influence, that they feel they have to defend. The little people are the people Thomas Merton is talking about too. Even Albert Camus had this same kind of idea, that if only one person stands up and says "No," the state is threatened. Merton said that maybe our hope is in the hands of only two people that are saying "No" and are consciously opposing this kind of dehumanization. They're the ones who are keeping the world from being annihilated. It's not the big people at all. Humanity doesn't rest with them, it rests with the little people. Obviously not everyone's a poet, yet I feel sometimes, somewhat, like I'm writing other people's poems, as if fulfilling a responsibility towards them. Artists are focal points for ordinary people. That's why they're important in places like B.C. and El Salvador. In El Salvador they shoot them; in B.C. they close the educational institutions, like David Thompson University Centre, that provide a focus.

INTERVIEWER

In your *Books in Canada* interview of a couple of years ago, you stated that "for me the poem approaches a truer state because it can account for movement in time, for numerous angles." What do you mean by "movement in time"?

MOURÉ

When I said that I think I was referring to photographs and the way they stop time and give you, not the truth, but one "angle." The way things occur, linear time is not the only kind of time, and so the poem can put things into truer kinds of time. Linear time is not real time, it's what people agree they'll run their watches on, so that when people say "I'll meet you at 3:00 P.M. on Sunday" everyone won't arrive at a different time on a different day. It enables us to conduct our lives from day to day, but to me it isn't a real kind of time.

INTERVIEWER

If it isn't linear time, what sort of time is it? Is there any distinction in your mind between past, present, and future? Einstein said that the distinction between past, present, and future is only a stubbornly persistent illusion.

MOURÉ

It is. I agree with that; there isn't really a distinction. The things you remember influence the present. The kinds of thoughts I have about the way this interview is going to go, or what we might talk about next, might be influencing what I'm saying right now. The fact that I first met you at a certain place might influence what I say. Whenever I see you I think about eating spaghetti on the floor at Ken's house in Banff. Things like that affect, if not actively, then passively, what I'm saying. The same process happens when you talk to anybody, or when you write a poem about what's happening. You're always talking about what might happen. Time is mixed up. Things in my poems that occur in vastly different times and different places end up in the same poem. Some people find this surprising. But I always see that there is a total unity to it. There are different kinds of logic about time and space; our generally accepted time and generally accepted conditions about space are only called logical because we all agree on them. But really, it's only convention that, for example, you have a map and there's an edge of a country and here's the country and here's the water. That's only a convention; you could make a map in a different way, perhaps extending the edge of the map to account for certain depths or reefs, and having *that* as your convention. But people get so used to conventions that they think they're *facts*, and they're *not* facts.

INTERVIEWER

Do you think it's important for you to either alter those conventions or to redefine commonly accepted definitions.

MOURÉ

I think it's important to remember that they're just conventions. When people start accepting conventions as facts, we start to lose some of our humanity. Conventions are just shared beliefs or prejudices. An extreme example of that would be in a country where all of a sudden the society systematically oppressed one group, such as Germany did Jews in the 1930s and '40s. All of a sudden a whole society started to accept a prejudice as *fact*, started to act as though this prejudice was a fact, and ended up with something deplorable. This way of thinking—taking conventions as facts—is embedded in the way we speak. We dehumanize ourselves. That's one of the things that allows Ronald Reagan to call Central America "the backyard of America." I thought I was going to have to stop writing in English after hearing that.

INTERVIEWER

Where does that Reagan comment come from, what was its context?

MOURÉ

He was talking about not allowing the "Communists" in Central America, because it is the backyard of America. To me this is very warped thinking. The American government has supported puppet governments in that region for years and years because they want to support their own corporate activities down there. Their corporate activities oppress most of the people. Over the years, in order to keep oppressing the people properly, they've had to build up a huge class of armed forces and security police and government people. Those people actually exist as a class now, whereas before there were just the huge landowners and the corporations. Now there is this whole class of people to oppress everybody. If the people get together and say, "This is bullshit," and get rid of them and have a government, then because they've offended American corporate interests, more than anything else, the Americans won't trade with them. Like Cuba or Nicaragua or Grenada. If you have to defend yourself or buy food or whatever, and the Americans won't sell you arms, then you have to buy them from the Russians, and then of course you're called "Communist." Ludicrous things begin to happen, including real invasions. You end up with a country the size of a suburb and thousands of Marines land there to take it over because it's the "backyard of America." This arrogant assumption, that these little countries are vital to the security interests of the United States, changes the meaning of the words "security," "vital," "interests," and changes the meaning of the word "backyard" for sure!

INTERVIEWER

Well presumably if Central America is the backyard of America, then Canada is the front yard!

MOURÉ

If we decided to do something drastic about American corporate interests in Canada, they'd be here too. But forget it. Too many people here benefit from American corporate interests, and the rest believe they benefit.

When you think of reality, for example the bananas in your kitchen, well you think of that as being normal, when in fact it's an incredible thing to have a banana up here. Actually it's very frightening. What is this banana doing here, how did this banana get here? It's actually quite frightening, and not ordinary at all that there should be a banana here.

It looks quite nonchalant sitting there on the table.

Bananas are something you grow up with and eat all the time. You think maybe there must be little people who live under these green plants and cut them down and mail them to Steinberg's . . .

. . . and we take the real history for granted.

I'm more interested in the history of the *people* who used to grow food to eat and who are now growing bananas, and they can't just eat bananas; and the bananas are to go somewhere else. Or people whose land has been taken over to grow coffee. The things the corporate interests are growing are things that people can't eat, or can't *live* off of. People used to be able to live and eat, and now all that has been disrupted. Gastro-nomical genocide. "Get rid of those lousy beans and grow some bananas."

I read recently that the second most important international commodity after petroleum is coffee, which is quite a remarkable statistic. Well, Erin, would you like another cup of coffee?

This is *tea*! Another story!

Where do your poems come from? The surfaces are concerned with everyday things—trains, drinking, family rituals—but there is an underground terrain as well, what you call in one poem the "subliminal code."

Yes! The surfaces actually are altered by the terrain underneath. I borrow or steal those surfaces as if they were mine, *because* they form clues to the subliminal code, the thing, the powerful force that is *under* the surface and *of* it. It's the real force of language in us. Content, for me, turns out to have as much to do with language as does form. The content exposes language. Raw words. Our bodies recognize it but our minds do not, because they are trained in a kind of acceptable logic that is collective and "normal." So I try to write from the body and not out of my mind or brain. Often I flop and hit upon the merely sentimental, but I have to keep trying to write this way. I know the words have a life of their own and try to share themselves with our universe. They have been in our bodies all along and we are just preparing ourselves to be ready to hear them.

My conscious poetic effort, then, is to be prepared to speak the code my body says, others' bodies say, the body says to the world's clutter of objects, and vice versa. I do exercises every day, and ride my bicycle because physical condition plays a part in this. What I write comes out of the ends of my arms, my hands. I can't write with my head, I'll get a concussion. Silliness aside, I believe the words can cause me actual physical pain and damage if the code is blocked; if I don't read what the words are actually saying in my body, I'll get sick.

INTERVIEWER

One of your reviewers called you a storyteller. Do you think of yourself as a storyteller? Is poetry different from storytelling; is it the same thing?

MOURÉ

I don't mind it when people call me a storyteller, because, well, I don't see myself as telling stories, but if people think of me as a storyteller . . . people *listen* to stories. A lot of my work has to do with narrative, those "surfaces" we were talking about before. Those who see my poems as stories recognize the events/surfaces in my poems and accept the poem in a linear kind of way; obviously that's not the only way to read them. But it's okay with me. If that's how they listen, then that's valid. It's nice that they listen. But I think my poems are narrative in the sense of co-relation, correspondence, rather than "story." The surfaces go very deep.

INTERVIEWER

In a recent issue of *Quarry* you say that writing is always about writing, about what it is possible to recognize and say. That would seem to me to be an anti-storytelling statement.

MOURÉ

Only in a linear sense, it is! I was reacting to the questions that *Quarry* asked, so my response was "re-action" rather than "action." They asked: "Why does so much contemporary creative writing self-reflexively mirror the creative process itself? Why do so many poems and stories today self-referentially make the language and form of poetry and fiction their subject of and object for discourse?"

In the first place, the answer is kind of obvious; the way language works/can work determines how we organize and explain our perceptions; it even to a large extent determines WHAT we see; in turn, this affects our actions. In my answer I was trying to say that even poetry that isn't visibly about poetry is still about poetry. It has to be. I think writing doesn't reflect creative process, it is creative process. Which doesn't mean you don't have to think about language all the time! I guess I have a different way of describing the relationship. That's why I said: "To talk of reflecting creative process is to erect a barrier between the work and its process, which are not divisible. It is to erect barriers between the work of art and our ordinary lives, which is to maintain cultural elitism." I think the work still *is* its process. I don't like *work* as a noun! I thought that the language of the questions was just as bad as the language of commodities that we've just been talking about—that dehumanizing language. Dividing things in order to explain them away. Well they're not going to go away. My answer was entirely defensive!

INTERVIEWER

Many of your poems end in what seems mid-thought. The reader is left with the reverberations of words and ideas. How do poems end? Or, *do* they end?

MOURÉ

Thank you! The poet pushes it off the page and into the reader. Real thoughts do reverberate. To add an "end" is a figment of the head. (Not the imagination.)

INTERVIEWER

Do you see writing poems and working on a train as similar occupations?

MOURÉ

No. I could quit the railway!

On the train, I have a meaning and duties that are very clear. It's wonderful because it's so simple. Serve the passenger! How many people are blessed like this! It takes a great deal of weight off my mind. It does exhaust me to the point of actual mental aberration—my inner clock goes off kilter, and very bizarre but observable things happen to me. It's a change!

INTERVIEWER

INTERVIEWER

There are poets who work more with the unconscious than the conscious, but you seem to work more with the latter. Do you think that's an accurate observation?

MOURÉ

The conscious and the unconscious? I don't think that I make a distinction. I don't think that I know what the difference is!

INTERVIEWER

How important is rhythm, the number of beats in a line? Are you more concerned with individual words than with the overall structure?

MOURÉ

Rhythm, which is the cadence of a voice, the recurrence of sounds, interdependence of parts in a whole, is very important! The number of beats in a line is metre, which I rarely think about. Rhythm has to do, I think, with breath and not with the number of beats. I'm concerned both with words and structure. But I don't want to force the structure into a grouping of words/lines that are finally arbitrary to the text itself. I learn about structure from the words themselves, I think.

I know the lines and rhythm are starting points because when asthma constricts me I can't write. My asthma returned to me a year ago after a fifteen-year remission. I'm still not used to it; at times I feel disabled poetically. The heart, by way of the breath, to the line (Olson)!

INTERVIEWER

A line which I think represents much of your work is "The short & bumpy sentences of the heart" from the poem "Sentences." Do you see that phrase as particularly important for someone wanting to understand your work?

MOURÉ

No. Maybe it forms a kind of inter-text by which you can read/hear the rest of my work and that's fun to do, it's legit, but probably, if I can say so, many other lines would do as well.

In other words, I neither forbid nor encourage you!

INTERVIEWER

Are there any individual lines in your poetry which seem to surface
again and again?

MOURÉ

No, I can't think of any.

INTERVIEWER

Do you have any favourite poems—of yours, that is.

MOURÉ

Like everybody else, my favourite poem is the one I'm working on
now. Another fish poem!

INTERVIEWER

There is optimism in your work, but it is desperate or frantic optimism.
Your poems are filled with talk of ambiguity—of work, words,
relationships, feelings. Is ambiguity the lesson of contemporary poetry?

MOURÉ

Ambiguity? There are no lessons. I'm interested more in what
something means, and why not, and why syntax is not working any
more in our world. When somebody can say "the backyard of America"
it becomes very hard to speak meaningfully at all. This is what I am saying.

INTERVIEWER

Many of your poems are political: "Post-Modern Literature,"
"Sanctus," "Certain Words, A Garden." What role does politics have for
poetry? What role does poetry have for politics?

MOURÉ

Poetry is on the side of life, the side of the Earth, out of the mother,
out of the deep Nature of beings. This rejects the world's overt, covert,
and invert political power and linguistic structure because the two are
opposed.

Politics has everything to do with poetry because it has distinctly
nothing to do with parties and legislatures and congresses and
constitutions and distinctly everything to do with the human body. Real
politics has to do with desire because being in a body has to do with
desire. Sexual, too, but not the way men have been writing about sex
for years. Desire is not about ejaculation. Which is why I was happy to

read Don McKay's book *Birding*. Finally, something different by a man! Reagan will not be able to use those poems for any of his purposes!

INTERVIEWER

Wanted Alive, as you were just saying, is about the body and desire. But it begins with an ending and a resigned question. What keeps the poems going?

MOURÉ

I'm on the side of life, that's all. Life is good. The earth is good. Trees and birds are good. Prayer, real prayer, exists.

INTERVIEWER

Is there a reason why there are four parts to both *Empire, York Street* and *Wanted Alive*?

MOURÉ

Maybe there are 5 parts and 1 is missing. But really, the poems asked for 4 parts. When 70-odd poems ask you for 4 parts and you are on the side of life, can you say "No"? I try to have respect for the poems once they are written. If they want to build 4 houses and live together, how can I stop them?

There are 4 directions, aren't there?

INTERVIEWER

What are you working on now?

MOURÉ

A book of poems called *Domestic Fuel*. Which is a chaotic mess right now. Today (22 January) I'm in Calgary at my brother's desk (my brother grew up and isn't here); I'm writing a poem about fish, and a short one about a funeral in Switzerland. Later I'm going out to the garage, to take down my brother's cross-country skis. We wear the same size shoes!

Interview by Peter O'Brien

Mavis Gallant

Mavis Gallant, nee Young, was born in 1922 in Montreal to Anglo-Scottish parents. When she was ten, her father died, precipitating her years of wandering. Starting in Ontario, she attended seventeen schools in eight years, finishing high school in New York in 1940. From there she returned to Montreal, where she was married for a short time, and where she worked for the Montreal Standard. *In 1944 her first two short stories were published in* Preview. *Six years later, in the same year that* The New Yorker *first accepted her work, she left Canada for Europe. After stays in Vienna, Sicily, Spain, Southern France, Italy, Austria and Switzerland, in 1961 she settled into her present apartment in the Montparnasse area of Paris. Although Mavis Gallant wrote enough fiction to support herself for three decades, she didn't receive the attention she deserved in Canada until the Macmillan publication (facsimilie of the American edition) of* From the Fifteenth District *in 1979.* Home Truths, *a collection of short stories, received the 1981 Governor General's Award, and in 1985 she published her seventh story collection,* Overhead in a Balloon: Stories of Paris. *A non-fiction book,* Paris Notebooks, *appeared in 1986.*

The following interview was recorded on 1 March 1984 in Mavis Gallant's office at New College, University of Toronto, where she was writer-in-residence for the academic year 1983-84. It was cold that Thursday afternoon, and Toronto was not behaving like Toronto at all because there was snow. In fact, our planned dinner had been cancelled the night before because Gallant had not wanted to go out in the snowstorm. On the way to her office, I stopped to buy white wine. Forgetting that I was in Ontario, where wine is often stored upright, I bought the most expensive wine on their list. I had counted on the cold weather to chill the wine on my way over, but it didn't. When I presented my gift, along with two store-dusty glasses and a corkscrew, it was received graciously. Gallant tried to make the best of it; she cleaned the glasses while I tried to open the wine so we could put it outside her window to chill. I couldn't pull the cork.

There was a lot of embarrassment at this point. We both tugged our hardest and oddly enough, we both held off laughing. I proposed getting a larger person to do it, perhaps someone in a neighbouring office? No, this would not do, she did not want them to know she was drinking in her office, with someone who appeared to be a student. Imagine the talk! In the end I snuck the bottle out, pretended I was a student surprising a friend on her birthday, and watched the first man I encountered push the dry cork in.

The interview began over two small glasses of lukewarm white wine with bits of cork floating in them, in an austere office (white concrete, and they had taken away her typewriter) chilled by the open window.

INTERVIEWER

I am not going to ask you when the Dreyfus book is going to be done, I'm going to ask you what you are doing . . .

GALLANT

Oh, no no no, lay off. I am absolutely sick to death of the subject.

INTERVIEWER

But, what are you doing on the Dreyfus book, what is your focus?

GALLANT

Oh, I can talk about the focus. The focus is simply what happened from the fifth of October to when Dreyfus had his second trial in 1899. It is what happened year by year, as best we know. At the beginning there is an essay that situates it in its time in Paris, and then at the end I'm having a short thing on what became of all the people afterwards.

But I've been on it a very long time and there are many reasons why I simply haven't had time to work on it as I would.

INTERVIEWER

About the focus. Not all works on Dreyfus deal with racism or antisemitism. For instance, the 1954 edition of *Encyclopaedia Britannica* does not mention that Dreyfus was Jewish until they describe the attempted assassination in 1908 at a ceremony for Zola, which is after they describe the arrest and trial.

GALLANT

It doesn't mention that he's Jewish? Well, what do they think the thing was about? Isn't that extraordinary? I don't think that it happened *because* he was Jewish. I don't think he was *arrested* because he was Jewish. I think that from the moment a newspaper published the headline "Jewish Officer Arrested For Treason" the heat was on. The press created the Jewish element, and once that was created, it was a snowball. Dreyfus himself didn't want to . . . he was horrified at the idea. He was very French and very patriotic and very army and . . . When he's still on Devil's Island, he gets a letter from one of his brothers, saying, "You're going to come back to a very changed France where people are at each other's throats." It is the last thing Dreyfus wants. He's horrified. And you know, the French were lucky that he was such a passive character, because he could have led a political party, he could have led a revolution, he could have led anything. The pro-Dreyfus force was so strong, and

253

they believed in that naïve way . . .

Is it naïve? The French—it's not like Canadians—the French believe that when they vote it is an existential act. It's going to change their lives. That's why elections take on such drama in France. It is not the kitchen politics of Canada, it is something else completely. They really believe their lives are going to be changed, with a sweeping movement. Then, two weeks after the election, their lives are as before, and they turn on the people in office—I'm not joking—saying, "You don't change my life, as I had thought." Mitterand didn't change their lives, except to raise their taxes. There was no fundamental change. They think that by doing this, the next day they will be different people.

INTERVIEWER

Is that what you were getting at in your May '68 Journals?*

GALLANT

I have not reread them, so I have no idea what I said in them. I had lent the originals to a friend who is at Oxford University, because he was writing a book about the thing. He kept them about eight years, and so during those eight years I didn't read them. He brought them back just last summer, and I reread a little bit because I presented them to the University of Toronto library. When I reread a bit, all that struck me was that there was a rapidity in it. I remembered that I was out in the street all the time, all the time, all the time.

There were a lot of pamphlets in it that people had given me and I had picked up and so forth, and these suddenly were all shabby and shoddy, and they looked like something that had been around fifty years. Suddenly all this was old old old—that's what struck me. But that's not what you wanted.

INTERVIEWER

After de Gaulle spoke, people were saying, "What was it all for?" and "Is this all there is?" and there was a sense of letdown because the revolution didn't change anything.

GALLANT

It's very hard to talk about now because it sounds so idiotic. But there

* Gallant's journal was published as "Reflections: The Events in May: A Paris Notebook" in *The New Yorker* 14 & 21 September 1968, and the journal itself is held in the rare books library of Robarts Library, University of Toronto.

was a moment, I don't think it lasted more than an afternoon. It was on the famous thirteenth of May, the day there was the great mass of people who came up from the Gare de l'Est and Place de la République. I, even I, and I don't succumb as easily to existential belief, thought that something was happening. I thought, "the French are going to do this intelligently, there's going to be no bloody revolution, and it is not even political. I didn't see it as political at that point. It was just a desire to stem and divert the awful thing that life had become since the last war, since 1948—the tensions, the ugliness, the materialism. It suddenly looked good for one afternoon. Even I was swept away by it.

But that was when I was standing in a crowd. I was in the middle of Boulevard Saint-Michel—I was on one of those concrete traffic islands, with a lot of other people who were all hanging onto this sort of pole [borne] in the middle of the road at the intersection of Boulevard du Montparnasse. Anyway, there we all were, and this crowd broke as it . . . There were people there saying "quiet, there is a hospital." So the crowd was silent because there was a veteran's hospital nearby, and it stopped. We could see way way way down to the Seine, because it was on a slope, and you could see the heads and banners and things coming up, and then silence would fall, and they would move silently. It was very impressive.

I thought, "My God, this is it, mankind, mankind is having a change for the better." It is hard to believe that I could have thought it for one minute, but I did. You know, when you're caught up, obviously. And I thought this was wonderful. But it lasted only . . .

The crowd went up to Place Denfert-Rochereau. At Denfert-Rochereau the Communist Party was weeding out their people and getting them into the factories to occupy them. It was back to 1934 or something. The Communist Party will always be mired in that, you know, 1934.

INTERVIEWER

You also mentioned in your Journal that you were afraid that the press, again, was going to make it into a racist issue, because the students at one point were saying, "We too are German Jews."

GALLANT

That was the most amazing thing that you can imagine.

INTERVIEWER

That they would say that?

255

GALLANT

"Nous sommes tous des juifs allemands." It was absolutely incredible. Well, now it is a catchword. Students will say we are all Arab Jews, and that's about the worst thing they can say of everything.

Long before, in the month of March, I had cut out, from *Le Monde*, this little article which said "The students of Nanterre are going on strike over a German Jew who is being expelled from France." That was the famous one, the one with the red hair, the one who was the leader of the . . .

INTERVIEWER

Cohn-Bendit?

GALLANT

Cohn-Bendit, yes; he is now a fat, tiresome man. I don't think his name was even in the piece. This seemed to me so un-French in behaviour, that they would *bother* about a foreigner, that they would *think* about a foreigner, that they would go on strike for a foreigner, that I cut it out, and I put it in an envelope. It's funny, I've still got this little cutting in Paris. So that was even before the month of May. I certainly did not predict or think that anything would come of it. I just thought, "Isn't this extraordinary, this is a mutation almost."

Well, I wouldn't think it odd now because since then there has been so much racism and anti-racism, and the students don't go one way or go the other. I think they are passive now, except about their own careers.

But don't forget, in 1968 there was still full prosperity, people could still drop out. They could bring the economy to a standstill and it would pick up again. It picked up for another four or five years, until 1973, when it started to decline. What was happening then, in '68, was happening in a very rich economy, everywhere, all over the Western world. It'll never come back, and it seems like a dream.

INTERVIEWER

It'll never come back? Isn't that pessimistic?

GALLANT

It's not pessimistic, it is realistic. How can it? The whole thing is kaput now.

256

INTERVIEWER

I picked up the last *Passion*, and read the reprint of the 1958 *Esquire* article about the Americanization of France, and I was wondering if, when you were in Paris, you noticed that at all, if that was an issue?

GALLANT

In 1958? No. It is now, but it's sort of a joke. When were you last in Paris?

INTERVIEWER

I've never been in Paris.

GALLANT

Oh. I see. Well, the whole Champs Elysées is just hamburger and fast food places. If you call that Americanization—but it's just worldwide modernization. I can't really get very excited about that. It would excite me, it would infuriate—I would react if they cut the trees down in the Champs Elysées and there were no more trees.

But you can't keep it a museum. You can keep something like Venice as a museum, but young Venetians have to go away to work, because there are no jobs in the museum, just the museum keepers. Not that I wish to see hamburger signs in Piazza San Marco.

In the May '68 Journal there were references to hostility to American ideas. For instance, J.P. explains to students that in Peking, the university programme consists of a major and a minor subject. When you told him that programme was the American university system, he replied that he couldn't say that it was American because they would never have accepted it.

GALLANT

Oh, I don't remember. Don't forget this is a long time ago, it was 15 years ago. You would probably get something else now. It is very easy to stir up anti-Americanism in France, among French. In Europe, at the moment, with the arms and the nuclear issue, this is completely different. It is very easy to stir up anti anything anywhere, though, isn't it?

INTERVIEWER

It is. It is too easy. I know you are interested in politics, so you have said in interviews, but I was wondering if that interest formed a broader vision, or made itself known in your work somehow.

Well, if it is known in my work, that is up to the reader to see. I would think that everything is political, in a certain sense, in people's lives. They don't always realize it; they're either the victims of it or not aware of it. I don't know, I can't say what readers see. They sometimes see the very opposite of what one intended, I don't think I could consider people, even in a small domestic entanglement—even if I didn't mention it or write about it—without saying what the structure was that they lived in, and what created it, and what at that particular moment was acting on it, and what that . . . Although one is writing a short story and not an essay. It is a different pattern. But I probably think like that very much. I'm wondering, when I'm talking to people, what they think, what they would say. It is much more difficult to discover in Canada what people think about these subjects. They often get very heated and angry, which is not fun, or they avoid it completely.

INTERVIEWER
I noticed in "The Pegnitz Junction" and in "From the Fifteenth District" that you were playing around with the form. In both of them there was more than one voice, or they had stories within stories within . . .

GALLANT
Oh, "The Pegnitz Junction" is just a story within a story within a story within a story . . .

INTERVIEWER
Yes, it's wonderful. What interested me was the play of voices, that there were several voices in one story.

GALLANT
It is more in "The Pegnitz" because you've got the voice of the woman who lived in Muggendorf, who hardly speaks German, and whose whole life history Christine gets. I did not mean that Christine was schizophrenic or anything. She heard it. In that story you have to accept that there were short circuits of thought. It is the story that I had the most enjoyment writing of anything I've written. I adored writing that. I wrote it in high spirits, and it was such fun to write because a great deal of it has some references to German writing—

258

parodies and take-offs and skits and all sorts of things that people didn't get—but it amused me to do that anyway. It is one of the few things I can ever reread. I don't reread. I sometimes reread that a bit, just a bit of it here and there. I don't know why, but I adored writing it. I wrote it very very fast.

INTERVIEWER

Really? Even though you were making allusions?

GALLANT

Well, I wrote the initial part very fast. I had a great deal of enjoyment writing it, and it amused me to write, and I wrote at a pretty good clip. I started it in Germany, one summer that I was there. I wrote constantly, and finally irritated the person who was taking me round to see the sights, because I just sat in the car scribbling. I didn't go out and look at the beautiful Renaissance statue or whatever.

INTERVIEWER

Do you know George Woodcock at all?

GALLANT

I met him only once.

INTERVIEWER

He said of "The Pegnitz Junction" that he thought it was all about how the war, how Nazism, put up a wall, and that the Germans you were writing about in "The Pegnitz Junction" were without memory, without a past.

GALLANT

Oh, absolutely. I don't think that is what it is entirely about. But that is true. I wrote that at the end of the sixties. The generation of the sixties, there was a wall behind them. Their parents were absolutely silent. They grew up puzzled and amnesic. In a place that had been bombed, everything that they were handling, practically, was new; cups, saucers. There was nothing, there was no reminder. I was fascinated by that, that there was no reminder. Yet there was a great deal on television. They could look at television and see. They were constantly running documentaries and documentation about concentration camps and so forth. It is not true that there was nothing. They could see it if they *wanted* to. But there was no connection between

259

that, present life, and their parents. Now they are making a connection, but they are making a connection with their grandparents.

INTERVIEWER

"From the Fifteenth District": you said many readers were baffled and irritated by it. Why?

GALLANT

"Many," I don't know about, but some people were. The other day someone who was interviewing me said it was fey, f-e-y. It is not fey at all, that woman isn't fey. The idea of the living pursuing the dead is not fey.

"From the Fifteenth District," I remember, was much longer originally. I had something in my mind and I never wrote it. There is an arrondissement in France that's an administrative . . . In the story, it's a place where the dead complain to the police of being haunted by the living. They were histories that could happen anywhere, those three stories, of the soldier, the Arab woman who wants her death to be described as something absolutely beautiful and not the horror that it obviously was, and Mrs. Essling. But I wanted to write . . . [interruption of telephone].

INTERVIEWER

Were you surprised then that some people would be irritated by it?

GALLANT

You never know what's going to irritate people. For a couple of years, '80, '81, into '82, I wrote in *The New Yorker* only humour, short humorous pieces, because I was writing Dreyfus and I just didn't . . . Many people didn't like it, they were irritated because it was satire. In fact, I remember in 1981 I was reading at U.B.C. and a professor got up, a teacher, and asked me most passionately if I would please stop writing this stuff.

INTERVIEWER

Why?

GALLANT

Well, "It isn't what you do, we don't understand it." Eventually I started doing other things again, so it was all right.

INTERVIEWER

I've noticed that your stories are open-ended. I want to know if they are open-ended because that is a form you choose, or if you think it is realistic, because in life situations go on, they don't end.

GALLANT

You mean it doesn't end with the line, "So he died, and his wife committed suicide, and his sister then got married and lived very happily in Mississauga, and she had two children called Kevin and Amy, and Amy was doing finger painting at the age of . . . " no, that's open-ended too.

I don't know what is meant really by open-ended because there certainly is an indication, at least to me, of what's next. I don't think there is any mystery of what's next, there is never someone saying "and I didn't know what I was going to do next." You know pretty well what the situation is from then on, or what it is bound to be. Or barring a miracle, happened to be.

INTERVIEWER

Yes. I was thinking of *A Fairly Good Time*, at the end, I wasn't sure if the character would ever change or if she would continue to be happy-go-lucky.

GALLANT

Well, I don't know that, but she certainly wouldn't be with him, would she?

INTERVIEWER

Yes, that is clear.

GALLANT

She does a very silly thing at the end to irritate him, sending a silly thing in the mail, and she obviously can't change, and he's not going to change either, and I think that is clear. There's a story I took out of that, it was longer, and there is a piece that I wrote as a story which ran in *The New Yorker*, where Philip is remarried, and he talks to his second wife about Shirley, but with a kind of nostalgia, and the younger, prettier wife is jealous.

INTERVIEWER

Why would he be nostalgic?

261

Because one is, that's life. He says she was absolutely awful, you couldn't do anything with her, she was absolutely hopeless, she was always . . . And yet the fact that on his honeymoon he will talk about her, makes the younger woman, although she is much more beautiful, younger, suddenly feel inadequate. But it is inadequate vis-à-vis the shadow of the first person. It takes place in an airport in Helsinki, they're on their honeymoon. "In Transit," that's what it is called.

INTERVIEWER

Because you don't reread your work, I'm going to give you an example for this one . . .

GALLANT

I have, excuse me, I have reread a number of things because I'm giving readings, so of course to give readings you do reread to the extent of finding out if the thing will read, so I've reread more this year, usually just the first page to see if it will read aloud, some things read aloud and some things don't, so I have reread more than I would ever normally.

INTERVIEWER

This has to do with the past. I'm trying to get at what the relationship of the past is to the present in your work. For instance, you have characters like Flor, and the woman in "The Moslem Wife," and Potter, Piotr, how do you pronounce his name?

GALLANT

Piotr. I think the Poles or Slavs pronounce the "r" differently than the French do. I can't really say it in a Slav way. It's just Peter.

INTERVIEWER

Those characters seem to be crippled or hampered in some way because they remember, they hang on to the past.

GALLANT

I don't think Piotr is a man hanging on to the past at all. I think he is trying to do everything he can to get away from it. He is not living with his wife. He's trying to get off with a younger woman. He's thinking of moving to a foreign country.

Okay, but I was thinking of the way he is puzzled and envious of
Laurie's . . .

GALLANT

Piotr is not hanging on to the past, his country is hanging on to him.
He can't get out of the country. How could he earn a living anywhere
else? How could he earn a living? What could he do? He can't just come
over with a suitcase. When he thinks of leaving and living with her, he
thinks wildly he's going to get into the French teaching system; he can't.
He is there as an exchange professor, don't forget. If he ever came back,
what would he do, sweep the streets? He couldn't even do that. Oh no,
he's trying, he's willing to do everything.

There is a part in the story which says his children even seem remote
to him. He's very much in love. He envies her her *freedom* . . . well, he
hasn't got it. He is not hanging on to the past, the political system is
hanging on to him.

INTERVIEWER

I see. Scratch Piotr.

GALLANT

Yes, well, scratch it, because you've got it wrong.

INTERVIEWER

But, Flor in *Green Water, Green Sky* and Netta in "The Moslem Wife" —
there is one point where Netta says she is haunted by a dark, an
accurate, a deadly memory, and is envious of her husband's lack of memory.

GALLANT

He has a lack of memory that can let him go from woman to woman,
and let him come back to her as if nothing had ever happened. But men
are often like that.

INTERVIEWER

You think so?

GALLANT

Yes, much more than women.

INTERVIEWER

Except for Laurie Bennett who goes from man to man.

GALLANT

Well I don't really know much about her.

INTERVIEWER

Your work often portrays refugees. Why this fascination with refugees?

GALLANT

Oh, I've written about that. I don't know. They just fascinated me. They seemed to me from Europe, from a different world, from somewhere, something fascinating.

The very first two little fragments I ever published in my life, which were in *Preview* magazine, were about a young Austrian refugee man. The second thing that I published was in the *Standard*, and it was also read over the CBC radio, and it was about a Czech refugee.

INTERVIEWER

That ties in with the war, which keeps reappearing in your fiction, as if you were fascinated by it also.

GALLANT

Fascinated? That was my generation.

It really was a great trench in life, before the war and after the war. Two worlds.

INTERVIEWER

Do you see it that clearly, in everything, even in families?

GALLANT

Oh yes, it was a deep trench. People's families meant nothing.

INTERVIEWER

But after the war?

GALLANT

People got together and tried the Great North American family baby boom thing.

INTERVIEWER

You did one play, and only one play. Why just one?

GALLANT

It is pretty recent.

INTERVIEWER

Yes. Will there be another play?

GALLANT

Yes.

INTERVIEWER

Do you have a favourite story that you wrote?

GALLANT

Perhaps "Speck's Idea." It was published in *The New Yorker* in 1979, and it was in *Best Short Stories 1980*, the American one and the Canadian one, and has been republished twice since. I've never been able to read it aloud because it it too long.

INTERVIEWER

Why would you say it is your favorite?

GALLANT

Because it's about Paris. It's a lot of different things that I've been observing about Paris, and I got them all into this story. It's about a man who owns an art gallery in Paris. Lots and lots of things about Paris.

INTERVIEWER

Just because you got them all in?

GALLANT

Oh, I don't know really.

INTERVIEWER

Have you ever had, or been afraid of, writer's block?

GALLANT

I've never had it. I've had fatigue. I've never been where I didn't have something that I was doing or trying to do. I've never had a period as long that I wasn't writing as this one now, here. Five months and just one book review. It is a change of rhythm that has upset me. It is not a block. It's just that I can't seem to get the machine going the way I'm used to. I'm used to having lots and lots of time to write, and not quite as many other things to do. On the other hand, it seemed pointless to come all these miles and shut myself up, lock this door permanently and sit here and not see anyone, because then I might as well be in Paris under rather more comfortable circumstances. So that's bothering me. Then I found that when I sometimes arrange this stretch of time when I think I can work, well you know, it's not a machine, you can't just turn the button on and say all right go.

No. No, the machine is backed up in some way. But it's not writer's block. I've heard people talk about writer's block. I've never had that, where they can't get anything down. The French call it the fear of the white sheet of paper: la peur de la feuille blanche. Why put a sheet of white paper in front of you if you don't have anything to put on it? That sounds completely idiotic. I wouldn't get anything out unless I knew what I was going to write. That sounds completely insane.

INTERVIEWER

What is your usual working pattern?

GALLANT

In Paris I work all the time. You mean when I'm on my own? I'm working all the time. Last year I was getting ready to come here in September; I was writing four stories for *The New Yorker*, four connected stories. I barely did anything else. I didn't go outside because I should finish it. Then there would be periods when I would relax a bit more, and take a quick little holiday, not even a holiday, I would just take the train to see someone.

The lovely thing is if you take a train, in a very short time you are in a completely different environment. That's the lovely thing about Europe. You take a train and you're in Holland, in Italy, it's completely different and you forget everything.

INTERVIEWER

Not like Canada.

GALLANT

No, certainly. I've tried to explain that to friends in Europe. One of the things that puzzles me and them is that Canadians don't take very many holidays. And they work very hard, god they work hard, long long hours, and they work all their lives here. Go into a store and you are waited on by what seems to me old women. They work all their lives.

I've had students who tell me their parents work all their lives. Why don't they take longer holidays? It isn't that they can't afford them. You just can't. It takes four to five hours of plane flight—it's like flying from Paris to Leningrad, or Paris to Helsinki, every time you want a holiday. Instead of being somewhere else in an hour, like the Mediterranean. This is geography.

INTERVIEWER

It's not just geography, though, because . . .

GALLANT

It is a different rhythm.

INTERVIEWER

Yes. But the idea of working all your life is very accepted here.

GALLANT

I've been working all my life because, in the first place, I don't conceive it any other way, and then, I have no choice. I live on my writing. If my writing stops, I stop. But that's not the same thing. People work and work here forever.

When you think of France, where they have five or six weeks of paid holidays a year, and a 34-hour week. The result is that the economy is different here. They start late in the morning here. Stores open early in France; you go out on the streets, stores are open early. You can go out and do your shopping at eight o'clock in the morning, and come home, it's done.

Banks here don't open until ten o'clock. It's just lunch hour, it would have to be one's lunch hour, banking.

INTERVIEWER

Have you always known you would write?

GALLANT

Yes.

INTERVIEWER

Did you ever doubt your ability?

GALLANT

Every writer does. Yes. Every writer does.

INTERVIEWER

Wonder if you have the talent?

GALLANT

Mmhmm. Yes.

INTERVIEWER

Is there a long—I don't know if this is the right word for you—gestation, from when you get an idea to when . . .

GALLANT

Yes, sometimes yes, sometimes no. Thinking of the four stories I wrote last year, really like a novel, I had the idea in the autumn, and I thought about it a long time all winter, and I suddenly started to write in the spring. I was writing other things too. But on and off. And then suddenly in spring I began to write, and wrote steadily into August. Sometimes it takes much longer. Some stories have taken three years. On and off. I put them away. Things I started twenty years ago I'll probably never finish.

INTERVIEWER

Imagination: is it inspired by memory?

GALLANT

I don't know. No. Because when you are a child you imagine. Your wild imaginings, what can they be based on: stories you've been told, your own desires, things you've read. So memory, to that extent, maybe, what you've . . . A little child will tell you the most fabulous story—what is it based on? What he wishes might happen, perhaps. Very often.

Lack of imagination is tragic. Lots of people have no imagination. I read somewhere in an interview with Philip Roth—I've forgotten where it was—in which he said the difference between a writer and everyone else, is that the writer can imagine.

I think it is more than that. I think the difference between a writer and everyone else is the ability to put yourself in someone else's place, completely. I think that's more than imagination. To actually think, "If I were in the next office seeing a student, would it be like this, like that?"

268

and so on. The most difficult thing, I think, for a writer, is when other people try to run your life for you. They say, "But why do you do that, why don't you do this and do that?" and go to places you don't want to go. Writers don't live like other people, and, it is evident, they can't. People will try to live your life for you, and you can't possibly want that. They are absolutely incapable of putting themselves in your place. But I can put myself in theirs, still thinking, "Why don't they shut up?"

INTERVIEWER

I think you just said what everybody who reads interviews wants to read; they all want to be reassured that the writer is somehow different, but yet not too different.

GALLANT

I don't really know. I never tried to approach writers when I was young, so I don't know. I had no idea what a writer was like. I know that the one writer I very much wanted to interview was Jean-Paul Sartre, when I was young. And I did. I was able to when he came to Canada. That was in what, '43? That was fascinating for me.

INTERVIEWER

That was for the *Montreal Standard*?

GALLANT

Yes. But I never tried to approach writers or anything. It never entered my head that that was the way to writing. It never entered my head that meeting a writer was a way to write.

INTERVIEWER

No. It's not.

GALLANT

No, of course it isn't. Of course it isn't.

INTERVIEWER

Can you think of any writers whom you would have read when you were very young, who might have influenced you, your outlook . . .

GALLANT

It is hard to say. I read a great deal. I'm amazed when people can say, "Yes, I was influenced by James Joyce." I really don't know. There were so many. I read a lot of Chekhov, as I've said dozens of times.

INTERVIEWER

What about Katherine Mansfield?

GALLANT

Yes, I read her enormously when I was young, I haven't read her for years. I admired her greatly.

INTERVIEWER

Do you think you learned from her work?

GALLANT

Well, I wasn't a student sitting at a teacher's feet, I was just reading.

INTERVIEWER

You could still absorb . . .

GALLANT

Yes, it's hard for me to say because I don't know.

INTERVIEWER

The reason I ask is because she appears twice in your fiction as a geographical landmark.

GALLANT

Yes, I noticed that, too. I read aloud a story called "Virus X," and it was a scene with two girls going to her grave . . .

INTERVIEWER

Oh, that makes three.

GALLANT

What's the other?

INTERVIEWER

"The Moslem Wife" starts off by locating the hotel, and the other one is—oh, sorry, not a story—the May '68 Journal, you identify a hospital as the one where Mansfield underwent a useless cure.

GALLANT

No, not a hospital, a hotel. It is not very far from where I live. And I read her journals, and I read her correspondence, but I haven't read any of that for years.

INTERVIEWER

Why is Proust your favourite writer?

GALLANT

Just because he's great, fascinating. I don't know. Maybe one is drawn to something that is concerned with the things that one is concerned with, but it's unconscious.

I don't read for anything but pleasure. If I read for information, I'm looking for information and that's the end of that. I could never be a teacher, because teachers read without pleasure. It's terrifying to think that they teach literature that they have read without the slightest pleasure. The concept of pleasure does not even come into it.

INTERVIEWER

No, I don't think that's true.

GALLANT

I think it is true.

INTERVIEWER

I think the first reading is always with pleasure, and the second reading is when they begin to do the teaching.

GALLANT

I think they make no difference between what they like and what they don't like. Everything is taught at the same level. They are looking for things that have nothing to do with the pleasure of reading. And writers— if you don't read for pleasure, forget it.

INTERVIEWER

How about influences besides authors, for instance film, directors, art, music?

GALLANT

I've often wondered about that myself, and I don't know. And then, I've often wondered how late, at what point influence stops, how late.

271

There is a writer I admire greatly called Joseph—not Philip—Joseph Roth. He's a Viennese novelist and journalist who died in 1940. I didn't come to him until late, until I was forty. Someone introduced me to this writer. I've read everything I can that's translated in English and French. It seems to me that we are almost . . . twins.

And yet it is not the same thing, we are not at all alike. He is writing about the Austro-Hungarian Empire before World War I. And he died of alcoholism; the most unlikely thing that would ever happen to me, you know. He was a refugee, I'm not. But there's something about his work that absolutely fascinates me. I was greatly flattered when a German I know, reading something I wrote, said, "There's something about it like Joseph Roth, Joseph wrote this." I thought, is it possible that I could, at my age, still absorb something? It's not the work, it's not the style, it's not . . . There's just something about the thinking. And I think one is drawn to someone who you think . . . I've asked people who knew him, would I have liked him, and they've said "Oh, no, he was always drunk and mad." But it's fascinating. Being drawn to someone who writes something that appeals to me. I read anything I could get my hands on, the way you do when you're an adolescent, but I was forty. It is amazing.

INTERVIEWER

Why not, though? There is no reason for you to be fixed and nonmalleable.

GALLANT

I don't think it's as simple as that. I think that it is something that you think, "Oh, I would have been interested in this subject, too," and you read it voraciously, this subject: frontiers, which fascinate me, people, foreigners. Anything that's different is interesting to me. I have at Massey a charming Chinese student, chemical engineer from Taiwan, who said to me, "Why don't you go to Taiwan, why don't you go to Asia, and then you'll have another setting for your fiction." I said I couldn't begin to even attempt to write about Asians. Even if I were to stay a year, I could never put myself in the place, I said to him, of your mother, your father, yourself, your anything. I could only be always an outsider looking on. That's something I dread, I'd never write, because I'd only be writing about myself. So that's not interesting for me. For example, he told me that he—we were talking about another Chinese person—could tell that he is the youngest son. I said, "How can you tell, how do you know?" He said, "Just as Chinese people can tell that I'm the oldest son." And I

272

said, "How? Because you're responsible and you're this and you're that?" It is something subtle. Now, I could never tell. I couldn't look at a Canadian and say he's the youngest in the family. You see, it is a question of looking for different things. I couldn't put myself in that place. I couldn't attempt to do it.

But I can get away with it with an Italian, with a Russian, with any European. It's close enough, the same religions are practised. You can start off with that, it is the basis of our culture. There is a certain similarity, and then there is a deviation. You have to take that into account. You have to try to think how it would be if you came out of a society such as the Swiss who write, speak, work in two or three languages. That's a different kind of mentality *déjà*, but it's not all that different. Basically, it's instinct.

INTERVIEWER

You said a Russian. Russia you would include as European?

GALLANT

I would think that I was taking a great risk. I don't think I could put myself in the place of a dissident, because they're all fighting among themselves. Unless it was based on things they had told me. Sometimes you only begin to guess or to feel what they are thinking.

INTERVIEWER

I know people always ask you if you know other writers . . .

GALLANT

I don't talk about my friends.

INTERVIEWER

No, I don't want to talk about your friends, but I want to know if you are part of a community. For example, in Canada one of the most common complaints is that there is no sense of community, no sense of people knowing each other and being able to talk about their work.

GALLANT

I'm told that the writers' community in Toronto is altogether too chummy, that's what people say.

INTERVIEWER

That's Toronto. I meant Canada as a whole.

273

GALLANT

Heavens, look at it geographically. How do you think that a writer in Vancouver can drop in for a drink with a fellow from Saskatoon? It can't be done. And writing is a very solitary occupation. Writers don't work with one another.

Any writer friends I've had, it has been a coincidence that they happened to be writers, and we never talk about our work. I have a very good woman writer friend in Paris, and we don't talk about our writing until something is finished. She will call up and say, "I've finished," a novel or whatnot, and I usually send her flowers or something. But it's a coincidence. I probably have more painter than writer friends.

INTERVIEWER

What about reading your contemporaries?

GALLANT

I read what comes through my hands. I don't have a systematic way of reading, unless something strikes me as marvellous, and then I'll try to find everything and do it all at once. But that's very rare. There is a great deal of almost good writing.

INTERVIEWER

What do you mean by almost good writing?

GALLANT

Competent.

INTERVIEWER

For example, would Doris Lessing be "almost good"?

GALLANT

Oh, no, Doris Lessing is a first-class writer. No, but there is a great deal of rather boring work.

INTERVIEWER

Do you remember much about your childhood?

GALLANT

You've read my work?

Yes, but I always assumed that it is not you in the fiction.

Yes, I remember a great deal. Coming back to Canada once, someone said to me, "Did you have an unhappy childhood?" and I said that it was unhappy like most people's. A couple of people I know said, "Well, mine was happy." Heavens, I'd rather have had mine than theirs. And I think they mean it.

In the introduction to *Home Truths*, you said that it was in New York City that you discovered for the first time at the age of fourteen that one could actually be happy. What did you mean by that?

Because I was in Ontario, and I'd had a very difficult—my father died and I was brought here, and I found it very strange and different. People were closed. I'm talking about before the war. I don't want to get into a great hassle with Canadians; I say this and that, and it's all taken out of context afterwards and thrown back at me. I really don't deserve it and I'm getting tired of it. Life was very different fifty years ago, which is when I'm talking about, and people were very tight and closed. I can't say that it was a very jolly place here.

I had come out of something perhaps livelier. I was coming to the conclusion that there was no way of being happy, and most of the people were unhappy, and that there was no solution. I didn't see anyone expressing joy or gaiety or optimism, or I never heard it, and I never saw it. I was thinking that the only happiness in life was just in books and imagining, and that people's lives were utterly drab. Even talking to you about it I feel bent down by that awful weight I used to feel, that there was no way out and life wasn't worth getting on with. I went to New York and that was a liberation. Simply because people were more cheerful—cheerful, that's all—they were just cheerful and happy. One of my first experiences was going to a movie in New York City, and hearing people, for the first time in my life, laugh in the cinema. I had never heard it.

You're kidding.

I'm not kidding. I'd never heard it. If you go to a movie here now, I can't say that people laugh all that much, but they talk all the time. They talk on the same level as we are talking now, and they eat popcorn, and they talk as if they were in their own livingrooms. I don't know if they do it in Montreal, but they do it in Toronto. That's very very different. If there's something funny, yes, people do laugh. If you read, and you read something funny, people laugh. They are very different, it's not the same. This is two generations on, don't forget. I'm talking about people before the war, it was fifty years ago.

INTERVIEWER

How long were you in Ontario?

GALLANT

Oh, just long enough. It was a liberation in that sense. People were completely different. Now, I don't think that Americans have the optimism they had fifty years ago, either, because they've had Vietnam, and they've had a recession. They were in the Depression, but they were coming out of it, and I suppose I was too young to talk to people about economics. They weren't in the war yet. There was a jauntiness and bounciness and cheer, and everything was just around the corner and everything was lovely and it was giddy. I saw that there was a possibility of happiness in life. That was the American creed then: life was happy. What was it in Canada? You can't even say Canada, because Quebec was different. In Ontario life was duty, life was earnestness. But that was a long time ago.

You're going to publish this and I know exactly what is going to happen. I'm going to give a reading, and somebody is going to throw it at me.

INTERVIEWER

I noticed in the Geoff Hancock interview that when he asked you what sort of childhood you had, you didn't say. You didn't talk about you, you talked about what other people said about you.

GALLANT

Because I don't know what sort of child I was. All children think they were ultrasensitive. All children thought they were sensitive creatures, tossed about by the storms of doubt, winds. I feel a certain pity for children. In fact, if I had a large fortune to leave, I would leave it for the protection of children against the savagery of adults. And there would never be enough.

You should see what I get in some of the stories here from students. There is a lot of savagery against children still. Even if you make allowances for fantasy, the cruelty . . . What goes on inside a middle-class house. Mothers, the descriptions of mothers . . .

INTERVIEWER

What about your parents?

GALLANT

They have nothing to do with my career or work.

INTERVIEWER

Not even the experience of death early in your life?

GALLANT

Oh yes, of course, I've a lot of curious material in fact that I've never wished to open.

Oh, of course. But then you know, the *difficult* is sometimes much smaller than the moments of difficulty you remember. It's awfully hard to say.

I've often found, when I was young, when I sometimes attempted to talk about things, that people would say, "Look, you couldn't have experienced that and that and that," and I'd think, "Yes, but I did," so I gave up.

INTERVIEWER

Why would they say you couldn't have experienced that and that and . . .

GALLANT

Because it was a great deal—it was a great deal—and that's probably why I became more careful when I was older.

INTERVIEWER

Thinking again of the time period when you came to Montreal in the 1940s and 1950s, all the women I can think of who were young adults at that time, became housewives and mothers. None of them would ever dream of doing something like working for a newspaper. Do you think your parents or teachers or even the class and milieu that you were in, would have had a certain attitude toward women that would have . . .

GALLANT

Well you see I was so young that I can't tell you about my parents. But the preparation, the life that was offered to me seemed to me to be very mediocre, and I had a great terror . . . I think my greatest fear is of the mediocre. Once I realised that life wasn't hopeless, and that there was a great deal to be had from it, I then thought that it was elsewhere, that it had to be in Europe or somewhere.

But I had a great fear. Because when I think of girls I was in school with, where are they now? But there were women working for newspapers. I wasn't the only one you know.

INTERVIEWER

But weren't those women dismissed with "Oh, that was because of the war"?

GALLANT

That was made very clear to us. Some very bright girls lost their jobs. In fact, a friend was in Toronto a while ago, we worked together when she was nineteen or twenty. I said, "Well, don't you know why you were fired?" She said, "I've never known." I said, "They were clearing you out to get the men in." She said, "Oh, I never thought of that." They fired her with no reason. She wasn't the only one; there was a batch fired. There were two of us they kept—I'm not talking about the women's pages—as journalist reporters because we spoke French. We were useful.

INTERVIEWER

Would you say that literature has a moral responsibility?

GALLANT

What exactly do you mean? Do you mean the writer is supposed to write uplifting things that are supposed to take people up? No, I don't think one has the right to say, just because one is a writer, what literature ought to be, any more than a painter has the right to say what painting ought to be. I think a social worker can say what social work ought to be, but that's completely different. Writing is entirely individual. You are responsible in the sense that anyone in society is responsible.

278

INTERVIEWER

Why do writers and artists feel they have to declaim about art and literature? They do, but why do we encourage them to? We do in our society.

GALLANT

Yes. Yes. Probably because what everybody else says is so idiotic that the writer finally feels, "Well, I'll get my two cents in, and I'll say something, and be a bit wiser about it." But it is completely individual. Writers are not a tribe. This is a completely mistaken idea. One belongs to a writers' union because of a kind of solidarity, for one thing, in Canada. I belong to an American union because it is one that helps writers when they are down and out, financially. I belong to that. And I belong to the PEN club because they help writers who are jailed in countries, who take up causes and things. I have no place in the communist union, they wouldn't accept me. I'm not a militant.

Writers declare because the society they live in accepts the declamation. In France it is considered important. I don't know whether in the United States and Canada the writer—I'm talking of North American society as a whole—if it is at all important what the writer has to say on the resignation of Trudeau, for example, or what it means to this, that, and the other. They seem to feel that other politicians have more to say. I'm not quite sure that that's true. Or generalists who specialize and have had the thing in the drawer for a couple of weeks, waiting.

INTERVIEWER

Do you see your fiction going in a new direction?

GALLANT

Oh, I don't know how to answer that. It is not that I don't wish to, but I don't think that I'm the one—it's for the readers or perhaps the editors I deal with to decide. It certainly isn't the same direction all the time, I'm aware of that. It changes, but I don't know why it changes. One doesn't simply get up in the morning and say now it is going to change. When I was writing, for two or three years, those little funny pieces for The New Yorker, and then when I began to write long stories again, they were humorous, and so I knew that something was being carried over from the shorter pieces. I didn't expect it to last, and it didn't, because last year I wrote some short stories which were anything but satirical.

I've started a lot of work since I've come, and some of it is Canadian, and I've noticed they are very short stories, short pieces, but they are not satirical. I wouldn't have the same point of view for Canadians because Canadians never strike me as people I would be funny about, probably because Canadians don't pose before the world as some Europeans do, such as the people in France. There is a position, "I am a Frenchman, I must do that." Canadians are mainly struggling for identity, to dutify.

INTERVIEWER

Is that a definition, or . . . ?

GALLANT

I don't know. There is a great deal of this "What is a Canadian?" I reread "Virus X" recently, I read it aloud. I read it in the '70s. I wanted to see if I could read it while I was here. It was almost like reading someone else's work, at that point. "Virus X" was written in the late '50s. The events it describes take place in 1952. In 1952 the Canadians in it are talking about national identity, so you see it was going on even then. That struck me. Here are these characters saying to each other, "Well, what about our national identity?" and we are still talking about it. This idea that Canada is a mosaic, that it isn't a melting pot, but the place is falling apart because where is the cement to hold the mosaic together? We should probably all have been made to learn esperanto. Is there an esperanto movement here?

INTERVIEWER

I've met esperanto teachers. I sat next to one on a train once; he was ready to sign me up by the end of the train ride. He had faith that this is the way to universal peace.

GALLANT

That's fascinating. They are very determined about what they are doing. If we all speak the same language we will all somehow . . . The Irish all speak the same language and they don't get along. The Irish are to me the most terrifying example. It's like a terrible haemorrhage on the edge of Europe. It goes on and on. No one seems to know what to do about it. It is just like a machine that keeps on, a bloody machine that keeps on turning. It doesn't make any sense at all. There it is on the edge of Europe, and blood is constantly flowing. They say if you take too many aspirin each one is a little internal haemorrhage and you end up being anaemic without knowing it, and it's like that, a tiny tiny haemorrhage each time. Vitality is flowing out of what's left of us in the West.

INTERVIEW

Are you working on anything besides Dreyfus right now?

GALLANT

I'm going to throw you right out that window. I'm not talking about it. I'm going to throw you right out that window [laughter].

INTERVIEWER

When you go back to Paris? Will there ever be another novel?

GALLANT

Oh, of course, yes. In fact I've got one that is almost finished. Everything I have is almost finished: a play, a novel, a book of history, short stories. Everything is almost finished.

INTERVIEWER

What are you going to do when they are all finished?

GALLANT

By then I will be a very old lady.

INTERVIEWER

Have you done what you set out to do?

GALLANT

You mean in life?

INTERVIEWER

Yes, or in writing, whichever you prefer.

GALLANT

In writing, it's never . . . I don't think any writer can ever say, I did what I set out to do. And then, you don't set out to do, nobody sets out with a thing, thinking that twenty years from now I'm doing that. I set out, I certainly did set out to live as a writer, and I managed it. I think that's absolutely grand. It was a great risk. I only realize now how much it was a risk.

INTERVIEWER
Only now? Really?

GALLANT
Because I kept coming back to Canada, and people talked to me about it.

INTERVIEWER
Did, or do, people keep asking how on earth you survived when you got there?

GALLANT
With difficulty. With difficulty. That was a long time ago. Even now, the students, not the young students because they don't notice, but those who are part-time, the mature students around twenty-eight . . . There was a student in here the other day who pointed out that I gave up a good job. I said, "Yes, of course I did, there was no other way of doing it." I wouldn't advise anybody to do it, because there is no job to come back to now, and not everybody is going to write better in Europe. Some people can write much better in Victoria, B.C., and some people can write anywhere. It just happened to work for me. And perhaps I didn't do enough, I don't know, perhaps I didn't. I wrote a lot, but I don't think that means anything either. I don't think it matters if you published twenty-two books or ten or three; it is the work itself.

Are we through with this? Let's unplug it and have another glass of wine.

Interview by Debra Martens

LEON ROOKE

Leon Rooke was born at 2:00 A.M. on 11 September 1934 in Roanoke Rapids, North Carolina. According to the "authorized biography" which appeared in the special Leon Rooke issue of the Canadian Fiction Magazine *(Number 38), the young Rooke had an interest in "dogs, tadpoles, chickens" and received his first book,* Terry and the Pirates, *for "Xmas 1945." Since then he has published plays, seven collections of stories:* Last One Home Sleeps in the Yellow Bed *(1968),* The Broad Back of the Angel *(1977),* The Love Parlour *(1977),* Cry Evil *(1980),* Death Suite *(1981),* The Birth Control King of the Upper Volta *(1982),* A Bolt of White Cloth *(1984), and three novels:* Fat Woman *(1980),* The Magician in Love *(1981), and* Shakespeare's Dog *(1983). His stories have appeared in many journals, and in anthologies such as* Best Canadian Stories *and* Best American Short Stories. *Rooke's novels and stories are bursting with fantastical characters and situations: miracles and angels exist alongside everyday events. Even the titles to his stories are nuggets of fertile imagination: "Saloam Frigid With Time's Legacy While Mrs. Willoughby Bight-Davies Sits Naked Through the Night On a Tree Stump Awaiting the Lizard That Will Make Her Loins Go Boom-Boom," "Adolpho's Disappeared and We Haven't a Clue Where to Find Him," and "Sixteen-Year-Old Susan March Confesses to the Innocent Murder of All the Devious Strangers Who Would Drag Her Down." Writing in* The New York Times Book Review, *Jerome Charyne called* Shakespeare's Dog *a "sculpted novel with a largeness of wit and imagination." Rooke has lived in Victoria, B.C. since 1969. He won the Canada-Australia Literary Award for 1981 and spent part of the Summer of 1983 in Australia.*

This interview was conducted entirely by mail from December 1982 to September 1983. The aim from the beginning was to maintain a colloquial flavour, despite the interview being written rather than spoken. Rooke was more than helpful in supplying short questions of his own to keep the tempo up.

I wonder if you could talk a little about how the writing process begins for you. It seems there must be a multitude of voices inside you jostling for position: how do they get onto the page?

ROOKE

The process often begins, of course, before a line goes on the page. One *thinks*. It's unnatural to us, but we do it anyway. At other times, yes, there are voices, a single voice, usually, an honest-to-God individual who somehow isolates himself from the multitude. The multitude, nowadays, is always there awaiting their entry, saying ME, ME, DO ME FIRST. Who is this creature, I ask myself, what's the story, what is he trying to tell me, what am I trying to tell her? So discovery is the primary process at work, and I wouldn't be interested in writing if that were not the case. One of the larger problems is in deciding when you've discovered enough. That's why revisions are so necessary. One is so easily fooled, first few times around.

INTERVIEWER

And the physical act of writing? How does that happen with a work like *Shakespeare's Dog*? I recall you mentioning sitting down and writing four or five pages and *then* looking back to see what you'd actually done. I wonder if you could expand on that idea?

ROOKE

Alright, I looked back and saw that it *was* a dog telling the story. But whose story? Up to that point it had just been a lot of squealing and yowling, a lot of dog-fighting, a lot of spear-thrusting. But a dog with things on his mind. It became clear, after a few minutes' thought—because of how he spoke—that here was Shakespeare's dog. I let him go on for another dozen or so pages, casting up the shadow of Will over the pages by installing the poet up at his scribbler's overhang. Off-stage, so to speak. But with entrance pending, while I got accustomed to the thought and while Hooker the dog was testing his leash. I then put it all aside and spent some months researching the subject. Getting the vivid sense in my head of what Stratford-on-Avon must have been like in 1585, and where dogs found themselves in that period. Formulating my own theories about this and that aspect of Shakespeare's life.

INTERVIEWER

You've mentioned that *Shakespeare's Dog* is based on factual material, yet of course we don't know if Shakespeare actually had a dog. Is the book an elaborate truth based on a simple lie?

ROOKE

The assumption, a reasonable one, is that Shakespeare brought his new bride back to live in his parents' house, which was a double-house packed to the rafters with little and big Shakespeares. It is inconceivable that there wouldn't have been a dog, or dogs, asleep somewhere in the yard. The lie is that dogs don't normally employ human speech. Yet if a low creature like a parrot can, and people insist they can, then why not a dog?

INTERVIEWER

Where did the name Hooker come from?

ROOKE

Hooker was Hooker in the first lines written, long before I had any inkling of what I was doing. The name stuck. It was quite a bit later—two or three weeks later—that I made any mental connection between Hooker the dog and Richard Hooker the Elizabethan theologian. That's the point at which I pounded on the table and let out a fine, gleeful howl. A gift bestowed. Such gifts often enter by the back door, which is one of the things that make writing a pleasure, and which is one of the ways that provide assurance that you're on the right track and that one day, months hence, it's all going to fit.

INTERVIEWER

The version of *Shakespeare's Dog* which General published contained more sex, juice, and frolicking than did the version of the story published in *Canadian Fiction Magazine*. The ideas or philosophies of the story did not get as much attention.

ROOKE

That's alarming, if true. I'd have said the proportions remain about the same. There's far less *frolicking*, I would have thought. I'm not arguing. Just surprised.

INTERVIEWER

The reviewer for the *New York Times Book Review* liked it but thought it could have been longer. What do you think of his criticism?

ROOKE

He should have started back over at the beginning. Clear to me, he missed much. My very secret suspicion is that he wasn't thinking of my book at all, but of his own new novel, *Pinocchio's Nose*. Mind you, I'm not kicking. The *Dog* has got blissful reviews.

INTERVIEWER

Shakespeare's Dog is a very complex book. Is it possible to understand everything that's going on in the book, or is that important?

ROOKE

I understand everything that's going on in the book, and I'm not that smart.

INTERVIEWER

Why are there four parts to *Shakespeare's Dog*? Is there an influence of *Finnegans Wake* hidden in his pages?

ROOKE

I'm going to go blue in the face, denying influences. No. The dog wanted four parts. It seemed to me he knew what he was doing. Beyond that, I cannot say.

INTERVIEWER

Is *Shakespeare's Dog* still gnawing away at your imagination?

ROOKE

Not gnawing. I've retained a few fleas. London does beckon. It's a faint beckoning, however.

INTERVIEWER

What about influences? Writers whose vision or style or idiosyncrasies have been important.

ROOKE

No single writer here. Nor have I suddenly had a vision, had my life clarified, by studying Monet's haystacks one rainy day at the Louvre, or by listening to water music, the song it makes rippling over stones. I've no doubt that hundreds of writers have influenced me, mostly temporarily, which is really about all I would want. Individual books, yes, certainly, but mostly long since forgotten. One is influenced by what one sees and hears—and reads, yes, reads—but there is no warm hand on my brow belonging to someone who daily says, "Follow me." Rather, there's the sweep of hundreds, a host, so to speak, that says, "Yep, it's worthwhile, happy to have you along."

INTERVIEWER
What's worthwhile?

ROOKE
Good writing. Excellence, whatever the form.

INTERVIEWER
Despite there being no single writer, are there a few you find yourself in conversation with—Apuleius, Gogol, Italo Calvino . . . ?

ROOKE
The list would be a lengthy one, and would include practically everyone I've ever read and liked. The list would not be notably revealing. Why is it essential for those who would be writers to read? You learn something about how a thing was done in the past, how it has evolved, how it's being done today. How it might be done. You learn that there are ten thousand ways of approaching material, and ten thousand methods of delivery, modes of styles, and a zillion different techniques. You learn to keep the mind open. You watch out for ruts and grooves. You pick up something about the elusive nature of language. You note and marvel at what some people, a great many, are able to do with it. You note that some writers, a great many, appear to have no use whatsoever for language. You consider the peculiarities of that puzzle. You do all that but mostly you know you're working blindly. You're swinging the axe and hoping the tree will fall and fall properly.

INTERVIEWER
What about the people you've read and disliked?

ROOKE
Disliked how much? I suppose it's possible that one could object so strongly to an author that one might be influenced by that author. Get a fixation? Brautigan-under-the-skin disease? Mike Hammer to the rescue? Red Ryder rides again? I don't know. Certainly the odd good book can come out of such violent dislikes, but these would be the result of the writer having had a good idea, or wanting to have fun, than there

being a question of influence. Not a very wide street, influence of this sort, I wouldn't think.

INTERVIEWER

Why the bit of Yeats in "Sing Me No Love Songs I'll Say You No Prayers"? I'm thinking of the line "Horseman, pass by."

ROOKE

I was beginning to get troubled by the story's length. I was looking to sound the first notes of an exit. I think now that this was a mistake, that I should have trusted the story and delayed those notes. But I wanted out. So I wanted a brief line for one of the story's numerous small chapters, a caption that would convey to the reader about sixteen thoughts simultaneously. That might gently and temporarily lift the reader out of the story. "Oh, here is a side street I am not to follow." A line that would serve as curious echo, and exist in space with its own reality, as Bingo's dream did on the previous page. Something that told the reader to get set, the story was ending.

INTERVIEWER

What about other influences, what's happening with contemporary painting, sculpture, video art, performance? Any influences there?

ROOKE

They take their places with tree, river, and mountains. Part of the scenery, which may or may not influence.

INTERVIEWER

And other sources? *National Enquirer*, things like that? Those writers really know how to keep the reader's attention in high gear.

ROOKE

Yes, for all of three seconds. Lots of rot in the exhaust pipes.

INTERVIEWER

And the Bible, its barrage of contradictory voices?

ROOKE

And therein, its merit, in large part: The attempt by many to extol its divine origins, the single thrust of crusading trumpet, is in fact anti-Christian. A mockery, really, of what sin and salvation is all about. We'll admit, though, that it draws a certain strength from its chorus, its refrains repeated over and over. And story, of course. And language.

INTERVIEWER

What is sin and salvation all about? In "Shoe Fly Pie" one of your characters talks about the "Holy unholy world stretching ahead of us." What's the difference between sin and salvation, between holy and unholy?

ROOKE

I don't know. That's what the search is about.

INTERVIEWER

Do heaven, hell and purgatory exist simultaneously?

ROOKE

Yep. With low walls to separate them and a busy underground railroad for shuttling people back and forth.

INTERVIEWER

Does good and evil have anything to do with morality, with religion?

ROOKE

I suspect morality would shrink and perhaps wither away altogether— and about at the same rate—if our sense of good and evil got mucked about with too much. Religion is a dog of another colour. It can be whatever enough people say they want it to be, and can have little to do with morality or with good and evil. "I worship the hedge. This is a nice hedge. Let's cut down all the trees."

INTERVIEWER

Many of your stories deal with evil: "Friendship and Property," "Biographical Notes," the list goes on. Does the writer naturally turn to this darker side for fuel?

ROOKE

I wouldn't want to state it so bluntly as that. Degrees and degrees, you know. But there is perhaps a misconception here. Hacks *choose* their topics; I don't know with what frequency a good writer does. The terrain comes largely unbidden. One goes where one goes, hoping for mercy.

Where did the titles *Cry Evil* and *Death Suite* come from? The stories inside are more optimistic than the titles of the books.

ROOKE

Both titles were mistakes. Yes, their contents are more optimistic, more energetic and joyful, and I'm delighted that you note it. Jack David and I and Robert Lecker tried out numerous alternatives to *Death Suite*, but got nowhere. I was more careful with *The Birth Control King of the Upper Volta*, including jacket affirmations of the upbeat drift of the stories. That book helped clarify matters a bit.

INTERVIEWER

Are you writing against the "shoddy evils" of the world?

ROOKE

Every serious writer is, I would hope. But it isn't absolutely essential that you do it by labelling things "good" or "evil" any more than you do it by saying, "well, folks, it's a grey world out there." I'd say that, to a certain extent, the creation in fiction of any authentic, living character is political. It is political, one, because it forces the reader to recognize that there are people different from (also similar to) himself, and two, what the author is then able to do with that recognition, is powerful, is an earth-shaker, really. Civilized people—readers—have an interest in entering other skins. So long as that condition holds, then all is not completely hopeless. That's the trouble with *bad* fiction; it confirms the shoddy, the superficial, the false. It affirms the tacky. Evil by itself, however, gets pretty grim. Joy, fun, *honour*, mirth, pleasure, love, integrity, all the higher pursuits—they get their run as well.

INTERVIEWER

So you see your stories as enlivening the reader's sensibilities, political and otherwise?

ROOKE

The careful reader, yes.

INTERVIEWER

Would you care to expand on your political commitment?

292

ROOKE

I'm not notably fascinated by the rich, the powerful, the affluent, the happily-adjusted, the contented, and I have a deep suspicion of all topics that are in vogue at any given time. That leaves nine-tenths of the world's population as story material.

INTERVIEWER

Together with these stories which I've mentioned deal with evil, there certainly are many entertaining, jovial stories. Do you see your reader chuckling along with you?

ROOKE

Faint chance! Well, it would be nice to think so. One of the problems frequently seems to be that most readers are unable to hold simultaneous thoughts in their heads. So if a line or passage—or entire story—is funny and sad at the same time, or beautiful and grim, they are apt to opt for one or the other. Usually, the other.

INTERVIEWER

I don't think I've ever read a story by you that could be called "quiet." The stories are full of words like "swirling," "foaming," "yeasting," "fermenting," "fluttering." Do you have any interest in your fiction in the quiet side of the world?

ROOKE

"Adolpho's Disappeared and We Haven't a Clue Where to Find Him" is quiet. It's quietly *told*.

INTERVIEWER

That's one.

ROOKE

Many have quiet *moments*. Quiet scenes? Endings? Lots of them have quiet endings. Don't they?

INTERVIEWER

A lot of your stories keep growing, metamorphosing. "Winter Is Lovely, Isn't Summer Hell," "Mama Tuddi Done Over," and *Shakespeare's Dog*, for example, have all gone through several published versions. When do you decide you've discovered enough?

ROOKE

That's the trouble, isn't it? We're always thinking we've discovered enough, then a year later or ten years later the candle gets relit.

INTERVIEWER

It seems that you follow the whims of your imagination more than many contemporary writers. What *is* the imagination?

ROOKE

Whims? These are driving compulsions. No, but I do follow leads, like a good detective. Imagination is what you wake with each morning. In fiction, it's energy made responsible.

INTERVIEWER

Marquez says that what he wakes up with every morning is fear. Is fear the same thing as imagination?

ROOKE

One is the bucket and the other is what the bucket holds. Which is which is probably left up to the individual person. Are they like reversible coats?

INTERVIEWER

Your characters have spoken at various times of narcissism, in stories like "Narcissus Consulted," "Shoe Fly Pie," and "Gin and Tonic." Is narcissism necessary for the writer?

ROOKE

No, not narcissism, though I can imagine a situation where it might be beneficial to peer over the edge and look to find the self in a pool of placid water. Is it the self one sees, or is it a host of others? In fiction, in my fiction anyway, I'm expecting to see those others.

INTERVIEWER

Many of your stories are about storytelling, the most obvious being "The Deacon's Tale" in Cry Evil. Does the writer naturally write about writing?

ROOKE

That the Deacon's tale is "about" writing is a bit beside the point. A side issue. Something *else* that was put in the truck when it was loaded.

It turned out, maybe, that this became the major shipment, but I wouldn't take much delight in the piece if his wasn't an interesting story. I get the feeling sometimes that what critics and readers want is "a good *boring* story." "Boy, that was boring, I loved it!" But I would not deliberately set out to write one.

INTERVIEWER
You have spoken recently of the need for "form" as a way of shaping what gushes out onto the page from your typewriter. Yet many of your stories seem to end in a sort of frenzy which threatens to break apart the form itself, stories like the "Murder Mystery" triptych, "Susan March," even "Adolpho's Disappeared." I wonder if you could speak about this creation/destruction of form.

ROOKE
What's a story, what is form? You have a river, you want to get across it. You ask yourself how. Well, you could nail a few boards together and go across on a raft. You could have someone pick you up and throw you across. You could swim. Go over on a rope. Hell, you could even WALK across it, assuming you're blessed with such dexterity. But what you really want is a bridge—the creation of a form—that will serve not only your own purposes, but those of others who follow you. A way that will serve all seasons and weather the years. So you study the tides, the soil, you learn all you can about the river, about your needs and the needs someone might have 30 or 40 years down the line, and you set to work. What you have when all this comes together and the last nail goes in—the last word written—is form. Or—let me be even more stupid: You are standing on a hill and you look down and see in front of you a huge tent. Beautiful, you think. What form! All *you* need to know is that it's a tent, repels water, will not fall down on your head should you choose to go inside. But the maker of that tent knows where all the stress points are, is aware to his soul of what it is that holds that tent up. What holds it up is what *allows* form, but the form that matters is what you see from the hilltop, or that you can sit inside the tent without any thought to its collapsing. The same with story.

INTERVIEWER
How would you apply this to stories of your own, such as those I mentioned?

"Susan March" is told in an utterly traditional form. Scarcely different, say, from Ring Lardner's "Haircut." Because the narrator speaks in a breathless voice, does that alter the form? No. Because it blends things that are really happening with things that the narrator desires would happen, and things that *may* in the past have happened with things in the present that may or may not be happening—not that it's nearly so difficult as that to tell which is which—surely this isn't destruction of form. Form is expansive. It's soft, like a vat of heated steal, and will take the shape you insist it have. I'd say, too, that Susan March, the way she thinks, the way she tells her story, is perfectly true-to-life. Interior monologue, drawing on events in the real world, retreating into the private consciousness—that back-and-forth dance—isn't some fanciful creation of fiction. In fact, that kind of dance, alternation, is probably the truest mirroring of ourselves that there is. Switch it over to a third person point of view and you'll probably find that this is what the bulk of our prose literature is in effect doing.

INTERVIEWER

Adolpho?

ROOKE

The point to note in the Adolpho story—for once noted you'll see that this story, too, is following its natural resolution and is as *formed* as the thing could be . . . the point to note is that about three-quarters of the way through, with attendant sign-posts all along and the note struck from the very beginning, the narrator has suffered a kind of stroke, that, in fact, a doctor might very likely pronounce him dead. And that the entire story (as I recall it) is being told by him while in that state. Thus at the end, when all his old subterfuges, diversions, whimsy—his innocence AND guilt (obviously he's done in his missing club-mate)—no longer can protect him, his lovely Orpha no longer entrance, his deceptions have played out, *then* he reacts with horror, for he recognizes that he's truly come to the end of the line. Orpha becomes vampire of the seediest type. Death, no return. Okay, that's tricky, no easy job to pull off, but I thought it worth the attempt. I wanted to see if one could describe that *passing over*. The narrator in another story of mine, for that matter, "The Broad Back of the Angel," does the same thing. Form can accommodate, and doesn't *always* destruct because the challenge is great or the going is hard.

INTERVIEWER

Do you see your stories as having a recognizable beginning, middle, and end?

ROOKE

Always, in anything over three pages. And sometimes then. But not perhaps in the standard notion of the term. Most stories, by their very nature, start, go on a while, then are over. That's the only way the term really means anything, and it's the way stories want to be told. It doesn't matter that much which comes first, except for the middle, which does like to be between things.

INTERVIEWER

You have written some very short pieces of prose, many short stories, and novels. Do you have a favourite length?

ROOKE

The short story is flexible enough to take in everything from a few pages up to short novel size. One can't complain about that. I'm fond of the short novel length. I'm especially grateful for brevity when I'm reading something I don't like. I have a sensible attraction to novels in the 160-180 page range—most notably those that deal with very few main characters over a brief period of time. Say, one day in the life of so & so, done so that it conveys a pretty clear sense of the full life leading up to that time. Without the use of spiritless, mawkish flashback and such. A good many writers, I'm saying, don't even consider technique. They've learned six or seven ways to get a thing onto the page, and that, they think, is enough. It's like the old "wipe" or "fade" or cut in film—cut from water swirling down the faucet to a river bursting its dam or a damsel soaping in the bath—hackneyed crap that any reader with two wits tired of ages ago. But we were speaking of length.

INTERVIEWER

Is the length determined completely by the subject.

ROOKE

Oh no, not completely, I wouldn't think. Style, approach, angle, language—the lean line as opposed to the more florid or languid one—determine length probably *more* than subject does. I want to be short-winded about big subjects, someone said. But wait, I get it, you're asking *me*. Well, some subjects ask to be treated directly; some—and perhaps

297

the same subject—take their power from a more circular treatment. Quite often the style a piece demands is set very early, and that determines length. All sorts of things, in fact, determine length. Fashion, for instance. "The novel this year, folks, must be no less than three hundred pages." Or *outmoded concept* does. *Size* itself does: big car, little car, toot-toot, look at what *I* have done!

INTERVIEWER

Philip Larkin, who at one time did write short stories, recently said: "I think a short story should be either a poem or a novel." What would be your criticism of that statement?

ROOKE

It's best left rotting on the vine.

INTERVIEWER

Yes?

ROOKE

The poets have enough trouble without my encouraging the mob to boil the rogues in oil—and quickly, too, before they multiply. Sure, I'd agree with Larkin. And sticks should be swords and raccoons should be pigs. Of course, they don't have a short fiction tradition in England; they gave it up largely; it proved too difficult. In England the sky is too foul, the eyes too close together; it's too rainy, too foggy, and now even the beer has declined. God help them if they hadn't had ships for plundering innocent little colonies.

INTERVIEWER

You've written poems, plays, short stories, novels, there's even some drawings in a recent story. Is there a difference between prose and poetry, between drawing and drama?

ROOKE

This is to confess the awful, stunted, prideful truth: the only difference that matters to me is that I respond more to prose. I take it more seriously.

INTERVIEWER

Are you connecting up the senses?

ROOKE

I'm going at it with bailing wire

INTERVIEWER

Do you think of *The Magician in Love* as prose or poetry, or does it matter?

ROOKE

I think of it as prose that knows what poetry is. No, in this instance it doesn't matter.

INTERVIEWER

Why is it that short stories seem so important to contemporary Canadian writing, more so even than poems or novels?

ROOKE

Because writers have learned how to write them well and a few readers have learned how to read them? God knows why. Is it true? If so, it's passing strange, and undoubtedly a brief phenomenon, like shoe laces with light bulbs attached.

INTERVIEWER

I was struck by the line "no trails made and herself alone to make them" in "Deer Trails in Tzityonyana." Is this trailbreaking the job of the Canadian writer? Is it different from the trailbreaking that writers from other countries make?

ROOKE

No significant differences exist that I've perceived. Ever onwards, upwards into light! The nose out of the cobwebs, yea!

INTERVIEWER

Is the rumble of history important to the writer? A national literary heritage which Canadian writers do not yet have?

ROOKE

The rumble is vital, otherwise, it seems, one wouldn't read *or* write— one would more likely be scratching about to find pure water, and maybe a lizard to throw over the fire. The wider the sweep is of what one inherits, the luckier one is. But much can be done out of a luckless, impoverished start. Writers are self-formed. That usually means they make up, while they are busy becoming writers, whatever heritage their situation or personality demands, with the result that a literary heritage of two weeks or two decades provides the same nourishment as one that has continued through five thousand years. Well, not the *same*. But the air can be fresher in the former. No shackles to liberate oneself from, except those attitudes of impoverishment. I don't know of any writer who has been destroyed by an absence of nationalistic literary heritage, while we could list scores who have been reduced by an absence of talent, or fortitude or staying power. A few are finally destroyed perhaps because no one buys their books or because the critical response to their work has been stunningly stupid. That's where the absence of a literary heritage hurts most, I would think.

INTERVIEWER

Are you saying it's possible for a writer to just burst into the world, without any heritage except his own?

ROOKE

I can conceive of such. Have you read Cormac McCarthy? Hauntingly beautiful, powerfully evocative novels about a place so dank and severe, so hard and sour you'd swear not even a rat could survive. Even from such a place a writer might come. Don't imagine though that I'm suggesting we turn back the clock — we're talking possibilities, not wishes.

INTERVIEWER

Is it possible to invent the world?

ROOKE

McCarthy's is half-invented; without that half, we wouldn't believe the half that's actual. Making the invention linger, hang on, have meaning and multiply, is the trick, I suppose.

INTERVIEWER

You recently stated that "the golden age is approaching." I wonder if you could elaborate.

ROOKE

I also said it's *always* approaching, because I think that's true, and because that's the healthy place for it to be. Think how nervous everyone would be — the critics, the readers, even some writers — if it were upon us. "Oh, another masterpiece, Saviour, protect me!" And how much gold does it take for the age to be accurately described as golden? There are quite important deposits all over the place

INTERVIEWER

Are your stories symbolical? Are they pure voice which attempts to deny symbol?

ROOKE

I'm not outlandishly symbolical. I'm sure that *pure* voice *would* deny symbol. Symbol is fine, useful, and dandy, when true to a work's texture. I wouldn't want to hoist it up on a pole and have it wave about like a red flag. If symbol is a thing to be noticed in the first place, I'd want to kick a big pile of dirt up over it. Then throw on leaves so you wouldn't know for sure that the dirt was there.

INTERVIEWER

In your stories, perhaps "Sixteen-Year-Old Susan March Confesses to the Innocent Murder of All the Devious Strangers Who Would Drag Her Down" being the best example, the mind controls the world. Is there such a thing as an objective, factual world out there, a world separated from the mind?

ROOKE

Oh sure, we can see that there is. Daylight or darkness, we can see that there is. But there is no way, dating from the first breath, we are ever going to enter that objective, factual world. Our control over it is more or less. One of degree, I mean. But Susan March, who rigidly maintains herself in that field to which she yielded long before the story begins, is not alone. Her way of seeing things is not that uncommon. She's super-suggestive within the certain iron rules set by herself and confirmed daily by her mother and by the few men she's known best.

INTERVIEWER

Are you a realist—are you setting a mirror up to the mind?

ROOKE

A curved mirror, like those put up to frighten shoplifters. Sure I am—sometimes—though it smacks a bit too much of the clinic. Of the couch. Of the Doctor From Vienna.

INTERVIEWER

You have said that writing is an escape from your own voice. Is that the same thing as escaping into the multifarious voices inside you?

ROOKE

I guess so. Although "escape" seems to suggest a state of urgency, of severity, that isn't that operative. The compulsion is largely benign. One goes to Rome because Rome is there.

INTERVIEWER

In your stories there are voices in the air, in *things*. Are these the same sort of voices that people have?

ROOKE

Can we make a case for that? I expect so. But it's a visual age, not horse-drawn anymore. People see ghosts in Bergman's wonderful *Fanny & Alexander* and they think, "Isn't that rich, isn't that the most marvelous thing!" They come across the same in a work of current fiction and they think, "Oh god, this author's weird, isn't this off-the-wall!" The ability to see and experience and enjoy fails when it isn't there in front of them in glorious colour and sound. But let someone drop a brick on your foot and you'll see it all right. So the ability is intact, it's just dormant all too often where the subtlety of fiction is concerned. Well, that's the dark side of the moon; there's a brighter side as well.

INTERVIEWER

You've written a lot of stories with a female voice in them—is there a difference between a male and a female voice?

ROOKE

Let men screech and women pelt me with stones. No, not a whit, where it matters. The eye of the whirlwind is neither male nor female, or rather it is both. The human heart in conflict with itself, to use Faulkner's phrase, is not exclusively one or the other. Does it matter so much that the heart is dressed up with stockings and lipstick or that it wears a Stetson hat? The male writer should be compelled by law to write from time to time from the female point of view. The female, being more generous by nature and more adventuresome, doesn't require the legal notice.

302

INTERVIEWER

I've also noticed that the mommy and daddy figures seem to be strangely absent, or present as spirits or troublesome visitors. Any special reason?

ROOKE

The special reason has to do, I expect, with the ages in which my characters are found. They are not often children, and not yet grandparents. They are at an age and in situations where mommy and daddy figures are not that central. At an age, that is, where parental figures cast as spirits or troublesome visitors is the most reasonable and the most realistic presentation possible.

INTERVIEWER

But also in "Never But Once the White Tadpole" the parental figures are important but in a strange way. Even Hooker talks about his "mam."

ROOKE

A dog howls, yodels, for his mam. Nothing so strange in that, especially if you're a dog and you've just seen your mother's bones by the roadside. You want mam back just as she was when you knew her best. I admit I have a fondness for the dog's howl. One, because it's speaking for and of—not just the dog's—but the human condition. Quality notes. It's lonely and plaintive, sorrowful or joyful, and it's beautiful, and it goes on being heard after the howl has quit. It's beautiful, too, because of what you hear in the silence between the howls. And because we know such howls were there from the beginning of time—the same howl—we're reminded of history and of the present and made to feel an eerieness, a wariness, about the future as well. An important chord is struck within us, I mean, to root us but also to lift us outside ourselves.

INTERVIEWER

"White Tadpole"?

ROOKE

Now that's an ancient piece. You've been rooting about in a very musty shelf. My first published story, I think. A grandmother had died, as I recall, and the child's world had gone a bit cockeyed. That grandmother, by the way, would have been the real-life wife of the old man in "If Lost Return to the Swiss Arms." He died, too. Death, death

303

. . . that also is part of the dog's howl.

INTERVIEWER
Dogs abound in your work and they always seem part mongrel, part philosopher, and part hedonist. Are they the true visionaries?

ROOKE
Old Howel the Good. Old Canine the Quick. Why not a dog?

INTERVIEWER
Do you think that contemporary writing deals more with the unconscious than, say, the writing of a hundred years ago?

ROOKE
I don't know. I'm inclined to doubt it.

INTERVIEWER
Are you more fascinated with the conscious or the unconscious?

ROOKE
I'm interested in what's alive and bears probing. The unconscious isn't a dead stone that stays dead stone. Once you turn it over you often discover it isn't dead and it isn't even a stone. I find that I have faint interest in things about which I'm unconscious; thirst is greatest when we're confronted with an empty bottle. There's a connection somewhere between those statements.

INTERVIEWER
It has been said: "If you want to be true to reality, start lying about it." What do you think?

ROOKE
Okay, we know, some of us do, that despite a world which insists on change—whenever didn't it?—and wouldn't tolerate anything else, that a limited number of (quote) "universal truths" remain dear; we also know that the truth turned upside down is still the truth, only we now have another way of perceiving it, a different perspective, maybe. Furthermore, we know that so long as it remains upright, cast in the form so familiar that we are blind to it, that many won't be urged to look in the first place. Lying about the truth can accomplish that.

Then you see no difference between truth and lying?

Well, some novels, poems, stories tell lies. They are not true to reality. Doctorow's *Welcome To Hard Times*, as I read it, is a lie. But useful, perhaps. Susan Musgrave's novel, *The Charcoal Burners*, is a lie, and a harmful one, in my view. But lie or truth, the writer's job is the same: to make the reader believe. Does one believe Henny Penny? Sure. I do.

How come the name Gore? There is a character with that name in two of your plays and in "The Broad Back of the Angel."

Gore made his first appearance, as the central character, in an early short novel called *The Line of Fire*—although at that point he was called Gode. Later on, in a story called "Field Service (dot dot dot)," he was called Codey. He was Egor the house-breaker in a story called "Leave Running." He was Gore again in the three stories contained in *Vault*. Elsewhere, too, I believe. And, yes, he was in the two plays and in "Angel." Ask me not why. You might also wonder aloud why a woman named Agnes has shown up, in oblique manner, in about 15 stories. Perhaps they are looking for each other?

Do you have a favourite story of your own? One that you can't stand?

I might be shocked, looking back at some of them again, but some of those I think best of would include "The Broad Back of the Angel," "For Love of Gomez," "For Love of Eleanor," "Wintering in Victoria," and old Adolpho. I have many that can't bear a second reading, though I've managed to keep these out of the various collections.

Does theme have anything to do with a book like *Shakespeare's Dog*? If there is any theme at all it seems to me that the theme is *words*, individual words which fit together and carry the story.

ROOKE

Language as affirmation, do you mean? Well, I'm certainly on the side of that. It's why we have to choose our authors carefully in the first place.

INTERVIEWER

In "Sing Me No Love Songs I'll Say You No Prayers" there is a remarkable scene, the one called "The Seven-Room House" in which you describe how the house that Crow Kay G. inherits came to be built. There is something so self-reliant, so crystalline about that scene that to talk about it at all seems to belittle it. Are you creating stories that want to live independently of all this questioning, of all this critical commenting?

ROOKE

That's the hope. Otherwise it's like going to a party where there is no liquor.

INTERVIEWER

Are answers slippery?

ROOKE

Not *that* slippery. The floor isn't so polished no one can stand up. Nor is the ground so swampy that man and woman and beast can't run.

INTERVIEWER

Where do the voices go after they hit the page?

ROOKE

Into the void. Into a very deep well. Drop a stone and after three lifetimes you'll hear a splash, and someone singing.

INTERVIEWER

Is Shakespeare listening?

ROOKE

If it isn't his ear, it's someone's ear. It's the same old untired, wonderful ear that comes alert every time it hears the rustle of paper.

INTERVIEWER

Were you writing while you were in the army?

ROOKE

Every day, or every day that I was sane. No, while in the army I possessed secret keys to several different offices equipped with typewriter and paper.

INTERVIEWER

Do you see that time as having a tangible influence on your work?

ROOKE

Not a lasting influence. All the influence there was to be had went into the short novel *The Line of Fire*.

INTERVIEWER

Did you have fun in Australia?

ROOKE

Absolutely. Australia is a superb place. The people at the Literature Board of the Australia Council—and those met across the country—were stunning in their welcoming, their planning, their generosity of spirit. Stunning in a great variety of ways, just as the geography of the place is. Those here who like books should know about writers such as Andrew Taylor, David Malouf, Murray Bail, Frank Moorhouse, Peter Carey, Rodney Hall, Roger McDonald, Elizabeth Jolley, Jennifer Strauss, Michael Wilding, etc.—a scratch of the flow, the mighty flow, for these and scores of others are not writers who will stop coming.

INTERVIEWER

How is the Napoleon book going? Can you talk about what you're trying to do with it?

ROOKE

It was going well when I last left it. No, I wouldn't care to talk about it just yet.

INTERVIEWER

Is there anything the imagination can't do?

ROOKE

It can't push a loaded wheelbarrow uphill. Or catch it once the wheelbarrow comes roaring down.

Is there anything the writer can't do?

They can't deny the potential of the next empty page, I suppose. They can't throttle a reader, or make an editor's jaw go slack. They *can* try prayer, but we know what comes of that.

Interview by Peter O'Brien

BIOGRAPHICAL NOTES
ON INTERVIEWERS

STEPHEN BROCKWELL did a BSc at McGill and an MSc at Carleton, and currently works for the Geocartographics Subdivision of Statistics Canada. He has published in the anthologies *Lakeshore Poets* (Muses' Company, 1981) and *Cross/cut: Contemporary English Quebec Poetry* (Véhicule, 1982), and has poems published or forthcoming in *Event*, *Rubicon*, and *The Antigonish Review*. He was the editor of *Short Poems* and is now the editor of *The Rideau Review*.

THOMAS GERRY has a BA from the University of Toronto and an MA from York. He recently completed his PhD at the University of Western Ontario. He has published articles in *Canadian Literature, University of Toronto Quarterly*, and *Studies in Canadian Literature*. He is currently Assistant Professor of English at Acadia University in Wolfville, N.S.

BARBARA LECKIE is doing her PhD in English at McGill University. She has published an article on women and madness in *Praxis* and has published book reviews in *Open City* and *Canadian Literature*. She has worked as an Assistant Editor of *Essays on Canadian Writing* and has been an Assistant Editor of *Rubicon* since 1984. She currently divides her time between Montreal and Paris.

DAVID MANICOM has been Assistant Editor of *Rubicon* since 1984. He has published poems in many journals, including *Malahat Review, Descant, Canadian Forum*, and *Shenandoah* (U.S.) and has published short stories, book reviews, and scholarly articles. He is currently completing a PhD on modern Irish poetry at McGill. A first collection of poems, *Sense of Season*, will be published by Porcépic Books in 1988.

DEBRA MARTENS has published fiction in *Descant, Room Of One's Own*, the anthology *Baker's Dozen* (Women's Press, 1984), and book reviews in *Rubicon, Books in Canada* and *Quill & Quire*. She has a BA from the University of Toronto and an MA from McGill. Originally from the Niagara fruit belt, she has lived in Toronto, Montreal and is currently living in Ottawa. She has a story forthcoming in the anthology *Celebrating Women*.

CLEA NOTAR is the Quebec editor for *(f.)Lip*, a national newsletter of feminist, innovative writing. An anglophone born and raised in Quebec, she has worked for CBC Radio's "Brave New Waves," as well as various arts and literary publications in Montreal. She has written educational material on the topic of eating disorders, political satire for film, and is presently writing a collection of short fiction. She has a BA in English from McGill.

PETER O'BRIEN is the founding editor of *Rubicon*. He is the coeditor of *Fatal Recurrences: New Fiction in English from Montréal* (Véhicule, 1984) and the coeditor of *Introduction to Literature: British, American, Canadian* (Harper & Row, 1987). He has a BA from the University of Notre Dame (South Bend, Indiana) and an MA from McGill. Born in New York, he has lived in Vancouver, Dublin, Medicine Hat, Montreal, and now lives in Toronto.

OTHER TITLES OF INTEREST FROM VEHICULE PRESS

WRITERS IN ASPIC Edited by John Metcalf

SPIDER BLUES: ESSAYS ON MICHAEL ONDAATJE
Edited by Sam Solecki

THE MONTREAL STORY TELLERS: MEMOIRS,
PHOTOGRAPHS, CRITICAL ESSAYS
Edited by J.R. (Tim) Struthers

CIV/n: A LITERARY MAGAZINE OF THE 50's
Edited by Aileen Collins

A MAN OF SENTIMENT: THE MEMOIRS OF PHILIPPE-
JOSEPH AUBERT DE GASPÉ, 1786–1871 Translated and
annotated by Jane Brierley